THE GENUINE ARTICLE

THE GENUINE ARTICLE

The making and unmasking
of fakes and forgeries

John FitzMaurice Mills
and
John M. Mansfield

UNIVERSE BOOKS
New York

Published in the United States of America in 1982 by
Universe Books
381 Park Avenue South, New York, N.Y. 10016

82 83 84 85 86/10 9 8 7 6 5 4 3 2 1

Printed in the United States of America

Library of Congress Cataloging in Publication Data

Mills, John FitzMaurice, 1917-
   The genuine article.
   Reprint. Originally published: London: British
Broadcasting Corp., 1979.
   Includes index.
   1. Art—Forgeries. 2. Art objects—Reproduction.
I. Mansfield, John M.   II. Title.
[N8790.M54   1982]   702'.8'74   82-8318
ISBN 0-87663-401-3   AACR2

CONTENTS

The aim in this book is to intrigue the readers with some of the more extraordinary true stories of fakes, frauds and forgeries and to describe how they were carried out, while at the same time enabling them to gain greater pleasure and even amusement from the occasional visit to such seemingly contrasting places as a local junk shop, market stall, jumble sale or a top West End antique showroom. As inflation spirals upwards and the attraction of higher and higher prices increasingly depletes the market of the genuine in fine art, antiques, stamps, coins and jewellery, the temptation to satisfy this growing demand for expensive rarities with cunning substitutes has escalated. The main targets of forgers are the very rich, but today almost anyone seeking a bargain is quite likely to become exposed to their criminal creations.

Water colours by little-known artists which seem a snip at £20 have turned out to be superb reproductions made by the collotype process, which can be virtually indistinguishable from the real thing until you know what to look for. Brass sun-dials bearing every outward sign of age including a seventeenth-century date are almost monotonously exposed as modern replicas, yet they are still found on many market stalls being sold as antiques. The examples are legion, but with only a little care and knowledge, most people could easily avoid being duped. This book does not set out to provide its readers with the definitive account of how to differentiate everything false from the true: to do so would require many volumes. Its intention instead is to help the readers to begin to look at the objects around them from a new viewpoint where they may be slightly less likely to take things at face value, and if they do, to know why, and enjoy genuine value that much more.

It has been said that part of the knack of the good connoisseur lies in remembering that only rarely does the forger attempt to make a perfect copy or pastiche of the original. More often the forger tries to create an object which his market will think contains all the attributes of the original which they find desirable. Much of genuine Chippendale furniture was too austere for the taste of the Victorians: such knowledge makes it easier to tell the difference between a real Chippendale chair and a Victorian fake. The Victorian piece is nearly always a trifle over-decorated with heavy carved embellishments which, although they are unlikely to fool many today, were exactly what the nineteenth-century buyer was trying to find. Often the most crass mistakes are made simply by our wanting to find antiques which are well suited to modern requirements. A good example was a most attractive 'Sheraton' coffee-table seen recently in a showroom window. It looked very authentic, but as coffee-tables are a relatively modern invention it had to be either an outright fake, or at best the end-product of some excellent but very recent carpentry which had possibly adapted some larger damaged antique to fulfil a modern role. Part of the forger's trap is the fact that most of us see what we want to see rather than what is actually in front of us. In fact the collector can be self-swindling and if what he wants to find is, let us say, a ruby ring, and one is offered to him at an extremely low price; greed can override normal critical judgement. The collector allows his mind to be swayed by his own covetousness and he fails to check authenticity. He is almost willing the object to be what he wants it to be, genuine.

The television series on which this book is partially based happened as a result of the weird juxtaposition of coincidences, priorities and budgetary considerations that only happen in vast organisations like the BBC. After long discussions with Professor Stephen Rees Jones of the Courtauld Institute it became intriguingly obvious that there was immense scope for a 'Horizon' film about authenticating paintings. It would show how centuries of copying, combined with a proliferation of fakes, make the task today of authenticating Old Masters a matter for considerable scientific expertise. At that juncture the 'Horizon' budget temporarily hit rock-bottom. However, the Controller of BBC2 had already become interested in the scientific detection of fakes, and asked that consideration be given to creating fifty ten-minute, studio-based programmes, each one focusing on a magnificent fake of a superb genuine painting.

The idea of collecting together such a large number of fakes would have appalled many, but also to bring to the studio week in, week out, a succession of the finest genuine works of art with which to compare the fakes, scared BBC2 and their insurers. To avoid, however, appearing unappreciative of the opportunities offered by such a proposal, the insurance problems involved were explained to the Controller and a suggestion was put forward for a more modest series of seven thirty-minute films ranging over a wide selection of fakes. The idea was accepted.

It was then found that remarkably few of the individuals who were intimately involved in this highly profitable trade were particularly anxious to give much help in the preparing of a television series whose object was not only to expose their dishonesty but also to show the previously unwitting viewer how to detect their tricks. Even the most reputable dealers, using the most politely plausible excuses, said that they were sorry, and, although they thought such programmes could be of enormous interest, felt that they themselves could be of little help. At last a little light began to come on the scene. Dr Stuart Fleming, a leading member of the Oxford University team of science-orientated archaeologists, and author of *Authenticity in Art* advised against immediate despair, suggesting a few incorruptible sources where research might be continued. Elsewhere other authorities became enthusiastic and very helpful. Mr Robson Lowe, for example, the doyen of British philately, said, 'I've been waiting for a long time for you people to do something like this. It's about time! Now look here . . .' and he proceeded to give an instant beginner's course on fake stamps, illustrated with examples from his albums, and never allowing there to be any doubt as to whether there would be sufficient material to make a thirty-minute programme wholly devoted to such a specialist hobby as stamp collecting. As he said, 'And then the seventh programme about stamps could focus on Sperati's work – that's if you've got the time to cram it all in!'

The small research team suddenly found that some of the portcullises of the antique business were beginning to lift, though perhaps accompanied by the creaks and groans of centuries of disuse, allowing entry into inner sanctums, to encounter a confusing array of priceless authentic treasures, incredible fakes, a maze of conflicting opinion about which was which, and quite where that left everything in between – for example, those grey objects called 'genuine replica', 'authentic reproduction', 'school of . . .', 'in the style of', 'autographed copy', etcetera.

This book is the authors' report on the strange world they found after months of exploring these inner sanctums.

CHAPTER ONE

THE ART OF
DUPLICITY

The pursuit of the rare, the beautiful, the genuine, has developed today into a game of wits played by the collector, the dealer and the faker, supported by equally interesting characters as restorers, middlemen, copyists, all drawn in by the lure of the final take. If the total annual turnover of large and small establishments, country sales, small auctions and the big international giants of the game were added up the result would be a conservative £1000 million and it is likely it could be far above that. What proportion of this is totted up by the sale of spurious copies fraudulently issued, marriages, reproductions with bent provenances, and outright forgeries? One expert opinion has expressed a figure of possibly twelve per cent.

The objects in the dealer's showroom or in the saleroom can fall into several categories. They can be completely genuine, backed by an honest provenance; they can be reproductions, copies, duplicates or facsimiles of works of art; they can be what are termed misattributions, cases of mistaken identity; they can be restorations, work that has had to be extensively restored; they can be questionables in which there is a genuine disagreement between recognised authorities as to their authenticity and their age; and they can be fakes.

Collectors of most periods have been plagued with this situation and it arises quite simply from a maladjustment of demand and supply. The problem is further aggravated when quite innocent copies or reproductions get into mischievous hands and are nudged in the wrong direction, then with a little adjustment perhaps of their appearance and a little falsification of records they can very easily be passed back into the pipeline as the genuine article.

The actual legal position is somewhat confused because if a fake or forgery is produced, the maker of it is not breaking the law. He only does so and becomes liable for arrest when he issues, or in legal parlance utters, the forgery; that is, passes it into the trade, or to a customer. Under English law, forgery first became a statutory offence in 1562 and there were a variety of punishments. These included a period of standing in the pillory, having both ears cut off, the nostrils slit up and seared and the forfeiture of land; also possible perpetual imprisonment. In the seventeenth century capital punishment was added. One of the most notable cases is that of a Rev. Dr W. Dodd in 1777 who forged Lord Chesterfield's name on a bond. He was apprehended and led off to the executioner's block.

Since that time there have been a welter of statutes but, strangely enough, the penalties seem to have dwindled. The same situation appears on the Continent. The most famous forger certainly of this century, Han Van Meegeren, made well over half a million pounds from his fake Vermeers and other Dutch artists. At his trial, on being found guilty, he received a sentence of one year.

The question is often raised as to why a forgery of high craftsmanship and quality in every aspect, where there doesn't appear to be any difference between it and a genuine work by a painter or craftsman, shouldn't be worth as much as the original. The answer seems to be an almost intangible one that lies in the area of aesthetics.

These craftsmen of the shadows are not a twentieth-century phenomenon. The first evidence of fake objects appears in the early Egyptian
tombs. During the heyday of the Romans there was an amazing wave of
forged antique specimens of Greek sculpture to satisfy the collecting
mania of the emperors, the generals and the leading citizens. The first
private galleries were erected to house the large collections. There is even
the case of the first recorded literary forgery when one Phaedrus wrote
under the name of Aesop, pointing out that he did this quite simply to
make more money. There were many more marble works signed with the
name of Praxiteles than the sculptor could ever have made in his lifetime.

During the Renaissance period in Italy and Northern Europe the seeds
were sown for further confusion. Not only were fakers active but also there
was a very large amount of copying undertaken, much of which was
entirely innocent. The practice then for art education was for one to be
apprenticed to a leading painter, sculptor or craftsman and, quite naturally, the style of the master would often be assumed and also he might ask
his apprentices to work into some of his pictures, costume or background
landscape details; they might even undertake complete copies of his works.
The great Raphael certainly attracted the attention of copyists and
imitators, intent on making money out of his name.

Giulio dei Giannuzzi, at times called Giulio Pippi but more generally
Giulio Romano, was born in Rome about 1492, and when quite young was
apprenticed to Raphael. He assisted the master with his work in the
Vatican and was probably one of the greatest of Raphael's pupils. He
copied a number of Raphael's Madonnas, and also used many of his
master's designs. On Raphael's death, his Will conveyed all his studio
equipment to Giulio Romano and another of his pupils, Gianfrancesco
Penni, with the instruction that they were to finish his incomplete frescoes
in the Sala di Constantino in the Vatican. The work of Raphael also
attracted the attention of a Flemish painter some time after he had died.
Jan Gillis Delcour, who was born in 1632 near Liège, travelled to Rome
where he worked with Andrea Sacchi and Carlo Maratti, and whilst there,
it was recorded, made excellent copies of many of Raphael's works. From
Madrid, Juan Bautista del Mazo, who had studied in the school of Veláz-
quez, travelled to Rome, where he too made numerous copies of Raphael;
from copies such as these have come second-stage copies where lesser

hands have worked their versions from the first copies. If you add all this up over the centuries, tracing the authenticity of a masterpiece can become a major feat of detection.

Forgeries of works of art and these fraudulently handled copies are a constant harassment, not only for the collector, but even more so for the curators and directors of galleries and museums who are spending very large sums of public money.

Is there a way that the collector can protect himself? Probably no, not entirely. The good and skilled forger is likely to beat the market, certainly with his early productions until they become recognised as such, analysed and classified. Training the eye, taking pains to investigate the particular field of one's choice, studying the genuine works of an artist or school or craftsman, can to a degree establish some form of protection. Then, it is possible that the longer the real thing is examined the more it comes to life, the more beautiful, the more satisfying it becomes and, contrariwise, the longer a forgery or a copy is looked at the more its quality recedes and it seems to die.

Today it would be very hard to pick a category of art objects which has not already been invaded by the forger. Nothing is sacrosanct to him, whether painting, a piece of sculpture, a jewel, a stamp, a document, or even a score by a well-known composer. If there is money, there he will be, putting forward his false wares. How does he do this? The avenues for operation are all too many. He might pick a dealer who has become a little dishonest; he might put an object into the collection of a needy person, who has a convincing old house in which it could be 'discovered' without arousing suspicion. Another route can be via the salerooms, working with a small gang and starting low down the pecking order for such places. An object can be sold in one country and then put into a saleroom in another, backed up by receipts and possibly catalogues of the first sale, and this process can be repeated until the object has attained a tail of convincing evidence and so multiplied its asking figure many times. It has been suggested that the world of the artist and the craftsman was invented to give a living to the dealers and the auctioneers besides satisfying the desires for ownership and possession by the collectors. Perhaps this is a little harsh, but the whole edifice undoubtedly does move along on the creative ability of the painter, the sculptor and the skilled craftsman.

When a collecting mania gets a bit out of hand, it's no coincidence that a spate of very fine forgeries appears. There is the example in this century when numerous fakes appeared to satisfy and back up the political doctrines of the Third Reich. The same situation arose in the times of other predators: Napoleon, Catherine the Great of Russia, Frederick the Great, and back to such as the Medicis, the Estes and other banker lords of the Renaissance. In the eighteenth century the new, culturally-aroused gentry went on their grand tour of Italy, scooping up enormous numbers of very fine works of art of every type, at the same time acquiring a disturbing proportion of outright fakes and lesser copies.

Is there some chink in the mental make-up of the forger? Is he a psychological misfit or is there some chip on the shoulder? Indubitably, Han Van Meegeren had a grudge against art critics, and this was amongst the reasons that initially motivated him to bring down, in his eyes anyway, what he saw as the pompous mouthings of the critic Bredius, the doyen of such people. There may be isolated characters who work away under lunatic guises, feeling that they are the reincarnation of a particular artist or craftsman; but very largely the prime motive undoubtedly is the very considerable financial gain, even if the largest helping of this loot does end up with a dealer or some shadow-agent used in the uttering. Very seldom indeed will the forger be in direct contact with his particular customer, for quite obvious reasons. There have been cases such as Alceo Dossena who in strict legal parlance produced large numbers of forgeries, but it is fairly certain that he did them in total innocence; the guilty person who labelled them and sold them being the intermediary agent.

The whole antique trade, in truth, exists to satisfy the desires of the collectors large and small. Fashion trends can be fabricated, encouraged, or discovered, and it is these trends which to a large degree determine the price structure across the market. The embryo collector can be sized up by a dealer, his aesthetic sense aroused, his urge to acquire encouraged and the whole range of human characteristics played upon – ambition, vanity, snobbery, display, personal standing. More and more today it is thrust into the ears of collectors that an antique is an investment. In fact, there are various establishments who are buying up first-line works of art of all types, salting them away and almost reducing them to sheaves of share certificates. A sad comment on objects of beauty and creation that lie mutely hidden away in the darkness of some banker's vault, supposedly to accrue more and more money.

The dealers inhabit a strange arena in which they too can become a prey for the crooked predator. Trials that expose a particular forger can equally well expose them as being a part of the swindle. This whole business of works of art and their values is proceeded with behind carefully arranged systems of veils. It is difficult for the man in the street and the average collector to penetrate the machinations controlling the movements of works of art, their discovery, decisions as to their price and their authentification. Provenances can be absolutely accurate to the best of knowledge of the expert art historian. They can also be as forged as the article they are backing up. A little bit of professional terminology, a display of art historianship plus details of supposedly celebrated collections, dates, sales and prices, can look very convincing on paper.

It is extraordinary the amount of waffle that an art lover will soak up and believe if it is presented to him by a person he trusts. He will also swallow grey lies that will build up the quality of the particular art object in question. If only he could have a glimpse of the make-up, the rehearsals, the manoeuvrings behind the scenes that have been set in motion to push forward a transaction. A part of this dark comedy may be played in front of the customer, who starts off as a spectator and all too soon finds himself in the cast and playing the part of the dupe.

Such an example could be of a dealer of well-publicised standing who sows a harvest for himself by choosing a line of a particular period of, say, Sèvres that has been out of fashion with collectors of porcelain. For several years he buys up all he can find of this type. Then he begins sending selected pieces to well-known auction sales where he has secret buyers who run them up to large figures. By this artifice he gradually builds up the reputation of this particular branch of his business. Now he trails these objects across the nose of some wealthy collector who he suspects will be interested. A little judicious publicity and a few hand-outs and this period of a Northern France porcelain becomes the rage, prices shoot up accordingly, and the shrewd dealer brings himself very considerable profit. He has done nothing dishonest.

One of the biggest come-ons the small-time faker produces for the young collector is 'a bargain'. There is something about that word that quickens the pulse of most people, but the knowledgeable know by now that there are very few bargains indeed. If a thing is cheaply offered, it is often for a good reason. It may be because a minor forger is trying to pass off some work; it may be an article that has been stolen. Exceptionally, it can be ignorance on the part of the seller. A bright forger doesn't attempt to underprice his objects. In fact, in many cases he will price them right up the market.

An inscription on an object can at times be highly misleading, particularly if it is backed by a certificate of authenticity from an expert on the subject. Sadly, this issue of dubious certificates for pocket-money for the expert has and does exist. One case of an inscription showing up a professional mind is a piece of pottery that was brought to a member of a select academy. It had a rather strange sequence of letters that puzzled a number of people. The pot on one side bore M.J.D.D. and it had reputedly been dug up near Dijon. As soon as the expert from the academy saw the letters he had no hesitation at all in pronouncing it to be an early Roman pot. Furthermore, he went on to say that it was a small amphora which had been used as an ex-voto object. The letters, he said at once, were the initials of the Latin invocation: MAGNO JOVE DEORUM DEO. His explanation was that the pot was a receptacle for a votive offering and therefore why not? – the inscription could read 'To the great Jupiter, the god of gods'. This gentleman, however, was somewhat taken aback when a rather lowly dealer examined the pot carefully and declared it certainly wasn't old, in fact it was a quite recently produced mustard pot and the initials M.J.D.D. stood for Moutarde Jaune de Dijon.

There is another example concerning a piece of apparently old worm-eaten wood, supposedly a sign-board. The inscription, evidently the work of a jester, ran thus:

```
I.C.I. . . . . . . . . . . . . . .E. . . . . . . . .S
T.L. . . . . . . . . .E. .C.H. . . . . . . . .E
M. . . . . . . . . . . . . . .I.N. . . . . .D. .E.
S.A. . . . . . . . . . . .N. .E. . . . . . . . .S.
```

A number of learned art historians came up with erudite explanations as to what the obliterated letters could be, and they reconstructed ancient inscriptions, verses and what have you. This riddle was eventually solved by quite a simple person who was completely unacquainted with the mystique of reading ancient inscriptions. He just read the letters straight off as they stood and came up, of course, with:

ICI EST LE CHEMIN DES ANES (This is the way for asses)

An impertinent little device, which apparently caught a naïve collector, was used by a dealer who offered the innocent buyer a large and impressive religious painting, saying that it was 'un tableau de sainteté d'après l'Apocalypse' (a sacred picture after the Apocalypse). *'D'après l'Apocalypse?'* exclaimed the young ignorant tyro, to which the completely unabashed dealer promptly replied, 'Yes, sir, Apocalypse; a German painter not very well known in Paris, but highly esteemed abroad.'

Since a study of the genuine can be one of the safeguards to prevent being taken for an expensive ride, so it would considerably help if there were displays of fake objects. Museums in some countries have already started the practice of having forgery collections where these frauds can be thoroughly examined and where possible compared with true objects in their same categories – a further process for training the eye. All too often museums and galleries that have fallen for a fake, hide them away in their basements in shame, a course that could do much more to encourage fakers than by publicly displaying them.

Essential to the faker or spurious imitator is a carefully rigged salon or setting where the disposal can take place. A contrived atmosphere of opulence, quality and a general feeling of being quite above suspicion is carefully created. In this environment the seller can use his inventive powers, his fertile imagination, working on his client with suggestion, salted perhaps with false information, misleading glamour with details of previous owners, a display of invented documents, an aura in general in which the artistic importance of the object is grossly exaggerated. In this context it is not always documents that are fitted to the faked art, sometimes the case is reversed and the faker invents in order to fit a genuine document. The same procedure is followed with the placing of signatures, guild marks and craftsmen's marks.

There have been numerous cases of mark and signature fiddling. There was the clay group featuring a satyr and a nymph by Clodion which was sold in perfectly good faith by Monsieur Maillet du Boullay to Madame Boiss, another dealer. This was to end with a lively scene in court. Monsieur Boullay had bought the group some years previously and when it went to Madame Boiss she had it for five years and found no buyer. Strangely enough after this rather lengthy period she found the clay statuette was not by Clodion, but in all probability the work of a well-known faker of Clodion's, Lebroc, and with closer examination she found that there was a small piece bearing a signature and date, both by the hand of Clodion, which had been skilfully inserted at the side of the group, the join being hidden by careful patination and some applied colour. The purchase money, however, was not refunded; the reason – the court accepted the theory advanced by Monsieur Senard, acting for Monsieur Boullay, that Madame Boiss had had the enjoyment of the possession of the group for a long time, and perhaps put forward her claim because she had not been able to sell it.

Some steps the neophyte can take to prevent an artistic robbery have been suggested earlier. To the previous advice can be added: searching in libraries, purchasing as many books as can be afforded, learning about the history, the manufacture and other technical details of the objects he collects, also finding books that can point to the types of deceipt that are around and show the traps that are laid. But if he chooses his sources and suppliers with care, he will find that there are certainly far more honest dealers in the antique market than one would think. The only snag is that it is the dishonest ones who seem to be in the fore and ever ready to meet and rob the novice. Yet this hazard of being taken in by a clever fake continues to exist. Sadly collectors rich or poor, untrained or experienced, will at times buy unpedigreed works, so also will directors and curators of museums and galleries.

The fact is that the demand, not just for any works of art but for works of art in a much looser sense, grossly exceeds the possible supply. The odd forger working in a little studio or some well-hidden workshop just can't meet this demand and so there have been factories for fake-making for several hundred years. They exist for paintings, weapons and armour, ceramics, furniture, almost any art object that can be named, and amongst the foundations on which they have been built are quite simply ignorant judgment and plain greed. Certainly, in the past centuries, particularly earlier, Italy held pride of place as the art object fake factory for the world. In the days of the early emperors there were the masons making excellent copies of early Hellenistic art for sale to the rich. But nearer our own time was a factory specialising in Etruscan works, which was run by the Riccardi cousins from Orvieto, who collaborated with Alfredo Adolfo Fioravanti. Amongst other objects they produced were the Three Etruscan Warriors exhibited at the Metropolitan Museum of Art in New York from 1933–61. Their work continues today, and in fact one of the leading craftsmen, who shall be nameless, has had notable conquests including some Etruscan paintings on terracotta that cost a collector well over half a million pounds.

Those who gather the extraordinary, the exotic, are very much a prey to the faker who specialises in such objects. Among other weird creations is recorded a basilisk, that strange volatile, mythological animal. One was made by a charlatan, a cheat called Tartaglio. Withered little mermaids have turned up pickled in bottles of alcohol and on inspection generally appear to be half a monkey sewn on to a fish's tail. Other curiosities include Abelard's jawbone and Samson's wig. Currently, there is the vogue for shrunken heads of the Jivaros of Eastern Ecuador. The genuine articles of these macabre exhibits are made by carefully removing the skin from the scalps which is then shrunk by application of hot sand over a period of weeks, and finally this skin is formed into a miniature face, almost completely hidden by the long hair. These objects were originally used by the Indians as part of a magic ritual: they believed that the power of a murdered enemy was inherited by his killer. Some Indians have realised there is considerable profit for them in this trade and are not only going in for murder to provide the raw materials, but are also faking the shrunken heads, using the skin of a certain long-haired ape.

It doesn't matter how strange or way out the object is. If a demand suddenly arises for it and the genuine supply dries up, the faker will very soon meet it. Collectors and museums have in the past, and are still today, coming across false exhibits in such various categories as bookbindings, paperweights, snuff boxes, customs stamps, share certificates, lace, locks and carpets.

Records show that the instructional literature for the faker is not all that far behind that for the genuine artist or craftsman. In the Stockholm Museum is an Egyptian papyrus of the pre-Christian era that gives workable recipes for imitating precious stones by using various coloured glasses. During Julius Caesar's rule in Rome there were a number of small factories for producing coloured gems and there exists information regarding the making of false pearls in pre-Mycenaean times.

Ever since the beginning of art forgery, both authorities and victims have tried to take steps to blot it out. Today this struggle is as determined as ever. On one side you have the scientists with all the up-to-date equipment for detection; on the other side you have the crafty faker who is trying to be one step ahead of the scientist and to produce yet another puzzle for him. In the middle you have the collectors, the directors of the museums and galleries, and sometimes to a degree they may unwittingly lean towards helping the forger. Is anyone who has taken costly advice, and perhaps spent a large sum of money in a blaze of publicity, going to admit publicly that they have bought a fraud? And here the public themselves appear to be on the side of the forger too, because there is something glamorous about someone who can apparently produce a work of art which to all intents and purposes is the equal of the work of one of the great masters of the past or today. After all, the public can salve its conscience, the crime of the forger is not violent, it is just cunning.

The struggle is further complicated by the fact that however brilliant an analyst the scientist may be in his laboratory, he first has to be alerted by the trained eye of the connoisseur or historian. What do these two go by? They will say things aren't quite right stylistically, and here is a very difficult barrier for the forger to pass. If the art expert is highly skilled and has had a great many years of study in a particular field, a forger who is setting out to produce a fake of a sixteenth-century painting has to be not only an accomplished art historian on period styles, but he must also know the exact materials, pigments, oils, varnishes, canvasses and woods which an early painter would have used. More than this he must be ever watchful that he doesn't include some small anachronism in costume, hairstyle, jewellery, furniture or domestic detail. Perhaps even harder, he must somehow insert himself into the mind and make-up of that long distant master. Today it is very difficult for him to see as that original artist saw, but if he is to succeed and get past the watchful eye, it is essential that this time-gap is bridged.

The hardest problem of all with painting is to be able to achieve the verve that the original artist can put into his work. The slashing, long-flowing brush strokes of Rubens were very easy for Rubens but not quite so easy for someone a century later or today. Often a slight hesitancy in the brush work or the modelling can alert a watchful eye, which picks out where the forger has had to feel his way along the lines and in so doing has squeezed out the life from a composition. There is yet another point: a true work of art, whether it is a painting, drawing, print, sculpture or some exquisite piece of craft, grows naturally under the hand of its creator through various stages until it arrives at its final form. To some eyes that final form may not appear totally finished, but the creating artist knows it is finished, for he is aware in some subtle way that if he goes any further he will, by 'licking up', adding little finicky details, suppress the excitement, the inspiration, which he has captured. Against this, the forger to a large degree works in a reverse manner, starting from the final result, and holding this in mind, without going through the growth development of the genuine work.

As well as his techniques the forger has two weapons which can cause a fair amount of confusion. The first of these is restoration. For some strange reason a work of art (of whatever type) which has been restored has an almost gilt-edged guarantee of authenticity as far as the public is concerned. If they look at a marble statue showing signs of hacking and mending, or a painting with obvious areas of damage that have been treated, they are well on the way to believing that whatever else is wrong the piece must be genuine. The forger here takes advantage of this situation and will, having created his fake, sometimes deliberately break it or damage it, and then put it through the normal processes of restoring.

A second trick is to make a pastiche; this means taking various parts from areas of other works by masters and putting them together as some sort of a whole. If this is not done with skill the pastiche can usually be picked up because it lacks a satisfactory harmonious composition; for instance, if it is a group of sculpture, the sense of rhythm may be broken. But skilfully done, it can very often mislead, because the expert may look at a picture or other work and feel that he sees in it the hand of such-and-such a master, and probably he undoubtedly does see a resemblance in certain areas. Then another expert will come along and think he sees the hand of a different master; he probably also sees a similarity to the work of his artist or craftsman; and so a great deal of confusion and argument can be caused and at times the forger escapes detection.

Among the principal weapons the scientist can use once he has been alerted are various types of photography: photomicrography and macrophotography, the former means quite simply taking a photograph through a microscope and the latter enables a life-size image of an object or area to be taken on the negative. This allows for a very high definition on a print.

Photography can also be coupled with ultra-violet and infra-red rays and, of course, with X-rays. This last is still probably the anti-fake device most feared by the forger; for under examination by X-ray everything that he has done in the way of preparing his support with its wood or canvas, early build-up layers of the ground and his painting method will be shown up. He may try various ideas to confuse the scientist; chemical salts can be scattered, metal foils can be inserted between the ground and support for the wood panel, although both these, particularly the latter, would quickly raise suspicion, as they would interfere with the passage of the X-rays. An advantage of the X-ray technique is that it is non-destructive and can be used to examine all types of object, from early frail antiquities to furniture, paintings, and textiles. The technique with corroded or grossly grimed specimens will show up hidden decoration and inlays. A skilled operator can very soon learn to 'read' the tonal densities and relate them to particular materials.

Ultra-violet rays are one of the simplest devices to use and are comparatively cheap and will readily show up recent restoration, retouching, alterations and additions, with not only pictures, but also ceramics and furniture. An ultra-violet lamp kit will be found with many dealers, as a first defence against deception. The ray is artificially produced by employing a mercury vapour lamp and the radiation is a band that is just beyond the visible range on the violet end of the spectrum. The examination or photography by ultra-violet radiation takes place in a darkened room, care being taken to protect the eyes. The photography using ultra-violet rays can be done in two different ways; the fluorescent-light method and the reflected-light. With the former a filter is placed over the lens of the camera which will absorb reflected ultra-violet rays but at the same time allow photographs to be taken of the visible fluorescence that comes up. The reflected-light method is carried out with the ultra-violet light being thrown back from whatever is being examined. A filter is used on the lens of the camera which this time will let the ultra-violet radiation through to the film but will stop visible radiation. It can be a quite exciting experience to take a suspect piece of art in for ultra-violet examination. Under a fairly strong hand-glass the object may appear quite all right, yet when the ultra-violet light is thrown upon it, alterations to the surface of ceramics, changes in inlays, retouches on pictures, changed areas of sculpture at once become visible as the areas fluoresce brightly.

Infra-red photography is particularly useful for examining paintings as it will penetrate the various layers of an oil and will quite clearly show up underpainting and initial drawing, both areas in which the forger very often comes adrift either through lack of knowledge or lack of patience.

The chemical analyst can often expose a fake; for example, of an ancient statuette, presumably of bronze that turns out to be some other strange alloy, probably one not known at the time when it was supposed to have been made. The same can apply to paintings, where with the use of various analytical techniques not only the entire range of pigments can be certified, but also the oils and varnishes and other substances that the artist mixed with them.

Probably, the one single most useful aid to the art historian is to have an accurate dating of his object, particularly if it is thought to be a hundred years or more old. Works including wood can be given a fairly accurate placing by dendrochronology, tree-ring dating. This certainly applies to furniture that is supposed to be three or four hundred years old: ring dating can produce a satisfactory and near-accurate answer. It works by counting the annual rings produced by the tree as it grows. These can be affected in thickness by dry and wet years, drought tending to form a narrow ring and a very wet year a wider one. The rings also tend to become thinner as the age of the tree increases. It was the American De Witt Clinton who did much pioneer work in this field. Early timber buildings in Germany were dated to about AD1300 by the work carried out on larch trees in the Bavarian Alps around Berchtesgarten. A bronze age lake dwelling at Buchau was dated in the same way.

Particularly in the field of pottery antiquities, which has been infested with forgeries, a dating method was badly needed, and this need was met by what is called thermoluminescence. To watch this being applied invokes a slight aura of the supernatural. In short, the method is this: there are traces of radioactive material such as uranium or thorium salts in most substances and some minerals have the property of being able to store in their crystalline structure energy produced by this radioactivity and it can be released in the form of light when heat is applied. One point against thermoluminescence is that a small portion of the object being examined has to be destroyed. Many of the substances need to be heated to over $640\,°F$ to produce this thermoluminscent faint glow. In fact it may be too slight for the eye to pick it up but very sensitive meters can measure the intensity, and the brighter the light given off when the sample is heated the older it is. This will not give an extremely accurate dating but will give a useful period band.

Probably the most celebrated method of time-telling is Radiocarbon Dating, which has been particularly successful on various artifacts from the past. This was developed by an American scientist Willard F. Libby just after the last war and is principally of use on archaeological objects of considerable age that have some carbon in their make-up. The method relies on the fact that carbon in the air and tissues of living organisms have a few atoms of what is known as heavy carbon. The amount may be very small indeed. Chemically the two carbons are similar, only differing in atomic weight: ordinary carbon is 12 and heavy carbon 14. Heavy carbon is radioactive, which means that over a considerable period of time its atoms have gradually broken down by the emission of Beta rays in the process that is termed radioactive decay. Research has shown that decay and loss of radioactivity takes place in a regular manner following the law of radioactive decay which is shown by the so-called half-life. With carbon 14 half-life is 5600 years. Libby found that by employing a meter that was very similar to a highly sensitive Geiger counter he was able to measure the radioactivity of heavy carbon in a sample of an ancient wood and then compare the results with modern wood and a very old known substance such as anthracite, which for all practical purposes has lost its radioactivity. By applying the law of radioactive decay to the findings he could find out approximately when the particular tree that provided the sample had been felled. Carbon dating will not exactly point to one year, though the results have a standard deviation and give an area of around 300 years in which the period will lie. Stonehenge I – the outer bank – was dated by this method to around 2750 BC. It is of interest that the late T. C. Lethbridge, by using a dowser's pendulum sometime before the carbon dating, came up with practically the same answer.

CHAPTER TWO

ANTIQUITIES

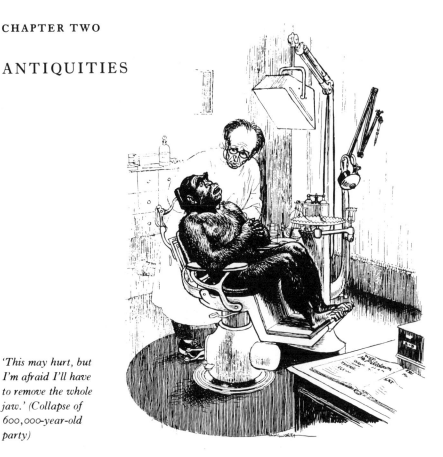

'This may hurt, but I'm afraid I'll have to remove the whole jaw.' (Collapse of 600,000-year-old party)

Until the nineteenth century, with the growth of archaeological activity, of privately financed 'digs' and government-sponsored expeditions, the collecting of antiquities had not been seriously followed. Now, with new conquests of the spade producing treasures and rarities, a demand for these early artefacts has mushroomed, and there has been plenty of evidence of the maxim that the market makes the forger.

Among the lines that became popular were flint tools from the old and new Stone Ages. The supply of the real thing soon became minimal and faking of these early implements started in the quarries of Saint Acheul near Amiens. But the master of this craft was an Englishman, Edward Simpson, who also went by the names of 'Flint Jack' and 'Fossil Willy', 'Snake Billy', 'Shirtless' and 'Cockney Bill'. He was born at Sleights, near

Whitby, in 1815, and in his early teens he worked for a Dr Young, a local geologist. This gave him a taste for collecting fossils and early artefacts; also for selling to the dealers. Flint Jack was a strange character; a mild, rather gentle-looking figure, and one who had his own personal and novel moral code. He found that there was a ready market for flint implements of different types and he soon developed a considerable skill in the fashioning of flints. He was to claim that his 'original fakes', as he called them, were so good that they had been bought by the British Museum. The products from the Amiens factory brought forth his scorn. He professed that he could pick them out, and also pointed to how poor they were. In one case, his anger was aroused when he found that the quarry workers in France were even altering original Stone Age implements to make them more saleable. Today it is unlikely that a 'Flint Jack' would get past an expert, because so much more is known about the characteristic patina on such implements, which is the result of thousands of years. The hard surface of the flint itself is almost impossible to patinate artificially; therefore a flint worked even a hundred or a hundred and fifty years ago is going to be a long way from the original in appearance. Different conditions of the ground in which the flints are found govern the resulting patination when worked. Flints from peaty areas have a dark brown patina; those from chalk deposits, when first excavated, show a deep black tone which fades after about ten years' exposure to the light; those in arid areas take on a soft sheen, largely produced by the action of wind and dust, which will be almost impossible for the forger to simulate.

But Flint Jack had a remarkable success in his own time, and latterly broadened out, producing such items as a Roman breastplate made from an old tray. He worked with a dealer in East Anglia, and claimed that together they sold a large number of forged objects such as urns and Roman milestones which found a ready market.

The search into the antecedents of prehistoric man brought some strange capers; perhaps none more peculiar than the so-called 'Piltdown' skull. Here there is a strange quirk on the part of a forger. In 1908 the fever for the search for early man was at its height and at Piltdown near Brighton a solicitor, Charles Dawson, a keen collector and archaeologist, stated he had dug out of a gravel-pit a portion of a human skull, which appeared to have great age. Three years afterwards more fragments were found, which were thought to belong to the same skull, and then a year later the English anthropologist, Sir Arthur Smith Woodward, dug up a portion of a lower jaw with two teeth still in place. Twelve months went by and Teilhard de Chardin, a Jesuit, found one human front tooth. About the same time Charles Dawson came up with a couple of nasal bones. In 1915 he found further fragments of the skull and another tooth, only this time a mile and a half away from the original excavation in the quarry at Piltdown.

The claim by Charles Dawson and Smith Woodward was that all the fragments belonged to one skull. Considerable argument was engendered as experts pointed out the difference in site of some of the fragments, and also that the forehead lacked the typical Neanderthal eyebrow swellings, and further, that there was a contrast between the ape-like jaw and the well-developed cranium. At a meeting of the Geological Society in 1912 Dawson addressed a large audience and put forward a case to back his suggestions. The quarry at Piltdown was dated by fragments of animal teeth and old flint tools. The supposition was that the skull could be no less than at least 500,000 years old. Dawson was supported by Smith Woodward, who at that time was working at the Natural History Museum in London, and in conclusion the skull was called *Eoanthropus Dawsoni*. Records of the Manchester *Guardian* at the time state, 'Piltdown man is incontrovertible evidence of the ape-origins of man. This must clearly be the oldest, the first Englishman.' To an extent the First World War halted the investigation. A number of experts expressed doubts and there were several attempts to reconstruct the skull in various shapes, using the bone fragments rather in the manner of a blind jigsaw. In the period between the two wars more and more doubt was cast; one of the theories being that the lower jaw didn't really match up with the cranium. One German professor was adamant that the skull could be human but the jaw was from an ape. Another German scientist, H. Weinhert, was convinced that the skull was authentic. He continued in this opinion and in 1952 published a book, *Primitive History of Man* in which he stated: 'The lower jaw of Piltdown man is not really so ape-like. It could be the jaw of a *homo sapiens* of similar type.'

Around this time scientific detection entered the field in the hands of two English anthropologists, Hopkins and Oakley. Amongst other tests they applied to minute fragments of the skull was that for fluorine. This substance will combine with phosphoric calcium in bones, gradually increasing in content, so that the older the bone the greater percentage of fluorine. Their findings showed that the percentage of fluorine present was minute; this would indicate that the age of the bones could be nowhere near 500,000 years or even 100,000 years. In 1953 a second fluorine test was run and the result pointed conclusively to modern bone. Further analysis showed substances such as gelatine, which could be expected in fairly new bones, and more than that the sample drill had brought an odour of scorching horn. It became clear that the jaw was not from a very early Briton but an orang-utang – a fact picked up by *Punch* with a caricature of an early ape-like Mr Piltdown sitting in a dentist's chair and the dentist saying, 'This may hurt, but I'm afraid I'll have to remove the whole jaw.' Mr Oakley went on to show that the jaw had been given a faker's 'restoring' treatment. It had been broken on purpose and then tinted a dull brown in an effort to simulate age. The only trouble was that the colour had remained on the surface and hadn't penetrated into the bone, as it would have done with a genuine article.

The interest then centred on the cranium. Fluorine tests here showed that the amount could indicate an age of several thousand years, but whether or not it was the skull of a Briton or some visitor from the Continent would be impossible to decide. The Piltdown skull had now been proved to be an elaborate pastiche, but to what purpose? Who was the faker and what was his reason? Obviously he must be a scholar with an advanced knowledge of anthropology. The pundits ruled out Dr Smith Woodward and suspicion turned on Charles Dawson, which was all rather disturbing for the specialist scholars. The Government had made the Piltdown quarry a national monument, and Dawson, who had died in 1916, had had a memorial erected in his honour in 1938 on the site of his famed excavation. Later digs there have found nothing more to corroborate the earlier findings.

The learned world of archaeology was split asunder; about three hundred papers were produced on Piltdown man. Some defended the name of Dawson against the accusations, stating that the man himself had been taken for a ride by another forger. Theories and accusations flew in all directions: Dawson had experimented in bone hardening; Dawson had found the fragments in East Anglia and buried them in the secondary layer of the quarry at Piltdown; and so on. Today most experts would say that it was Dawson who had produced this rather sour joke on the anthropologists. His reasons? Exhibitionism, or to attain a recognised quality of scholarship; his name had also been quoted in connection with the sighting of a sea serpent and the discovery of a petrified toad; he had been caught up in the writing of a thesis on a fake Roman statuette, and he had tried to cross a goldfish and a carp. Like a number of famous forgeries, the Piltdown puzzle is not yet completely solved in some minds.

In September 1978 a recording was played to a learned assembly attending a seminar at Reading University. In stunned silence they listened to the voice of a dead man. It was that of Professor James Douglas who had died earlier in the year, at the age of ninety-three. He had been the assistant to Professor William Sollas, Professor of Geology at Oxford from 1897 to 1937. Douglas claimed that Sollas had carried out the Piltdown hoax as part of a personal feud with Sir Arthur Woodward Smith, former Keeper of Geology at the British Museum. Sollas apparently knew Charles Dawson and it was suggested they had collaborated in the hoax; Sollas having more detailed knowledge, Dawson had, in fact, supplied Sollas with the chemical for staining the 'skull'. The feud between Sollas and Woodward Smith must have been long standing, for there had been another hoax played on the same victim. This was a semi-fossil bone on which two boys from Sherborne School had scratched a horse's head. They told one of Sollas's assistants it was to fool their science master, who had been taken in and sent the bone to Woodward Smith. Sollas allowed Woodward Smith to publish a paper on the engraved bone, which was read to the Geological Society in London. The truth was only revealed ten years later in Sollas's book *Ancient Hunters*.

An earlier adventurer into fossils was Johann Adam Beringer, a Doctor of Philosophy and Medicine, at Würzburg. He was to be one of the earliest respected scholars to be taken for a ride by forgery. In 1725 three boys from the village of Eibelstadt near Würzburg came to see him with a number of what appeared to be small fossilised creatures. Beringer's excitement encouraged a hoard of these early 'fossils' to be collected, with a seeding of the genuine ones amongst them. They came from soft sandstone beds and included some rather strange examples of small fishes and animals; also insects such as spiders with their webs, and even the sun, moon and comets. It was fairly blatant forgery; in fact there were still marks of the tools that had been used which would, of course, be totally absent from genuine fossils. But at first Beringer was so carried away by his thrill at the finds that he produced a learned paper which was published and dedicated to the Prince Bishop of Würzburg. Perhaps in this there is a slight sign that he was not a hundred per cent certain, as he included the sentiment that he was now leaving his discoveries to the experts, and would be glad to have their opinions on this strange business. It seems no sooner had he written his book than the murky secret was out. The fakes had been produced by some local 'craftsman' at the instigation of two brother professors of Beringer's, Ignaz Roderique and Johann Georg von Eckart. The purpose of their deception had been nothing more grandiose than to show Beringer up as a fool. The unfortunate man tried to buy up all the copies of his book, but after his death a second edition was published. The tailpiece here is that his fossils, like many another fake, became eagerly sought after as collectors' items.

Amber has been used as a form of jewellery and adornment from very early times, and particularly during the Renaissance and late medieval period lumps of amber which had enclosed tiny reptiles or small animals, insects and the like, were very much sought after. Again, the forger saw an opening for ready cash, and early in the sixteenth century one of these craftsmen produced a lump of amber apparently enclosing a small frog. The target was the Duke of Mantua, but it was rather a bad fake and was shown up in 1558. The method for these false enclosures within amber is quite simple. A lump of this material is cut in half with a fine saw and then the two halves are suitably hollowed out. Into this space is put the insect, or object, to be enclosed, the remaining space being filled with a resin similar to the amber; then, the two halves can just be stuck together again. Examination with a magnifying glass can very often disclose the cut; also some of the fakes are so carelessly made that bubbles of air have been left inside, a fact which gives them away at once.

Early man had a liking for engraving drawings of animals – perhaps as a memento of his skill as a hunter. An example of this early art form was discovered in a cave at Le Chaffaud in the Department of Vienne by an archaeologist Brouillet in 1845. Another learned gentleman, Monsieur Lartet, published a paper on this bone engraving in 1861 which produced a somewhat unexpected result. Forgers are, on the whole, very wise to the trends of fashion, publicity and the rest, and one nineteenth-century fellow must have sensed that here was a coming market. Within three years of the publication of the engraving of the genuine Old Stone Age work a small cache of engraved bones came to light in Le Chauffaud. The possible success of the forgeries was somewhat spoiled, for included with them was a bone engraved with Sanskrit symbols.

The discovery of caves as possible sites of the art of early man brought a wave of examinations of such places. In 1874 a teacher, an amateur archaeologist, Karl Merk, began looking in a cave near Thayngen, known as the Kessler Hole. Very soon he found a number of flint and bone artefacts which dated from the Magdalenian period. He also found bone engravings of a deer and a wild horse. But Herr Merk showed his excitement too freely in front of his workmen. He also made the mistake of paying them a bonus of two francs for everything they found that was worthwhile. The work in the cave itself was apparently complete; there remained, however, at the mouth of the cave and outside a certain amount of debris from the excavation, and in this one of Merk's workmen 'found' some rather strange bone engravings: a recognisable seated bear and a seated fox. Merk was taken in and published his findings in the *Transactions of the Zurich Antiquarian Society* in 1876, which brought a riposte almost at once from a Professor Lindenschmit, who happily pointed out that he recognised the engravings of the fox and the bear as being copied from a children's book *Zoos, Menageries and their Inmates*. This particular case and others like it so much upset the academic and learned experts that when the Altamira cave paintings were discovered near the village of Santander in Northern Spain in 1879, the fount of wisdom in such matters dismissed the discovery as a fake and a trap. In fact, when copies of the paintings were laid before the International Congress for Anthropology and Pre-Historic Archaeology in Lisbon, the assembled gentlemen put them out of court as an amusing joke. They have long since been proved beyond question as dating back to the Upper Magdalenian period from around 12,000 BC. These and other cave paintings of a similar nature are remarkable for their spontaneity and accuracy, particularly in depicting movement. The materials the long-forgotten artists used would have been very simple; not much more than mineral-coloured clays, and charred sticks from a fire, put on perhaps with chewed twigs or pieces of fur as well as fingers, and possibly bound with fat or blood.

A still earlier art form produced by man which has drawn the attention of the fakers is that of the Venus figurine. The earliest known of these small objects date from around 25,000 to 22,000 BC, the Aurignacian period. One of the most celebrated is the 'Venus of Willendorf' from Austria. This is a carving in limestone measuring only $4\frac{3}{8}''$ in height. Stylistically these are difficult sometimes to detect as forgeries. There is the apparently clumsy engraving of the so-called Venus of Bautzen; this is worked on a piece of flat Silurian quartzite. It was found at a depth of about 13' in a sand quarry near Bautzen. In many ways the protuberant stomach and short, squat, figure resemble the genuine articles such as the Willendorf example. This fraud was shown up when a geologist examined the area from where it was supposed to have been excavated and found that the deposits pointed to a period around 500,000 years ago which rather speedily put the Venus of Bautzen out of the running.

Another odd deceit that could only bear fruit in some scholastic jousting was concerned with Neolithic cremation-graves. The first of these rather strange places came to light in 1907 when Gustav Wolf came up with the fact that in South Wetterau he had found incinerated remains of the later Danubian civilisation. His so-called cremation-graves were little more than flat round holes with rather minute amounts of ash. Undeterred he went on and just before the First World War he had 'identified' a hundred. In so much esteem was his opinion held that his findings were included in the syllabuses of schools and universities and they had a long run; it wasn't until 1954 that doubt was expressed. Then it was pointed out that this whole method of very ancient corpse disposal was really the brainchild of Wolf. But he too had also been deceived; his co-excavator, Bausch, had been pulling a fast one on him. Sadly, Wolf was totally taken in by his collaborator. Late in his life he gave, in writing, the credit for the 'discovery' of these cremation-graves in the area between the Lower Main of the Weser to the sharp eyes of the excavator Bausch.

There was another burial place mystery. In the 1920s a small shallow oval pit about 9' long and 3' wide was excavated near the little village of Glozel in the Madeleine Hills about twelve miles south-east of Vichy. It contained fragments of pottery and also glass, some of the broken pieces showing signs of having been melted. Nearby was found a small stone pickaxe and a stone slab with what appeared to be ancient man-made marks on it. The discovery was made on 1 March 1924 by Emil Fradin, a farmer, when he was ploughing. On 15 March Mademoiselle Picandet, a school mistress, brought her pupils to the site and expounded her theory that here had been discovered an immense incineration grave, and thus she set in motion the making of a far-reaching fake. She told her professional superiors, and on 9 July the President of the Société des Amis des Bourbonnais heard of it and sent a Monsieur Clément to inspect. He returned supporting the incineration theory of Mlle Picandet. Gradually the area became notorious and was visited by numbers of people, some wanting to carry on a dig. The canny farmer saw a possibility of a little easy money and started asking a fee of fifty francs, somewhat extortionate, for two days excavation. On 28 July, a Monsieur Viple visited Glozel and when he saw the remains of the pit came to the conclusion it was an ancient glass kiln. In fact he sent samples for examination. Next to enter the picture was a Doctor Morlet of Vichy. He visited the site and decided that it must be pre-Gallo-Roman. He was told by the Fradins of other finds in the same area; a clay pitcher was included. The good doctor became so excited that he told the Fradin family they had a most important property in their possession and advised them to put a fence around the land, as they could make a good deal of money and might have international scholars coming on pilgrimages as they did to Java to see *Pithecanthropus*, the ape-man. On 28 April 1925 Morlet entered into a contract with the farmer's family which gave him sole rights of excavation for up to nine years at an annual rent of two hundred francs. He was careful to see that the agreement included rights of photography and publication in respect of all articles found, and found they were. As the digging progressed, there appeared carved bones, strange stone slabs with indecipherable markings, pebbles with crude drawings of reindeer, and bits and pieces of pottery. The arrival of the reindeer engravings now persuaded the excavator that the site dated back to 30,000 years BC, because it had always been taken for granted that reindeer became extinct at the end of the Old Stone Age.

A Dutch specialist entered the arena and took impressions of the inscribed characters, and after examining them carefully, he announced that the characters gave intimate details of the lives of an early people.

These people he felt were likely to have been Jews of partly Aramaic descent who might have worked in the turquoise mines of Mount Sinai. They could have been brought to France by the Phoenicians, as slaves, and then settled in the Phoenician colony of Sen at the mouth of the Rhône. From there they probably migrated northwards, at first up the river and later by land, finally establishing themselves in the Glozel district.

The French government was so impressed by the findings that it declared the site to be of the greatest importance and prohibited access to it; then the cast involved in this charade started to grow. A surgeon, an amateur archaeologist, was certain the Glozel finds were fraudulent and he made a rather loose accusation of deceipt against some person or persons unknown. The police now entered the act, searched the house of the farmer and took away a large number of excavated items. Other objects, such as stone axes, engraved bones and slabs, were exhibited in a nearby barn. The forces of opinion continued to gather. An international committee was arranged for the specific task of carrying out a thorough investigation of the site and of the objects found. Included in this were experts such as the Parisian archaeologist Salomon Reinach, the geologist Dépéret of the University of Lyons, the British early Greek specialist Dr Foat and a Latin scholar, Audollent, of Clermont University.

Once again the laymen had the somewhat disturbing and sometimes amusing experience of witnessing top brains disputing what seemed to be an unimportant case. The Swedish expert criminologist Harry Söderman felt that, as there was no sign of disturbed layers of soil where the objects were found, their authenticity must be proven. The committee satisfied themselves that all was in order and Glozel could be recorded as a genuine site. But now came the crunch; the findings of Monsieur Bayle of the Paris Police Laboratory. He announced that amongst other things a piece of aniline-dyed cotton thread had come to light on one of the clay slabs, also a potato seed. Chlorophyll had been identified in the clay, an impossibility if it had been fired. Pottery, including some of the inscribed tablets, was unfired; in fact, on being placed in water it very soon fell apart. A tablet with a root showed that the forger had bored a hole and then inserted the root and filled up the hole. The expert examination indicated that metal tools had been used in the decoration of the pots. Now one side of the

Top: Glozel investigations under way. Bottom: The Fradin family in front of their museum

scholastic argument declared vociferously that the finds at Glozel were one of the biggest frauds in history. But the opposition were adamant that all was genuine. Dr Morlet and Salomon Reinach were amongst those who were certain that the Neolithic culture coming to light at Glozel was absolutely authentic.

Little Glozel became notorious. The press had a field day with such headlines as 'A community fights for its honour', 'Bayle's irresponsible dilettantism', and even the cabaret singers of Montmartre referred to it in cheeky ballads. But still, as with many other such, mystery hangs over it. There are some unexplained facts. Undoubtedly, the objects found were forged, although some of the villagers who were making a good thing out of the barn museum continued their show. Experts for the authenticity asked 'Could a simple peasant labourer, so young, make these objects? Where did the reindeer bones come from?' Dr Morlet kept bravely on, even publishing in 1955 accusations against the professors who were for the total forgery. In November 1927 poor Dr Morlet had had another rebuff, because the Leipzig museum of local history came up with a rather weird clay box, said to be dug up in 1914. When he saw this he was convinced that it could be related to the finds that had been made at Glozel; but this little fake was shown up when a Dresden schoolmaster proved that it was a prank of his whilst a boy. But Morlet, still unconvinced, carried on with his belief in the authenticity of Glozel and its bits and pieces.

At the beginning of this century there was a story floating round the cafés of Paris concerning an example of how the eager and unwary collector can at times be very easily duped. There is no question that many fakers look upon their trade as not only a craft and even an art but also a kind of sport in which they play their moves to cheat and deceive the collector, the unwary dealer, the police and the rest. Many forgers are passably good psychologists and they can read the mind of a collector, often with surprising accuracy. This story that was current at the beginning of this century concerned a forged Rameses. A certain Parisian collector was the owner of a complete collection of Egyptian fine art objects, but he had let it be known that it wasn't quite complete and he would very much like to have an example of those huge Egyptian statues in basalt that can be found around the Nile. He was very rich and he had sent forth the information that this was what he wanted – two dangerous ingredients in the world of antique dealing. Notice of these facts came to the ear of a faker, who, to gratify this collector's longings, despatched an informant to report to him that a beautiful statue of heroic size of Rameses had been discovered near Thebes. The middleman wouldn't say where it was exactly, but he did say that the owner of this statue would give the collector first refusal and the statue was ready to be shipped at the very reasonable price of 100,000 francs. He accompanied this verbal information with a show of provenance, documents, stamps, letters, descriptive memoranda and the rest. The collector swallowed the bait. He made the middleman promise that the statue would be brought straight to his house and the whole thing would be conducted in secrecy, as inwardly he felt that if somebody else heard of this, then he might be outbid and might lose the fulfilment of a great desire of his acquisitive heart. Later the middleman gave him the information that the statue had reached the Paris railway station after its long journey via Naples, Genoa and Marseilles. The collector, nervous now, insisted that it should be brought to his house during the hours of darkness. He paid over the money as soon as the giant figure was delivered. But suspicion soon pointed to something drastically wrong. It was too new looking; the style was incorrect; modern tool-marks could be seen. Most of all, Rameses was made from not Egyptian basalt but clay-slate from near Angers.

'Finding' first by burial and then exhumation is by no means an uncommon trick of the forger. There have been two well-publicised examples. Just before the last War on 2 May 1937, a Monsieur Gonon, a farmer of St Just-sur-Loire, near Brizet, reported that whilst ploughing his turnip field a large block of stone started to appear. He had cleared away more of the earth and discovered a marble statue which became known as the Venus of Brizet and, more popularly, 'Venus of the Turnip Field'. Gentlemen of standing in the world of early Greek work, such as Georges Huisman and Noel Thiolier, examined the statue of the Venus and were ecstatic, saying that it was indeed genuine and dated from about the first century BC. It was bracketed together with the Venus de Milo and wild claims for the sculptor included the Greek Praxiteles. The farmer did well, exhibiting it for a small charge, and extravagant figures were quoted as to possible selling prices. But then came the disclosure, for, in 1938, a young Italian sculptor, Francesco Cremonese, hearing the city of Paris was about to buy this beautiful Venus, admitted that he had made the figure, using his young Polish girlfriend, Anna Studnicka as a model. This he had done apparently for the age-old reason of trying to convince the unbelieving that he had talent. With the help of his brother he buried the statue in the hope that it would somehow be discovered. But, yet again, the experts refused to have their scholarship confounded and stuck to their disbelief of the claims of the young sculptor. It wasn't until the end of 1938, when Francesco produced in the presence of reputable witnesses part of the nose, the lower part of the figure and also the left arm, which he had broken away before burial to give greater authenticity, as well as his girlfriend, that the professional historians had to admit defeat.

Just over a hundred years ago on the other side of the Atlantic, in 1869, near the small village of Cardiff in the State of New York, another buried figure turned up. This time a farmer said he was digging a well and claimed that he came across first of all a very large foot and gradually unearthed a figure of about 9' high which was afterwards found to weigh a ton and a half. As with the other finders of buried treasure in this category, he and his wife made quite a nice thing out of admission money to a tent which he erected over the place where the figure lay. He even produced a Red Indian who told stories for the eager ears of the crowds of how his forebears had battled against giants and captured them rather like wild animals in deep holes which they had dug. Once again the voices and opinions of experts cried out against each other. Was it a fake? Was it of a great age? Was it modern? It was Professor Marsh of Yale who was among the first to call it an outright fake and a friend of his, A. D. White, obtained a small fragment which was given a thorough analysis in a laboratory. This produced a surprising result. It was shown to be plaster of Paris and of very recent manufacture; moreover the giant had been skilfully patinated and stained. One would think that this discovery would have put an end to the belief of authenticity, but once again, as with some other forgery cases, those who have initially been duped are extremely reluctant to give up their opinion. The great Barnum himself became involved and bought the so-called Cardiff Giant for 37,000 dollars, promising the farmer a cut of future takings. When the story came out it showed that the farmer had a brother-in-law, George Hull, who had approached a craftsman, Edward

Burckhardt, in Chicago, and it was he who had made the figure of the giant. It had been carefully aged using amongst other substances sulphuric acid and eventually Hull, with Newell the farmer, had buried it in the field.

To complete a trio of strange disinterments there is the celebrated Irish Giant. This huge figure, 12′ 2″, with a chest of 6′ 6½″ and 4′ 6″ arms was supposedly dug up by a Mr Dyer whilst he was looking for iron ore in Co. Antrim in the 1870s. The giant had six toes on his right foot and weighed 2 tons 15 cwt. Mr Dyer found his discovery was more profitable than prospecting for ore and exhibited the figure in Dublin, and then brought him to England for showing first at Liverpool and Manchester and later in London. He got involved with a showman, Mr Kershaw, and a general fracas ensued as to the rights of exhibiting and ownership. The giant himself by contemporary reports was a weird sight, being partly draped. Whether this drapery was to protect the prudish Victorian eyes, or whether it was a part of the supposedly fossilised figure does not appear certain. The final whereabouts of this huge man seems lost as with many others behind the curtains of time. Undoubtedly Ireland is rich in giant legends and at several places graves for these super-beings are to be found, including one near the village of Drumcliffe, Co. Sligo, which is 38' in length.

There seems little end to the variety of antiquities to which the forger will turn his attention when he sees a market. The nineteenth century, amongst other fashions, called for Roman objects. It became almost a status symbol to possess something from the times of the Emperors. Excavations in Germany in the early part of the nineteenth century were undertaken by a builder by the name of Kaufmann, and for his ready customers he unearthed copies of the gods, Mercury, Minerva, Vulcan, and an eagle once purporting to be in the possession of a Legion, and later he produced literally sheaves of swords for the gullible.

In the district of Ascoli in Italy a huge hoard of Roman sling-shots came to light and the Berlin Museum bought more than four hundred of these. Here another international battle of know-how began; this time between the German authorities and the French. The production of the Ascoli sling-shots had been done with care. What had actually happened was the forgers had been in on the discovery of a Roman foundry for these missiles, which contained not only a large amount of lead, but also the moulds and other necessities for their manufacture. So the fakes were given a very authentic look indeed. In this instance, as they were using Roman lead, chemical analysis would have proved nothing. The deception, however, was finally uncovered, because the deceivers had followed a document that pertained to give instruction with regard to the stamping of the various names of the Legions and other details on the shots; these instructions were faulty, and the forgers repeated the errors that the earlier writer had made.

In the field of mass production of somewhat mundane objects, there is the collection of the unfortunate Italian antiquary Giovanni Battista Passeri, who lived between 1694 and 1780. He assembled the world's greatest collection of Roman terracotta lamps. These humble domestic items are very common and it is only when particular ones have some exciting characteristic or unusual decoration that collectors go for them. Strangely enough, practically every lamp in Passeri's collection was unusual and displayed novel symbols and signs. He was very pleased with his work in accruing this large number of 'unique' lamps, and he published a three-volume catalogue of the collection, which was used by scholars as a definitive authority on the subject. Suspicion, however, was later aroused by some of the inscriptions, especially in the case of one that was in the form of a bull's head. Earlier opinions had said that lamps made in this design had been dedicated to the goddess Artemis Taurobolos. The clue here was that the forger had been lax with his spelling of this lady's name.

Now and then, rather extraordinary cases come along where experts fall over one another to 'prove' the authenticity of a forgery. There was a case of an early Christian lamp which was in the shape of a fish and on one side it bore Christ's monogram and on the other a cross. Some historians put forward the theory that it stood as a symbol of Christ. Actually the faker had gone a bit further, he had put a tiny fish in the mouth of the larger one. But the scholars were ready for this, and explained that there was clear influence from the New Testament words, 'I will make you to become fishers of men'. This to some experts was final evidence as to the genuine quality of the lamp. The rather impertinent little forgery had passed the test and must originally have been made in quite a large edition, for it was purchased by a number of museums including the Berlin, which actually, somewhat unthinkingly, bought two.

Still dealing with clay antiquities, as recently as 1971 Turkish police arrested a man on the charge of producing forged pottery of the Anatolian Neolithic period, pertaining to be 7–8000 years old. In the previous years a number of museums in Europe and the United States, including the British Museum, the Ashmolean at Oxford and the Metropolitan Museum of Art in New York, and also numerous private collectors, had made purchases of these objects. The luckless buyers thought that they were purchasing genuine antique pottery that had been dug up at Hacilar in

South West Turkey where a prehistoric settlement and cemetery was being excavated. The site had been discovered in 1956 and excavations had started in 1957. Apparently the method the fakers had used was to infiltrate their forgeries into the excavations or to mix them with the genuine examples when they were en route to their new homes. Someone cast a doubt on these pieces and some sixty-six objects were submitted to thermoluminescent dating. These included painted bowls, figures and anthropomorphic vases. The result was a bit shattering for the buyers, as, out of the sixty-six pieces, forty-eight were shown to be modern fakes. Chemical analysis indicated that the clay they had been made from had a composition which was quite different from that of the authentic Hacilar pottery. A further clue was that some of the fakes had a white crusting which was soft and which could not have been acquired in the district where they were supposed to have been found.

The British Museum, like many another leading museum and gallery in the world, has bought its share of the spurious. In 1873 the BM had the chance to buy a sarcophagus which had been reputedly dug up at Cerveteri, the old Etruscan capital. It displayed excellent modelling in the manner of the fifth century BC. There must have been quite a lot of persuasive talk from a Roman middleman dealer which the English experts swallowed. The sarcophagus journeyed to London and was displayed with pride in the museum until 1935, when somewhat secretly it was removed from its place of honour and deposited in one of the voluminous cellars under the museum. What had come to light was that the Pinellis, a family of Italian stonemasons, had made this sarcophagus and others like it. Pietro, the head of the family, disclosed his knowledge of the deception, not only where the British Museum was concerned, but also the Louvre.

Tanagra figurines have for a long time been a favourite with forgers producing faked claywork. There seems to have been an uninterrupted line of deceivers since the time when the Tanagra work first came into fashion with collectors. These small figures were produced in the style of the late fourth and third centuries BC; many of them actually being cast from top-class originals. Some can be difficult to tell, particularly when they have been cast; but one way is that the cast which is being passed as a fraud will be slightly smaller, owing to the fact that the terracotta shrinks during the drying-out and the firing. Some of the more intelligent fakers have got round this give-away by a mechanical expanding of the moulds, but where this has taken place the work is not so perfect.

On 16 February 1923 the Metropolitan Museum in New York bought an accepted fine example of Greek art at its height. A bronze horse. The seller was a well-known dealer in Paris. The horse was said to date between 480 and 470 BC and was well backed up by scholarly writing and opinions and was in no way doubted either from the technical production of the cast or stylistically. For thirty-eight years it held pride of place in one of the galleries, It had been photographed, it had been reproduced in plaster, and thousands of copies had been sold. Then, suddenly, in 1961, someone raised a doubt. They pointed to two holes, one in the mane and the other in the forelock. These were supposedly for harness and would appear to be misplaced because the harness perhaps would have tied behind the ears and what the purpose of the forelock hole was, was uncertain. One expert put forward the theory that the casting was wrong and that the horse was a fake, and moreover, the forger, in doing his research, could have looked at the statues on the Acropolis, where the horses and female korai have similar holes at the top of their heads. Perhaps, it was suggested, the holes were intended to carry ornamental plumes and similar holes in the bronze horse were meant for this purpose too. This idea was somewhat shot down, when it was pointed out that the holes in the head of the sculptures on the Acropolis were meant for nothing more than to hold iron spikes to prevent pigeons perching.

Although these original doubts had been disposed of, there was still some unease, and a bronze founder from Brooklyn was called in. After examination, he put forward the theory that the horse could have been cast with a core of sand and clay which would have been held in position with iron wires while the molten bronze was poured. He added that a skilled forger, in order to hide his traces, would have cut back the ends of the wires and filled the surface with small bronze plugs. Magnets were used and they did indeed trace the direction of some internal iron or steel wires. This was backed up by radiography, which again pointed to the fact that the Met's bronze horse was a fake. But the evidence is not regarded as final and scholars and scientists work away; in fact, later examinations of the composition of the alloy and other factors, suggested to some that after all

45

The Greek bronze horse purchased by the Metropolitan Museum of Art

the horse was genuine; and so for the time being the little bronze horse can't be quite sure whether he is genuine or a bastard.

The fast growing collections of America and the numerous museums springing up all over that still expanding land must certainly provide the forger with his richest fields for harvest; yet it is not only the museums of the New World that can be taken for a painful ride by the faker. This is the story of yet another pastiche, this time in gold. At the end of February 1896 a Rumanian merchant, Schapschelle Hochmann, appeared in Vienna with an exquisite collection of antiquities which he said had been excavated from the ruins of the early Greek settlement of Olbia on the Black Sea. The finest of these was an exquisitely worked tiara. The provenance included the facts that in the second century BC the people had presented Saitaphernes, the Scythian chief, with this tiara, and there was a citation which was between the decorations: 'The Senate and People of Olbia to the Great Invincible Saitaphernes.' Other items included hornbook clasps, ear-rings, necklaces and rings. Yet again, the two teams, one for the genuine and the other for the fake, started to line up. The connoisseurs Count Wilczek and Baron Nathaniel Rothschild were certain it was genuine. Otto Benndorf, a well-known archaeologist, backed them up, and he concluded that it was an excellent piece of craftsmanship from pre-Christian times. Against the piece being genuine, amongst others, was the Director of the Museum in Vienna, Dr Bruno Buchner. He pointed to a certain oddity; that was that damaged areas were in parts which were free from decoration, while the exquisite repoussé work was undamaged. He pressed his opinion, stating that it was unlikely for a delicate piece of gold work like this to have been buried for two thousand years without overall damage, and told his governors he was against purchase for the museum.

Not disheartened, Hochmann got hold of two agents and sent them off to Paris with the tiara. Here he had better luck. The tiara was examined by two of the Louvre's top experts, M. A. Kaempfen and M. E. Héron de Villefosse, who both declared it to be genuine. They felt that here was an outstanding chance to snap up a great treasure for the Louvre, and very soon money was provided and the purchase consummated before the Russians might have time to raise objections about this historical treasure being taken away from their country. The Tiara of Saitaphernes was first

The Tiara of Saitaphernes

put on display in the Louvre in 1896 on a somewhat ironic date, 1 April.

More historians and connoisseurs entered the arena. Among the first was Professor Wesselovsky from the University of St Petersburg. He said – modern fake. He spoke from experience, as similar examples had turned up in Russian and Polish museums. The German archaeologist, Adolf Furtwängler, from Munich, was concerned by the fresh look of the gold; that very soft warm patination, typical of excavated gold articles from the distant past, was absent. He also pointed to what appeared to be anachronisms in the handling of the figures, the treatment of the anatomy, clothes and other details.

This question of anachronisms in forgeries of all types very often trips up even the most skilful forger, because to succeed in an elaborate piece such as this his knowledge and research must be considerable and, more than that, he must try somehow to see as nearly as possible as the craftsman of the period saw when making the original. He needs to understand the construction of the materials, how the gold plate was hammered out, what type of tools were used for the engraving and repoussé work and even how the craftsman held them, as this governs, to a high degree, the personal characteristics of a piece. Professor Stern of the Odessa Museum backed up Adolf Furtwängler. The opposing team of the genuine were joined by one of the keepers from the Hermitage in St Petersburg. The wordy skirmish went on for a number of years. Papers were written for and against; learned lectures delivered. Then in 1903 right out of the blue came an admission of manufacture from an Odessa goldsmith Israel Ruchomovski, who was born in Mosyr in 1860, and who had moved to Odessa in 1892. Apparently, he had been self-taught in the tricky art of gold and silversmithing and had attained a quality of workmanship equal to the best. He even volunteered to go to Paris to show his prowess, rather in the manner of Van Meegeren painting yet another Vermeer in prison. When he was questioned about the construction of the tiara, he accurately described his technique and the methods he had used, and also pointed to the original articles from which he had copied various pieces of decoration and motifs, thus making the tiara a pastiche, which had caused so much argument and confusion amongst the experts. He had created a master-piece of such quality that when the Louvre bought it they paid out 200,000 gold francs. The case of the 'Tiara of Saitaphernes' probably caused more waves of fear and uncertainty through the world of museums, galleries and collectors than any other fake.

In the field of antiquities how many more objects, great and small, are smugly sitting in the cases of our museums and in the windows of the dealers quietly keeping their illegitimacy to themselves, fairly secure that unless the intellectually-awakened eye pierces their guise, the tools of science are not going to rip apart their fraud?

CHAPTER THREE

CERAMICS

*A genuine stoneware bird
made by Martin Brothers.*
1903

Faith in rituals of connoisseurship can cause buyers of ceramics to make
serious and occasionally very expensive mistakes. Either on television, or
in the showroom, many will have seen the way in which the acknowledged
expert carries out his study. Whether it is an austere blue and white
Chinese bowl, a lavishly painted gilt vase, or just a plain cup and saucer,
the ritual remains the same. First the piece is handled and possibly given a
surreptitious tap to discover if it is cracked. Then follows a thorough visual
inspection to confirm that the design is appropriate, and to see if, for
example, it is a hard or soft paste porcelain. Finally it is turned upside
down to read the china mark. It can take considerable expertise to tell the
precise date of the enormous variety of china marks from every period of
Meissen, Sèvres, Chelsea, Lambeth, Bristol, Worcester, Spode, Wedg-
wood, the list is long.

But even the most experienced collector must keep his guard up as the field of ceramics is one of the most rewarding and varied for the forger. There are so many different types of ware, periods, potters, factories and techniques that he can simulate. A maxim for the novice could be 'the object is guilty and must prove its innocence.' Take nothing on face value, nor pay too much attention to the dealer's sales talk.

Unfortunately far too many people have complete faith in the reliability of china marks, and many mediocre books about collecting ceramics encourage that faith, assuring their readers that once they have mastered the hundreds of marks they will be expert enough to pick their way through any collection of china and pottery with absolute confidence, thinking that the recognition of the mark guarantees positive identification of the genuine. Achieving such knowledge takes months and it can be a waste of time, for even if every European china mark that has ever existed is learnt there will still be the complexities of the oriental marks. The history of ceramics is a story of copy, copy, and copy again, with, for example, Germany copying the orient, Britain then copying Germany, and then the orient copying the British copies of the German copies of the orient. The real connoisseur never relies wholly on china marks; even if his knowledge is truly encyclopaedic, it is still possible to be fooled. It is not as widely known as it should be that marks are comparatively easy to fake or alter.

The forger, whose target is the buyer who places total reliance on these marks, generally seeks to upgrade a relatively humble piece into something of much greater value by first removing the original mark. This can be done either by using a special acid solution, or by employing a hard abrasive stick to rub through the glaze and remove the mark. He then paints on the new mark and, to camouflage his work, covers the entire base with a special lacquer to return it to its previously hard smooth surface. If it is suspected that a piece has been 'improved' by this method, it is easily checked by wiping the suspect mark with acetone which should quickly dissolve both the lacquer and the mark to reveal the original glazed surface underneath, together with the tell-tale signs of scraping in the place of the original mark.

Some forgers, however, go to greater pains in creating china marks which are well-nigh impossible to detect. For example, if they set out to fake the famous Chelsea gold anchor they will paint on the device with a mixture of real gold, mercury and oils. After this application has thoroughly dried out, the whole pot must be gently heated until it is very hot indeed; this may be done by using a blow-lamp or placing it in an oven. When thoroughly heated, the blow lamp can be set with the flame at a fine point and as hot as it will go, and then a brief caress with this flame over the fraudulent mark and the original glaze will melt and allow the phoney gold anchor to fuse into the whole to such an extent that when the pot has cooled it cannot be felt with the finger tip, nor will there be any sign to arouse suspicion.

Again one of the safeguards can be wherever possible to employ comparison; the genuine will nearly always be an uncomfortable neighbour for a fake. This can apply especially to rarities; for example, Hispano-Moresque, a ware which is a synthesis of European and Near Eastern styles. The glazed work seemingly offers a good chance for the faker; the lustrous glaze of varying colours is quite within reach of modern potters who understand something of the intricacies of smoke acting with the so-called muffle glaze. Yet with all their fraudulent skill the final result will be threatened with exposure when put beside the genuine.

As far back as the Italian Renaissance, plagiarism between the old factories, many of which are now extinct, was raging. Pesaro aped Urbino, Faenza copied Cafaggiolo. In the twenties the latter factory was most successfully faked by a potter tucked away in Florence, whose work fooled eminent collectors around the Continent. The same ware has also been imitated by the factory of Caltaginone in Sicily, although their offerings in this style had a rather unpleasant dark grimy blue look which was far removed from the pure colour of the real Cafaggiolo.

Another of the popular targets for the forger was the work of the Della Robbias. Many are the false productions of these great craftsmen which have taken in the unwary. The position becomes complicated as there are large numbers of reproductions that are made and truthfully initially sold as such, only later to enter the crooked side of the trade, perhaps after being given a convincing false patination and a little 'damage from age'.

An Italian ware that has been a late starter with many collectors is majolica; among the first well-known figures to buy this was Goethe. By the mid-nineteenth century the fashion caused prices to rise and many began to compare the quality of the potter's art in this manner with the work of the great Renaissance artists. Contemporary craftsman sought to rediscover the art of the earlier majolica. One such was Torquato Castellani who was of the celebrated family of Italian dealers and imitators. Torquato may not have intended his work to be deceptive; in fact many of his pieces he signed and dated. But to see an example by itself can be very misleading, for he had the ability to capture the feeling of the earlier potters.

The work of Italian potters, particularly that of some of the earlier ones, seems to almost mesmerise the judgement of some who should know better. Not only have native fakers done well in this field but also those from other countries. Joseph Devers was master of the production of imitations of Italian faience, in fact, in 1851 he sold some of his efforts to the Sèvres Museum.

In France the decorative and highly imaginative work of Bernard Palissy drew the attention of fakers even in his own lifetime; his own pupils were not above a dabble in the trade that could bring good rewards. Palissy may have died in the Bastille with his secrets for glazing and the constitution of his clay, but that has in no way stopped the hordes of imitators who as Palissy himself said 'grope in the dark' for the formulae of success. Today practically all genuine Palissy pieces are off the market safely in the cases of museums or in well-guarded collections, and the would-be collector should be aware of this. During the reign of Louis XIII, a studio near Fontainebleau was active in producing fakes in this manner. In 1852 Alfred Corplet, a restorer specialising in repairing Palissy ware, swamped the market with imitations. In 1878 A. M. Pull joined in this lucrative pastime, and at the same time the Barbizet Brothers were active. A number of the imitators of this period were either careless or had little regard for their clients; they modelled sea-fish and other creatures never used by Bernard Pallissy, who confined himself to fish and animals he knew existed around the French capital.

In 1845 the celebrated factory of Edmé Samson et Cie was founded in Rue de Beranger, Paris, with the intention of providing help for clients whose dinner services had suffered damage. Samson would make replacements for these depleted sets, and in this way the factory became expert at matching the different wares. Over the years Samson produced

53

fine examples of various types, including Dutch Delft, Meissen, Chelsea, Bristol, Marseilles, Derby and many others. All pieces made were supposed to have been marked with an 'S' to show their origin, and generally alongside this would be the mark of the factory imitated. But as mentioned, marks can be fiddled: a drop of hydrofluoric acid and it is all too easy. Samson imitations are now sought after, and the price would probably be only half that of the piece copied.

It is the sheer variety of Samson that can appeal, not only with the emulation of many factories, but also with his apparent command of modelling and complex decoration. He had particular skill with small figures such as in a monkey band – very close to similar groups from Meissen, each little musician bearing the crossed swords of Meissen. The products of the Chelsea factory in the mid-eighteenth century, when it was run under the direction of Sprimont, attracted the versatile Samson, but although his pieces were delicately coloured and marked with the gold anchor they can generally be picked out from the originals because Samson always used hard paste for them. With Chinese ware such as blue and white K'raak of the Wan-li period and the Japanese Imari, the brilliant imitator could often come far too close to the original for the comfort of collectors. All too often highly specialised knowledge is required to expose the deception. Today the faker has to aim at achieving very high prices, because the cost of duplicating the workmanship in, for example, fine European porcelain of the eighteenth century, has become prohibitive.

A visit to the Royal Worcester factory, to see the creation of a replica of a small 1760 fruit bowl with blue decoration on a pierced basket design proved the point. It involved a series of highly skilled operations often using the kind of costly equipment which no forger could afford. First the bowl was moulded, then the holes in the basket pattern were individually incised by hand. The transfer designs of flower sprays were printed on to tissue, and each one cut out to be fixed on the bowl, another time-consuming hand skill. The bowl also underwent several firing and glazing operations, all to make an admittedly beautiful object, but one which would only sell for around a hundred pounds, or, as far as the faker is concerned, too little reward for too much effort. Although it may not be worth anyone's while to fake such pottery today, it definitely was in the eighteenth and nineteenth centuries, and deceptive creations of that

A Chinese hard paste porcelain tea pot of about 1755 (top) and a Worcester soft paste imitation of about 1760

period still abound. Henry Sandon, author of *Worcester Porcelain 1751–1793* and curator of the Dyson Perrins Museum at Worcester, gave us a guided tour of his unique collection of not just fakes but cleverly altered originals.

Two tea-pots were produced, which at a quick glance looked identical. The first was made in China in 1750 of hard paste porcelain; the second made only five years later, but in Worcester. It had a less glassy look about it than the Chinese pot, and Mr Sandon explained that this was because it was soft paste porcelain. The big difference, however, only became apparent after spending some time staring at both tea-pots. On both were figures of Chinese ladies, one painted with a rather austere elegance, the other more flamboyant, almost a caricature of how Europeans thought the Chinese looked. They appeared as Europeans dressed for a comic opera, a sort of Gilbert and Sullivan effect in porcelain!

In the eighteenth century there was a great vogue for everything Chinese, but particularly for porcelain; the famous German factory, Meissen, was quick to take advantage of this market, while at the same time not making exact copies, but modifying the refined simplicity of Chinese designs to fit the more garish tastes of Europe. The Chinese rarely added gilt to their porcelain regarding it as exhibitionist vulgarity. Meissen however realised that in Europe there was a big market for ostentation and added gilt to many of their wares. Their market analysis must have been correct for Worcester followed and splashed even more gold on to its dinner services with the result that, in 1788, George III saw one he ordered a king-size set for himself and gave the factory a Royal Warrant.

Possibly as a direct result of this royal preference for displays of gilt, several factories in Britain and elsewhere took a second look at their stocks of unsold, discreetly decorated, chinaware, and 'clobbered' them. It is a technical term which means attempting to make an original simple decoration look richer and therefore more appealing by adding, for instance, to a blue and white pattern, extra ornamentation in red, green and gold. It also started off the first wave of European faking. Mr Sandon produced a typical example. Originally it had been a Sèvres plate and still bore the original 1770 Sèvres factory mark underneath. A Shropshire potter named John Randall imported thousands of rather plain Sèvres

Top: two late eighteenth century tea bowls with the same transfer pattern. The bowl on the left has been 'clobbered' – had more decoration added

Bottom right: a Royal Worcester Ewer, of about 1889 and, on the left, a German fake of about 1890

A Worcester soft paste porcelain basket of about 1775 (top) and an imitation of about 1890 from A. Booth's Tunstall pottery

plates, removed the simple decorations with acid and 'clobbered' them to make a handsome overall profit.

A similar treatment had been given to a Worcester cup and saucer; the plain white had originally been sparingly gilded with a few elegant swirls. The faker had removed this pattern and replaced it with complex multi-coloured flowers and motifs. However, by viewing the surface of the saucer in a raking light the indentations, made in the clay by the now obliterated thin gilt lines, could be clearly seen.

Much easier to detect are fakes where the wrong material has been used: lift any piece of porcelain to the light and it has a beautiful pale translucency. However superbly accurate the detail of its earthenware copy, a quick check against the light will reveal it as opaque and therefore wrong.

More difficult to detect are fakes which have translucent bodies. Two apparently identical vases, both obviously magnificent examples of the finest late-eighteenth-century Worcester porcelain, were shown, both exquisitely decorated with panels depicting extravagant peacocks and strange insects. Here again it took some time to tell the difference, but once seen, the fake was so unmistakable that it was difficult to recall that, only moments before, the illusion of similarity had been completely convincing. There was an element of careless abandon in the real Worcester vase which indicated the uninhibited pleasure of an artist trying to portray the movement of some insect with free and effortless ease. This may sound like somewhat pretentious art criticism, but the fake had a certain deadness and lack of freedom about it, the stiff formality which comes from copying. It is suspected the bogus vase had been made in France by the firm of Samson. But, as Mr Sandon pointed out, 'it's worth remembering that the costs of making these fakes would now be so great, with the present-day costs of handwork, that you would have to pay for a new one to be made as much as it would cost to buy an original – so perhaps the days of these outright fakes of this quality are numbered!'

But are they really? Signs are appearing that costs of production are now being off-set by the greatly increased prices that the customers will pay – so great is the fascination for antiques, and in many cases so inadequate the level of knowledge about them.

Roam about junk-shops, side-street dealers, mixed-lot auctions, and it is quite likely that Staffordshire pottery will be in evidence. The rather quaint characteristics of this ware have always had a keen following since its inception. The naïve and simple style has an irresistible attraction. For a number of years now this field has unfortunately been invaded by the faker, the prime prize being the Victorian examples. One rather strange point here is that the fake instead of selling for less than the original often is priced higher. The target for these objects is not in any way intended to be the knowledgeable collector, but rather the amateur adventurers into the magnetic world of antiques.

How can the imitation be exposed? Superficially it may have an ephemeral appearance of quality. The first weapon is that stand-by, regularly repeated in this book, experience, which is only obtained by study, examination and discussion with someone who knows his subject and where possible, handling an actual piece and having the points of recognition explained.

The forgers help a little by being fascinated by a particular type of subject. Many of these pieces will be of cricketers, shepherds, shepherdesses, sailors and girls. More specialised subjects include Dick Turpin, Tom King, Fred Archer the great jockey, Generals Havelock and Campbell, the boxers Heenan and Sayers, Grace Darling with a Lighthouse, Garrick in his tent as Richard III, and the Death of Nelson.

The foregoing fakes in varying degrees of quality are made quite legally by the hundred thousand, and although they are manufactured openly as reproductions, some are liable to be offered as originals. Large cargoes of them end up in America, where to help satisfy the rich buyers extra value is imparted to some of the pieces by the addition of the Chelsea Gold anchor. It is the first thing inexperienced eyes look for, and on sight it will be decided that the piece must be genuine. Perhaps the final insult being that each one will be plainly marked GERMANY; this is to comply with the American law that the name of the country of origin be clearly shown.

The better fakes have the surface treated to give an appearance of age; the glaze can be artificially crackled, and staining applied in certain areas; also smoking with tapers may be used, which is then rubbed into the cracks. The true glaze should feel smooth and slightly slippery, whilst the fake glaze has a tacky touch to it.

The tricksters will attempt almost any ruse to answer what they may well feel is a 'legitimate' demand from the market. At one time or another ceramics from almost every part of the world have been faked, which leaves an increasing maze for the buyer to find his way through to the genuine.

By its fragile nature pottery is apt to be one of the most restored articles, and craftsmen have been remarkably adept at this. One method of restoring a broken pot with a piece missing is to model the lost fragment in clay, then fire it and glaze and colour to simulate the rest of the object. Finally the finished fragment is stuck into position. This is a very expensive operation and thus it is reserved for pieces of high value. Between the wars there was a Florentine potter who was so expert that the finished mend would be almost imperceptible.

The cheaper process is to replace missing fragments with a mixture of plaster and glue, which is sand-papered smooth when set. The surface is prepared for painting by applying an isolator of glue or shellac and then an artist using ordinary oil colours can give a convincing illusory effect that is completed by a coat of varnish. A quick sniff at the article may give this method away, as oils and some varnishes retain a smell for a long time.

Signs of deterioration in the glaze appear to be satisfactory evidence of age for some. Unfortunately this presents no problem to the faker. The simplest way is for him to apply judiciously a little hydrofluoric acid, or, if he is more thorough, to experiment with firing and glazing; for if these two are worked together properly, so that there is a contrast between the shrinkage of clay and glaze, a quite splendid surface cracking will result. To add to the insults the faker can heap on his customers, there are now lacquers and enamel paints that have some ingredient mixed into them which causes a near-perfect net-crack as they dry. One such device has probably been included in the manufacture of some quite convincing apothecaries' jars that have started to appear, the country of origin in many cases being West Germany. At first glance they seem to be most attractive, but a closer look shows that the cracking in the glaze is perhaps a bit too even, and then, as it rises to the top of the jars, it magically stops, and the glaze inside is perfect without blemish, although not quite, because the careful German generally puts in a small notice warning the owner not to put liquids in them as they will leak! Fun perhaps and not too much harm at around ten pounds, but not so amusing after more trickery, adding craquelure, staining with greasy soot, and then at least one nought added to the price tag.

If we jump from the bottom of the market into the heady atmosphere of the really big money we will see that unfortunately the days of outright fakes of the much rarer forms of pottery seem to be by no means numbered: instead they are enjoying a major boom. Ming, Sung and T'ang have become names synonymous with the finest ceramics. T'ang was the dynastic name of the pottery of China in the eighth century AD. The custom of the early Chinese was similar to the Ancient Egyptians who buried the finest of their art with their dead. A good T'ang horse today fetches about a hundred thousand pounds, a good camel seventy thousand pounds and a small twenty-centimetre figurine of a dancer, upwards of ten thousand pounds. Not surprisingly, with such tempting prices, the market is now polluted with a large number of fakes. The worst are easy to identify: like the examples of eighteenth-century Chinoiserie mentioned earlier, they exemplify the exaggerations typical of the bad copyist who only achieves a caricature of the original. But some modern fakes are deceptively superb.

Old pottery absorbs moisture which, whenever it freezes, expands and cracks the glassy surface of the glaze into a random pattern of tiny fissures. As in old paintings, this 'craquelure' is highly appreciated by the connoisseur as an obvious indication of antiquity and therefore, for his benefit, is carefully re-created in any superior forgery.

Thousands of people visit major auctioneers like Christie's and Sotheby Parke Bernet every year in the hope of achieving the top prices for their antiques: among those thousands are always several who have unwittingly bought fakes, and several who wittingly are trying to sell fakes. As a result Sotheby's for one, possess an impressive collection of unsaleable items which their experts detected as fraudulent, and which either caused great distress to their unsuspicious owners, or for which their owners have never dared return.

Among these is a typical T'ang figure which had been detected as a fake by what is called the thermoluminescence test. Like other fakes already discussed it was more a caricature of T'ang than the real thing, with exaggeratedly mobile drapery and strangely acrobatic, yet very un-Chinese gestures. But this one exquisite figure looked well nigh perfect: it was elegant, and demure in its posture, with the kind of subdued brown, green and blue colours entirely appropriate to that kind of pottery. Moreover there was some evidence of the craquelure which would tend to confirm the antiquity of such a piece. Without scientific tests Sotheby's ceramic experts were unable to say whether it was true or false, although, even if false, it was agreed to be a superb piece of craftsmanship.

Dr Stuart Fleming of the Oxford Research Laboratory for Archaeology was called in to examine it. He admired its good looks but abstained from further comment until he had tested it in his laboratory.

When a sample of genuine T'ang is subjected to thermoluminescent testing a typical upward curve and plateau is traced on a graph which reveals a long exposure to radiation. Once any piece of pottery is fired all the history of centuries of its clay being exposed to radiation is obliterated like wiping a slate clean, and from that moment on, the clay begins afresh to absorb radiation. This level of general exposure to radiation has been much greater since the nuclear explosions of the twentieth century, but even before our modern interference with the atom, there were always tiny levels of environmental radiation. Because this annual dose of radiation can be measured, the years of exposure can be totted up for any specimen which is known to have been wiped clean of radiation history at any given moment; for example, a pot fired in AD 1000 today will have a radiation history of 979 years. Heat a sample of such a specimen in a vacuum and measure the radiation given off, and you will know how much it has absorbed in the years since its clay was originally fired, freeing it of previous radiation history. Count the years of exposure and you have its date of manufacture.

Dr Fleming drilled a tiny sample of pottery from underneath the figurine to avoid possible restoration areas which would have confused his results. He compacted the resulting powder into a small tablet and heated it in his thermoluminescence apparatus to over five hundred degrees Centigrade, until it glowed red-hot, enabling the light level to be recorded. The pen on the graph, despite a few minor mechanical hiccups, traced a horizontal course, well below the plateau registered by the genuine sample of T'ang. Dr Fleming took one glance at the record of comparison, picked up the figurine and stated with an authority impossible only a few years ago, 'I am confident this is modern'.

CHAPTER FOUR

COINS

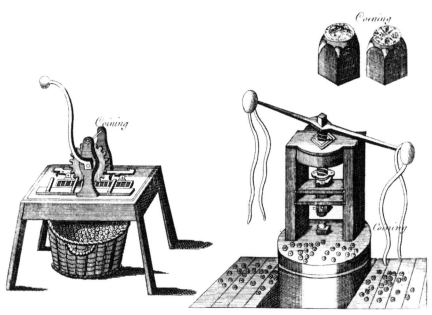

*Eighteenth-century
coining machinery*

The word counterfeit or a rumour of the circulation of faked money can send a chill through certain circles. The mention of the possibility of the passing of fraudulent cash, signals an attack on financial stability. Coinage nearly always carries the image of a sovereign, a president or patriotic symbol. Money to fulfil its duty must, in the eye of authority, be inviolable. Counterfeit coinage is not just defrauding a few individuals, it is undermining the economy of nations.

There are two distinct classes of coin forgery: the first is where the forger attempts to defraud the general public by duplicating common currency; the second is where the forger tries to pass off fake rarities to the collector. The latter only requires the forger to succeed in making relatively few coins to gain a potentially very high return; for example, the

1887 Victorian five-pound piece is today worth around five hundred pounds; it was struck in large quantities at the time and fairly recently copies of it have been discovered which must have given their creator a handsome profit. They were superbly made and deceived the experts for some time before scientific examination revealed their falsity. They were forged by a technique called pressure casting. The process involves centrifugal machines normally used for making dentures. Heat and centrifugal pressure expand and force the metal into all the cracks and contours of a mould. Striking a coin, on the other hand, means hammering blank sheets or strips of gold, silver, or whatever metal is appropriate, with the engraved die of the required design. In a standard mint this die is normally cut on a reduction machine: the original design is about the size of a dinner plate, and a sensor traces the contours of its surface relaying every indentation of the relief to a cutting edge which simultaneously engraves the design in miniature on to the surface of the die. Until 'pressure casting' was invented the forger's task was very difficult, for he had to cut his own dies by hand, and to do so had to achieve a perfectly accurate reverse image of the often very small original.

Fortunately for the forensic expert, when the forger uses hand-engraving to create his die the subsequent process of striking his forgery generally lets him down unless he is clever enough to strike only one single copy for each die he cuts. Considering the extra work such duplication of effort would involve most forgers are too greedy and almost always strike too many copies from one die and thereby get caught. The reason is glaringly obvious: it is virtually impossible to make an absolutely perfect copy of the genuine die, and if there is even only one microscopic error on the resulting fake coin (for example if the top of the 'o' in the date 1901 is slightly blurred, scratched, or lacks uniformity) that error will also be seen in every subsequent copy.

In the early 1970s there was such a spate of coin forgeries that dealers and collectors clubbed together to protect themselves against this growing menace. The International Bureau for the Suppression of Counterfeit Coins decided to publish a regular magazine which would contain detailed illustrations of all 'reproduction' coins which came to light. In January 1976 the first edition of this *Bulletin on Counterfeits* was published with clear indications to the collector of how to perceive defects in a series of suspect coins. Notoriously difficult examples were given a whole page each, with photographic enlargements of both faces of the coin, and suggestions about key defective areas. For example, 'a pimple below the centre of the harp in the third quarter of the shield, and another behind the middle lion in the fourth quarter of the shield'. For the connoisseur with scientific testing equipment, comparative details are also given about mistakes in the metallurgy of the forgery, its weight, and specific gravity.

Since 1950 a number of skilled hands have been tempted by the reward for counterfeiting coins of this century or the latter part of the last. At the eastern end of the Mediterranean there has been a flourishing concern known as the 'Beirut Mint' that has lined its coffers with 'replicas' of sovereigns, Russian platinum roubles and Roman solidi. Around twenty years ago in Italy Jose Beraha Zdravko, known as Behra, was at work on sovereigns. Somewhat stupidly he made avoidable mistakes. For instance, on the reverse of coins with dates prior to 1917 he had the South African Pretoria mint mark – which did not open until 1923. The nine in the dates tended to be larger than the other three figures and was also slightly out of alignment.

A more ambitious attempt at major financial returns came from America, and also from the hand of a very skilled craftsman. It involves a seemingly humble coin, a United States one dime piece, dated 1894. At that time there were four mints in the USA, San Francisco, New Orleans, Denver and Philadelphia. In 1894 San Francisco struck only five single dimes: on these it put its mint mark as 'S'. Philadelphia in 1894 did not have a mint mark. The craftsman in question took a dime of a later date minted in San Francisco, chiselled off the 'S' mint mark, and affixed this 'S', probably with laser beam welding, to a Philadelphia 1894 dime. The coin now jumped in value to some $50,000. It was brought to London and offered to a dealer, but suspicion was aroused as to why an attempted sale should be made on this side of the Atlantic. Under an expert examination and high magnification the fraud was exposed.

As with all antique items where rarity makes some of the finer objects unobtainable, the collector of coins is often attracted by the only possible substitute for the genuine article, namely the *bona fide* replica. They even used to be made on behalf of the British Museum, using a technique called electrotyping where impressions of each side of a coin are joined together with a copper core in the middle. Unfortunately, but not altogether surprisingly, many of these replicas began to be passed off as genuine and the Museum discontinued their manufacture. However there are still several companies today who offer replicas of rare coins on the open market. Mostly such replicas carry tiny precautionary inscriptions saying 'Replica' and give details about their maker, date of manufacture, and with gold replicas, a minute description of the fineness of the gold ('750' or '1000' – i.e. 18 or 24 carat). There was a case where among genuine medieval coins offered for sale a reproduction of a coin called the Bona of Savoy (extremely rare when authentic) was on display. The maker's mark and the mark of fineness had been skilfully removed; quite how many similar pieces have been bought by the unsuspecting is not known. Five hundred years or so ago even His Holiness Paul II was marking the fakes in his coin collection catalogue. Sixteenth-century books on numismatism had lengthy contributions on counterfeiting.

Fortunately for coin dealers, because sometimes only two or three examples of a rare coin exist in good condition, the whole trade is instantly on the alert when several more examples come on to the market. One international dealer, Douglas Liddell, has said how his suspicions became aroused at one time. A certain 'gentleman' from Switzerland already well known to Mr Liddell as a *bona fide* collector, having bought several coins quite genuinely from him, suddenly began to ask for very rare coins. Mr Liddell sold him a few great rarities, from which this man was later found to have made copies. But when he tried to sell these copies he was soon detected because, with only two or three known examples of the originals, his copies were automatically suspect and therefore exposed to much more rigorous scientific examination than any potential buyer would normally undertake.

At the other extreme of the counterfeiting industry the danger for the public sometimes comes more from lead poisoning than financial embarrassment. In 1976 a petrol station attendant in Camberwell was watching the Cup Final on television. He was distracted from the game by the curious sound made by two fifty pence coins as they were paid out on to his counter. With the instincts of a budding Sherlock Holmes he bit them. To his considerable surprise, his teeth went clean through. As the car of the customer drove off the attendant took its number.

The police traced the car. In their subsequent investigation it transpired that the counterfeiter had made his coins with a teapot full of molten lead which he poured into plaster casts. He was quite open about his lack of finesse, saying; 'If they had come out well I would have passed more, but most of them were terrible. It was a mug's game'. Judge Charles Lawson, QC, wholeheartedly agreed, sentenced him to six months, suspended for a year, and said, 'This is not one of the most serious of counterfeiting cases. But it is one sphere of human endeavour to which the law does not permit private enterprise from individuals. The Mint has the monopoly. Ordinary people are not allowed to set up in opposition to the Mint even in a small way as you did.'

Not all forgeries of the British fifty pence piece have been detected so easily. In early 1975 cities in the North of England were flooded with more examples. Although they were relatively easy to detect visually, the forgers evaded capture for some time by using their counterfeits in fruit machines. Regrettably such forgery is by no means a dying art. In 1976 it took the police twenty-four hours to count a hoard of three tons of counterfeit fifty pence pieces, worth more than a hundred and fifty thousand pounds, discovered in a disused factory in Chiswick, London. As a Scotland Yard spokesman said at the time, 'There is no apparent way of distinguishing them from the genuine article. They are extremely good fakes. It would take an expert to tell the difference.' Until that statement several attempts at the large-scale forging of fifty pence pieces had been quickly detected simply because the counterfeits were badly made. Today however Scotland Yard's fraud squad is devoting considerable attention to the possibility that skilled counterfeiters who previously aimed at creating rarities for collectors have been forced out of that lucrative market by the new *Bulletin on Counterfeits* which is constantly exposing their efforts; it seems highly possible that such forgers are now specialising in the mass production of relatively low value currency which, when they try to pass it off as genuine, will mainly escape detection because of initially only coming under the largely uncritical scrutiny of the general public, and not a numismatic magnifying lens.

Those forgers who still try to pass off expensive fake antique coins are now more devious in their tactics. The soil of Sicily has long been regarded as a happy hunting ground for archaeologists interested in ancient coins.

Left: Denarius of Augustus
Top: the genuine coin
Bottom: a forgery

Right: Decadrachm of Syracuse
Top: the genuine coin
Bottom: a forgery

69

The export of such coins is illegal, but despite that, authentic examples regularly come on to the open market in Switzerland. Dr Kent, Deputy Keeper of Coins at the British Museum, described how Sicilian peasants, before somehow disposing of their authentic finds, make casts and moulds of them, allowing the rumour to circulate that a hoard has been found. The police descend on them, extract the false coins, which then pass from policeman to policeman until they finally end up in the Museum of Syracuse where they are recognised as forgeries. Dr Kent complained that in the problem area of combating coin forgery the law is, to say the least, unhelpful. As he said, forgers can hardly be touched by the law as it stands: the forger of coins has only to claim that he is making replicas and not forgeries and the law cannot touch him, so we can hardly speak of forgery as something illegal: it's very doubtful if it is illegal in this or any other country. If the manufacturer of false coins gives you a certificate of falseness with them, who is to say he had any intent to deceive anyway?

One of the complications of trying to be dogmatic about what is and what is not a genuine coin is the unsavoury custom of many official national mints to restrike coinage years after the original date on the coin, in order to cash in on the bullion market by buying gold at one price and minting it into coinage to sell at twice or three times the original price. Even our own Royal Mint has been guilty of such behaviour: until the late 1950s it continued to strike its 1925 sovereign. Their reason was that in Arabia a sovereign coin with the head of a king fetches a shilling more than one with the head of a queen. As Dr Kent commented, 'It's a nice point – we can hardly say that the Mint forged its own coin – or can we?'

Probably the most notorious of all modern forgers was the American ex-priest, ex-airline pilot, Harry Stock. Douglas Liddell related how, after being introduced to 'The Reverend' Harry Stock by another English coin dealer, he had had the embarrassing misfortune of being taken in and actually buying some Victorian five- and two-pound pieces from him. Mr Liddell then became suspicious and after the coins had been double-checked at the Royal Mint it was confirmed that they were forgeries. Mr Liddell pointed out that Stock's undoing was when he started to forge extreme rarities.

Stock had made a rather hurried exit from the United States where, in 1969, he was released on bail after being charged with selling forged

An Edward IV groat
Top: the genuine coin
Bottom: a forgery

three-dollar gold coins. When you ask dealers which group of fake coins has given them the greatest difficulty, most have little hesitation in saying 'Beirut Sovereigns'. Untold numbers of these superb pressure cast forgeries now adulterate the market. It was therefore no coincidence that Stock's next port of call should be Beirut where he set about finding a master forger. Said Chalhoub was an expert in pressure-casting and Stock obtained from him some of the coins he later offered Mr Liddell. But he was too greedy and by putting so many remarkable coins on the market within a very short time he alerted suspicion, and paid the price of several months on remand in prison. It was then decided to deport him. With the benefit of hindsight it would seem to have been an amazingly crass decision on somebody's part to choose, out of all the cities in the world to which he could be deported, the one most infamous for his particular criminal speciality. He was sent back to Beirut and within days was in business once more. In 1974 he again went too far: 'They flooded the market' explained the Chief Inspector who led Scotland Yard's investigation. 'They had to withdraw by 1975. Too many coins were suspect.' Stock was eventually caught in Zurich selling forged platinum roubles, posing as a jet-setter with Russian trade interests!

Hopefully the final chapter in Stock's nefarious career closed in October 1976 with the trial in Manchester Crown Court of eight dealers and two others, all accused of conspiring to utter counterfeit coins and to import or receive them into the United Kingdom. The fact that a forgery of a £20,000 gold coin was only discovered because all three genuine coins minted are in national institutions must have come as disquieting news to those wealthy collectors who stake major investments on their own ability in being able to differentiate between what is authentic and what is false. Mr David McNeill, QC, on that occasion must have caused many numismatists to have a second very careful look at recent acquisitions when he said, talking of Said Chalhoub, 'Provided he was given a genuine coin from which he could make a die, his skill was such that he was able to produce virtually unlimited quantities of copies.'

Douglas Liddell has stated that he finds the problems posed by fake coins are becoming steadily worse, with good forgeries appearing several times a month and detection becoming progressively more difficult. He has admitted after having been caught out on several occasions, that he is extremely wary. Like Mr Liddell, Dr Kent is also in the unenviable position of regularly having to make major value judgements on potential fakes. He even sometimes receives them from their actual forgers who presumably hope he will guarantee their value by authenticating them. When he was President of the British Association of Numismatic Societies he lectured to collectors on how to tell the difference between ostensibly similar coins.

When Dr Kent was asked how much reliance he placed on scientific tests when authenticating coins, his reply must be almost unique for any recognised contemporary expert on authentication. 'I probably need the scientists' help less than one per cent of the time, and even then it's only to give an official back-up to what I already believe.' Moreover, he has found it extremely rare that any scientific report or analysis has caused him to change his views. However, despite his often not needing, for example, the assistance of a specialist metallurgist, his approach to any coin is rigorously methodical and one might say eminently scientific in its discipline.

First he examines the coin to see and feel if it was cast or struck, and his historical knowledge tells him if that is correct. Even with his first glance at a coin, if it looks odd he has to find out why, and then prove it. He tosses it from hand to hand to see if it feels right, and then checks if its weight is correct. He balances it and taps the edge: if it rings true it is more likely to be genuine; if it does not, it may be cast, an electrotype, or perhaps merely damaged in some way. He studies the colour, as oxidation of debased alloys causes obvious colour changes. He notes whether the coin is gilded and relates that finding to his experience of the genuine; some eminently genuine coins are gilded and look fake, and some fakes are gilded to make them look genuine. Only then will he begin to explore fine detail with microscopes, and he finds the occasion very rare indeed that he has to study a single letter on a coin under the two hundred times magnification of the department's binocular microscope. However, only five 1933 pennies exist and when one was shown to him it was only under that binocular microscope that he was able to see that the '5' on a 1935 penny had been removed and a '3' soldered in its place. Dr Kent commented to the person who had invited him to inspect the coin that it was a marvellous piece of work. Perhaps it was the forger himself, for he left very angry, and at top speed.

By no means all coin forgeries are modern. Almost as soon as coinage was invented as a substitute for barter, fakes were created as a substitute for coins. Dr Kent cited the classic age of coin forgery as the late eighteenth and early nineteenth centuries, with John White in Britain, and Becker on the Continent as the greatest exponents. Becker's work is still sold unrecognised, at highly reputable auctions. Just such a sale was being filmed in London for the television series which prepared the way for this book, when there was a mild hiccup in the clockwork precision of auctioneering patter: it was discovered afterwards that a certain coin had been withdrawn after whispers of doubts 'upon its being absolutely right'. Dr Kent alleged that Becker's coins are still to be found, unrecognised, in major collections even though they have long been published. 'They are very dangerous and should never, never be underestimated.' There was considerable laughter in that particular lecture when he added, 'I'm a great admirer of Becker!'

One of Becker's specialities was his highly successful technique for ageing his coins: he described it as 'taking his old men for a drive'. By 'old men' he meant his counterfeits which he used to keep in a special box on the axle of his carriage. The box was filled with iron filings and the jolting and abrasion of only a short journey gave his coins the appearance of centuries of age.

Another easy, but rarely applied test for forgery, is a magnet: some forgeries of Charles I coins are plated, and regularly fool both the public and many dealers. If the envelope of precious metal is not damaged there are few grounds for suspicion. But pass it under a magnet and if its core is of iron, it will jump up to disclose the fake that it is.

Only when testing the most cunning modern forgeries which use alloys does Dr Kent have to rely on sophisticated techniques like X-Ray fluorescence and in this area he and his colleagues are having to pioneer detection methods which still need catalogues of comparative standards that as yet do not exist.

Only the wealthier collector or museum curator is ever likely to be offered the best fakes which are largely designed specifically for that market, and not merely to dupe the man in the street. The general public is, however, very much exposed to offers of two less expensive types of collectable item which merit taking careful precautions before buying.

It is generally, but erroneously, believed that collecting coins is automatically a profitable hobby: with the exception of very rare top quality coins there is no guarantee of any profit whatsoever except possibly in the long term. Even with rarities, coins can be a dubious investment: if you had bought an Elizabeth I gold sovereign in 1975 you would have had to pay about £1400. In 1978 such coins are still selling at that same price. If at the same time you had bought a Charles II two guinea you would find the sale price has actually dropped over that short period by £25. A sample portfolio of seventeen coins sold in 1975 for £3661; the same coins are on sale in 1978 at £4003, giving you the illusion of an annual profit of 3.1 per cent. But if you take inflation into account your purchase would have caused you a loss.

The quality of good coins is graded as 'fine', 'very fine' and 'extremely fine' and it is the dealer with whom you buy and sell who grades your coins. As the difference between just 'fine' and 'very fine' can sometimes mean a price differential of a hundred pounds or more it is most important to deal exclusively with reputable companies, members of either the British Numismatic Trade Association or the International Association of

Numismatists. Another point worth remembering is that fine coins literally do deserve kid-glove treatment. Just fingering a pristine mint condition coin for even ten seconds will transfer sufficient grease and acid from the skin to damage the surface of the coin. Like handling a film negative, coins should be held by the edge to avoid corrosive finger prints which can quickly degrade an 'extremely fine' piece to only 'very fine'.

The second precaution advised is concerned with medallions. Medallions made in limited editions and specially designed by allegedly famous artists to commemorate some unique event are heavily advertised as collector's items, guaranteed to repay the original outlay as their rarity increases. Unfortunately only very rarely does this alleged rarity bring even a minimal increase in value; far more often such medallions not only never regain the price originally paid for them, but are only saleable at the price of bullion. In a similar fashion, official government mints regularly produce commemorative coinage to attract the collector as an investment. Here again it often takes many years for such coins to accrue significantly in value; sometimes so many are dumped on the market that no buyer is ever likely to achieve a profit in his lifetime.

A fifteenth-century bronze medal cast from a gold original of the Roman Emperor Heraclius – its true origin was not recognised until the seventeenth century

75

CHAPTER FIVE

DOCUMENTS

'The Doctor's Dream' by Thomas Rowlandson, 1756–1827

The practice of tampering with letters and documents has been known throughout history, and has produced some extraordinary stories and involved people from all walks of life. For the collector the way is strewn with the strange convolutions of time and ancient intrigues which are now often unsolvable.

In the ninth century appeared the so-called *Isidorian Decretals*; the author was apparently one Isidore, an Archbishop of Seville who died in 636. Contained in a bundle were about a hundred letters which were supposed to be from early popes, and with these was the celebrated 'Donation of Constantine'. In the fifteenth century these were exposed as forgeries by Laurentius Valla, a leading Humanist.

Ironically it has often been members of the religious fraternities who seem to have been drawn to faking. In the chapter on Miscellany, there is a listing of 'relics' which were sometimes concocted by monks. In the fifteenth century at Viterbo in Italy, a monk named Annius forged 'Berosi Antiquitatum libri quinque', supposedly a document concerned with Berosus, a priest at Babylon in the reign of Antiochus Soter (280–262 BC).

In the late eighteenth century cupidity gave rise to the odd tale of the 'Queen's Necklace', a mixture of melodramatic farce, double-dealing and violence. The Queen involved was the ill-starred Marie Antoinette and the necklace a massive affair of 647 brilliant stones of nearly 3000 carats in all, which she never wore nor apparently wanted. It was designed by the Court jewellers Böhmer and Bessenger in 1774 with Louis XV's mistress Madame Du Barry in mind. The value of the necklace today would be around £3,000,000. When Louis XVI came to the throne the jewellers showed the necklace to Marie Antoinette who, despite a love for diamonds, turned it down. A plot was hatched to assist the near desperate jewellers and involved another lady who liked diamonds called Jeanne de St Remy de Valois, a supposed friend of the Queen. She was approached to act as an intermediary for a second attempt to sell it to Marie Antoinette and offered a large commission if she was successful.

Jeanne's background included descent from a bastard son of Henri II, and a mother who in later life worked in a brothel. Jeanne had been adopted by the Marquise de Boulainvilliers, had run away and married a soldier to give her some security before she bore twins sired by the Bishop of Bar Sur Aube. After this she and her husband took the titles of Countess and Count. She made up the story that she was a confidante of the Queen, and also of the influential Prince Louis-René-Eduard de Rohan, Bishop of Strasbourg, Cardinal of the Holy Church and a senior member of the Académie Française. Jeanne, to convince the Cardinal of her friendship with Marie Antoinette, suggested he eavesdropped on a meeting between herself and the Queen. This he did, but unbeknown to him the 'Queen' with Jeanne was a prostitute. The idea was put to him that the Queen wanted the necklace but did not want Louis XVI to know about the acquisition. So Jeanne initiated a correspondence between the Cardinal and the 'queen'; for this the services of Marc Antoine Rétaux de Villette, a skilled forger, were used. Amongst other productions from his adept hand was a document telling of Marie Antoinette's acceptance of the price for the necklace. A contract was signed by the Cardinal, to which the forger added 'approved' to each paragraph and Marie Antoinette's signature at the bottom of each page. The Cardinal then asked the jewellers to bring the necklace to him; the faked contract was shown them, and they handed over the gems. In his turn the Cardinal took the diamonds to Jeanne's rooms and handed them to a disguised messenger who was supposed to receive them for the Queen. Jeanne's husband, self-styled the Count La Motte, then left Paris for England with the necklace; Jeanne received a two hundred thousand francs commission from the jewellers. These unfortunates, thinking the Queen had the necklace, wrote to her for a settlement. The upshot was that Marie Antoinette had the Cardinal thrown into the Bastille, as well as Villette and Jeanne. A trial in front of sixty-four judges lasted nine months. The Cardinal was popular with the great mass of the people, who cried out for his release, which action could have turned their rage and suspicion against the Queen. The judges allowed him to go free but also free of all his titles and revenues.

Jeanne did not escape so lightly. She was stripped naked and flogged outside the Palais de Justice and branded on each shoulder with a 'V' for *voleuse*, a thief. Next she was incarcerated in the grim Salpétrière prison from which she escaped to England to die squalidly in an orgy. The furore which arose as a result of the forged letters is credited by some as the final spark that set off the French Revolution.

The eighteenth century was a vintage time for literary pretenders. Between 1747 and 1757 at the naval school in Copenhagen, the English teacher, Charles Julius, prepared a faked transcript of a manuscript on Roman antiquities by Richard of Cirencester. It alleged it was an itinerary of Britain which supplemented that of Antonius. It was accepted for over a hundred years until a Mr Woodward exposed it as a fake in 1866.

At about the same time in England, Thomas Chatterton (1752–1770) lived his life in a romantic semi-trance, seemingly roaming through an earlier age of literature. Amongst his fake productions were a number of poems supposedly from the hand of a character he had invented himself, a fifteenth-century poet, Thomas Rowley, a monk. Chatterton made Rowley into a kind of literary doppelgänger. For all his own brilliance as a poet the young man could find no success in selling his fakes, and in desperation even tried to interest Horace Walpole, saying he had found the manuscript in a chest in St Mary Redcliffe, Bristol. But he failed. On 24 August 1770, at little over the age of seventeen, he swallowed a lethal amount of arsenic.

Another picaresque literary forger in the eighteenth century was one James Macpherson, 1736–1796, the son of a Scottish farmer. In 1760 he published *Fragments of Ancient Poetry collected in the Highlands of Scotland and translated from the Gaelic or Erse language*, these were followed by a six-volume epic poem 'Fingal' and then another epic 'Temora' in eight books, said to be a translation of Ossian. Despite the admiration of Goethe the authenticity of the works was challenged by a number of scholars including the redoubtable Doctor Johnson. In answer to these doubts Macpherson produced his fake originals. He was never totally discredited, and lived to be the MP for Camelford, Cornwall, and when he died was laid to rest in Westminster Abbey.

In 1777 a son was born to an engraver Samuel Ireland, called William Henry, who was to become known as the boy who wrote a play by Shakespeare. Unlike other forgers of the Avon bard who produce fragments, such as verses, letters and deeds, William wrote a complete play *Vortigern and Rowena* and garnished it with the supposed locks of Shakespeare's hair. His impertinence was rewarded with not only public but academic approval. On 2 April 1796 his play was produced at Drury Lane by Sheridan, with the celebrated Kemble in the leading role. Its failure, however, led to the exposure of its real author, who confessed his guilt, publishing a volume entitled *Confessions* in 1805. Ireland's forgeries formed the theme of James Payn's novel *The Talk of the Town*, 1885.

Gradually these fallacious literary productions gained in status and became collectors' items, or became confused with the genuine and bought unknowingly as the real thing.

In July 1972 Sotheby Parke Bernet sold one of the most extraordinary collections of manuscripts ever assembled by one man. He was a wealthy Victorian eccentric called Sir Thomas Phillips, and unlike many collectors who fall prey to bargains, but are deterred from paying top prices when there are even the slightest grounds for suspicion, he was so mesmerised by antiquity that he bought almost anything if he considered there might be a chance of it being authentic. Of one item he wrote, 'Is it not possible that this Homer may be a Relic of the Alexandrian Library which burnt down twelve hundred years ago? . . . is it not possible that the Librarian might have put this roll into his pocket prior to the assault of the Caliph on Alexandria and carried it off?' The answer to that somewhat rhetorical question was supplied by the buyers at the auction, for the bidding for the 'Homer' stopped at £750.

J. G. Kohl, a German writing about Phillips, recorded the collector's first encounter with the 'Homer' scroll: 'The object obviously fascinated him; the vellum attracted and charmed him as a piece of jewellery would a woman.' Phillips had fallen under the spell of an arch literary faker, a Greek called Constantine Simonides. He had come to England armed with a poor selection of not very old but genuine manuscripts, and several superb but fake scrolls of Homer and other classical poets. The British Museum bought almost all his genuine wares, and turned down all the fakes. Simonides then learnt about the curious uncritical enthusiasm of Sir Thomas Phillips, and was rewarded by selling him the remainder of his genuine scrolls and almost all the fakes.

As Phillips explained to Kohl, after having just paid £50—a princely sum in 1854—for the Homer scroll,

I kept revolving the matter in my mind all night long. Should I allow the earliest manuscript of a Homeric rhapsody to escape me? The Greek may possibly prove once again to be a rogue and to have brought me merely a remarkable forgery. But it is also possible that the document may be genuine. This morning he threatened that if I did not close with him he would take it away and let the British Museum have it. Should I risk that? I preferred to risk my £50.

Today, at the end of the 1970s, fakes, not so much in the esoteric areas of literary documents, but in the field of signatures, phoney cheques, and faked executive expenses, are alarmingly widespread. Twenty years ago the head of the United States Federal Bureau of Investigation, Edgar G. Hoover, reckoned that the annual loss in the USA from forged cheques alone was over five hundred million dollars and most experts today consider the situation has not improved but deteriorated. Often even evident forgeries now pass inspection simply because the vast majority of signed documents are unquestionably authentic and their verifiers are out of the habit of verifying.

For the programme about fake documents one of the easiest ways of forging a signature was demonstrated. A hard-boiled egg was shelled and skinned and then rolled over an ink signature. The egg retained a distinct impression of the original. It was then rolled on to a blank sheet of paper and it transferred a clear shadowy print of the original. With a pen with both the ink and nib shape closely similar to those used initially, the printed signature was traced over. Even on close inspection by the naked eye the reproduction looked extremely plausible. Yet when examined under a microscope the near misses of the pen as it tried to follow the pale grey line printed by the egg were very obvious. But the fact remains that when a fake signature is only likely to suffer a cursory inspection and without the aid of any magnification, it is unlikely to be detected.

There are, however, many clues which can help even the most un-scientific judge of handwritten mischief to detect fraudulence. A simple example is the classic proof of authenticity of any document where the signature is written across a postage stamp. Everybody, including all forgers, knows about the custom of steaming letters open, and steaming stamps off letters. But if the stamp is steamed off a letter or any document it is almost certain that any nearby writing in ink will run, or at best, become slightly blurred, thereby alerting suspicion. Forgers prefer to peel the stamp off carefully in its dry state, and close examination of both the stamp and the surface to which it was previously adhered nearly always reveals fibres torn from either surface. If the stamp is then re-affixed to another surface, the fresh adhesive will often discolour the edge of its perforations, giving an obvious warning that someone has tampered with it.

The various clues largely demand a small element of commonsense for instant detection: but the best forgeries are aimed at those whose common-sense is either distracted or temporarily held in abeyance. When a pen nib passes over a stamp on to paper to which it is adhered it tends to splutter its ink very slightly. When a ball-point pen makes a similar manoeuvre, there is a clear change of pressure as the point falls off the edge of the stamp and indents the paper below. Such traces are notoriously difficult to fake, but most people do not even look out for them.

Even folds in paper can give away the forger's activities. Try folding a sheet of paper then drawing a line across the fold: do it with pencil, ball-point and nib. In all cases you will perceive a change of thickness in the line immediately the top of the writing instrument hits the fold. With pens, as opposed to ball-points, there is a tendency for the ink to spread slightly up and down the fold where the line crosses it. If you compare a page of writing which was folded afterwards where the folding has, inevitably, caused no change to the flow of the writing instrument, you will begin to understand how only a few of the most elementary checks which are routine to the forensic scientist can greatly help you in authenticating a suspect document.

For example, it is generally assumed that the advent of the ball-point pen made forgery much easier. Using carbon paper to print the forgery, it was assumed that any signature could be traced through it on to a document making an undetectable duplicate. However, ball-points have a nasty habit of 'gooping', a forensic term which describes a particular, easily discernible characteristic peculiar only to such pens. Draw a straight line with a ball-point and the ink should flow with uniform regularity as the ball revolves. However when the pen makes an abrupt change of direction the ball stops and reverses, leaving a slight dot in its track, as all the accumulated ink on one side of the ball-holder is suddenly transferred on to the ball and thence on to the page. When you draw through carbon paper with a ball-point the carbon copy will never show this 'gooping'. Another factor about ball-points which may seem blatantly obvious but which nevertheless has caused several expensive mistakes is the fact that they only came into the shops at the end of the Second World War, so any ball-point signature dated before then is likely to be wrong.

Perhaps the most celebrated story of anachronisms in forgery concerns Vrain Lucas, a skilled document and letter faker in nineteenth-century France. He duped a certain Monsieur Chasles, a respected member of the French Académie des Sciences, for many tens of thousands of pounds. This scholar had a great weakness for collecting autographs and letters. Lucas worked out the complete treatment for him. With some brilliance he recounted to Monsieur Chasles that he had acquired the collection of the Comte de Boisjardin, a noted collector of letters,who had sailed to America in 1791, but had been shipwrecked and drowned. The Comte's collection had somehow survived and been recovered in a chest, little the worse from a soaking.

The items Lucas thrust on the learned scholar included: a lengthy letter to Lazarus from Mary Magdalene, a letter from Cleopatra to Julius Caesar telling the great Roman that their son Cesarion was flourishing, a passport signed by Vercingetorix, and letters from such as Attila, Alexander the Great and Joan of Arc, also love notes from Laura to Petrarch and a poem by Abelard. More surprising than all this was that all the letters, except one from Galileo, which was in Italian, were in eighteenth-century French. Mary Magdalene's script began:

'*Mon très aimé frère Lazarus, ce que me mandez de Petrus l'apostre de notre doux Jesus*'; furthermore this epistle was supposed to have been written from Marseilles. Lucas was exposed and after his trial was left with a two-year sentence to serve and a fine of five hundred francs.

The failure to take sufficient trouble over the type and texture of paper he uses often gives the forger away. Texture tends to reveal the fake where an alteration or substitution is involved. No good forger would consider just erasing, for example, a signature and writing a fresh one in its place. After erasing the original, he carefully rubs the surface of the paper with an agate burnisher where it had been erased to restore its previous smooth sheen. Unfortunately for him, if you are suspicious, you can easily show up the newly-burnished area by sprinkling it with powdered graphite, and then shaking the powder off. It will only adhere to that part of the paper which was burnished, leaving a tell-tale grey patch on the otherwise pristine white page.

Another oversight about paper which sometimes gives away even the most technically adroit forger of documents is the watermark. See a watermark and the paper can immediately be dated to the years when that particular mark was used by any given paper mill. But a quick glance is not enough. Using a well-known household disinfectant it is possible to paint a copy of a watermark on an otherwise unmarked sheet of writing paper which can look highly plausible to the inexpert eye, especially if that eye sees it against poor light. A successful forger, adept at using a fine tipped paint brush, can with sufficient time, produce an excellent watermark, and he may place a mark using a bent wire stamp, having first bandaged the wire so that it will hold the disinfectant.

One regular practice in forging documents is not so much the addition of fraudulent items but the elimination of undesirable ones. Often this means cutting off an inappropriate letter heading, a contradictory last paragraph or signature, or a revealing note in the margin of any given page. Despite the continuing lack of conformity about page sizes, caused by the painfully gradual acceptance of the metric system, it is relatively easy to find the original dimensions of a given sheet of paper and compare the suspect page with them. If it is smaller, something must have happened to it. Often however that 'happening' is easily perceived without reference to paper makers' catalogues. Using small scissors it is virtually impossible to cut paper in a straight line, and even with large ones careful inspection will reveal the tiny notches between each cut. If, however, the size of the page is correct the faker will have had to insert his fraudulent information among existing print or handwriting. Unless you make a mistake you are very unlikely to squash two lines of script together, or squeeze a signature into the very bottom of a page. However ill-educated or mean about writing paper, most people have an ineradicable sense of proportion when it comes to filling a page, and this sense is at its extreme when it involves official documentary records like cheques, important letters or wills. You are very unlikely to compress either your signature or your normal writing when you know that you have plenty of space. If several people are asked to sign a document they too will space out their signatures, one after the other. If, however, you find three signatures below one another with the second one squeezed between the other two you have very reasonable grounds for thinking it was probably added at a later date. Similarly if, for example, the number of noughts on an IOU or a cheque seem curiously cramped together you may well question whether there has been a fraudulent addition. If the last paragraph or sentence of some written agreement looks uncomfortably compressed and at the same time completely alters the meaning of everything before it, although it could be an innocent correction or afterthought, it is much more likely to be evidence of criminal tampering.

Lest the reader consider in this age of television scanners linked to super-intelligent computers, that technology must by now have mastered the detection of fraud committed by mere humans, it may be added that it is only two years since the police discovered an international team of fakers operating on such a vast scale that they made the Great Train Robbery look like petty larceny. Mr Kenneth Richardson, speaking for the prosecution, told the Central Criminal Court on 19 February 1978, 'It was a fraud, the Crown say, which really knew no limit. If it had not been checked, and if it had gone on, there can be little doubt it would have undermined the banking system of virtually the whole civilised world.'

Using concealed cameras, the police had built up a dossier of over five thousand photographs before pouncing. On 13 August 1976, after lengthy preparations, a series of dawn raids were mounted on various London addresses, and thirty people arrested. At 9 Vere Court near Queensway in West London, the police found quantities of forged passports, driving licences, vaccination certificates, and traveller's cheques, together with several stolen credit cards. In another room they discovered the actual presses and printing equipment used in creating the forgeries. From this apartment and other premises raided at the same time the police retrieved a total of nine and a half million dollars' worth of forged bankers' drafts. One of the accused held so many passports it was impossible to tell his true nationality; when questioned earlier by the police he was alleged to have refused to reveal any details about the operation, saying, 'I cannot tell. My life would be dead! Please sir, I kiss your hand but do not go on or they will kill me. It is very bad for me.'

Although the Crown had prepared two and a half tons of exhibits and 490 witnesses to call if needed, it was admitted that some of the biggest fish had escaped the police net, being in other countries at the time of the raid. The prosecutor said that those in the dock were only representatives of an international criminal conspiracy called 'The Organisation'. No British bank had suffered from their activities, but London was the operational centre of the conspiracy, whereby forged bank drafts were presented to banks throughout the world.

The 'Organisation' case was largely concerned with the wholesale faking of printed and handwritten documents. One of the major ironies of the current revolution in micro-miniaturised electronics, particularly in the field of computers where a single 'chip' the size of a pinhead can store a whole library of information, is that it was originally hoped such advances would eliminate the possibility of fraud.

A celebrated case of computer fraud occurred in the United States over the last few years where a failing insurance company staged a miraculous recovery on the stock market by literally inventing new clients and their new policies within the computer. The public auditors had no access to the paper-work at the various branches and relied on the computer's read-out to show the company's financial situation, which seemed to get healthier and healthier. Only when the company chiefs realised that, on the law of averages, some of the fictional clients must occasionally be dying off and their equally fictitious beneficiaries would require payment, did the enterprise run into trouble. Such cases alerted financiers to the possibility that anyone with access to a computer terminal and a knowledge of computer languages like Fortran or Algol might well be tempted to break their codes and type in a much improved balance to a current bank account, or even transfer money without their immediate knowledge. Banks are naturally reticent about publicising such cases, but it is known that the computer revolution has been accompanied by a considerable tightening in bank security precautions.

But somewhere in the great banking edifice there are probably loopholes still waiting for the bright faker to find them. It is reported, for example, that an American called Robert Roche, who for convenience occasionally assumed an English accent, had been cashing copies of traveller's cheques which he had cut out of old National Geographic magazines.

'Doctor Syntax at an Auction' by Thomas Rowlandson 1756–1827

If bank clerks or others remarked that the paper of the cheques did not feel quite right Roche's powers of persuasion were such that they invariably handed the cash over.

CHAPTER SIX

FURNITURE

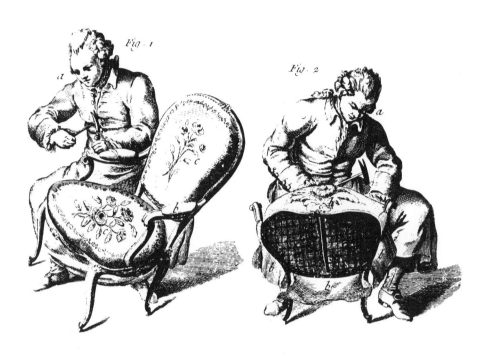

During the research stages of preparing *The Genuine Article* a number of leading experts in antique furniture were consulted. Some of these were based in fine premises in St James's and Bond Street in London. Their showrooms, discreetly patrolled by immaculate staff, with opulent clients to match just back from Yves St Laurent or Savile Row, were a treasure trove of exquisite veneers, ormolu and everything from Jacobean splendour to William Morris fantasies. Ask the actual price of even the most insignificant side-table and your question is politely ignored while you are told that the object under review, 'is rather charming, isn't it?' That reply quickly puts you and the capacity of your wallet firmly in place.

'As you obviously well know, it's a rather pleasant little bit of Hepplewhite. I can't immediately recall its precise date, but I've got the full provenance in my files. Just look at the elegance of those legs, and then that decoration, that's marvellous I think—No, not that bruise nor that chipped piece—although that's the wonderful thing about this delightful little table: to our certain knowledge it's been in the Duke of What's-his-name's home at some period, in fact I suggest ever since it was made; and no one's ever restored it. It's absolutely perfect!'

If you were foolish enough to retort that it does seem to have suffered rather brutal treatment in his grace's household you would probably be informed either that,

'In that case you are more likely to find cabinet work of your taste in Oxford Street,' or that, 'We'd, of course, be only too glad to have it restored to its original condition for you.'

Repeat the query about the price and the murmured reply may well be,

'Oh, I'm sure it's well under fifteen.'

'Well, that's not so bad after all . . . let's forget the bumps and bashes, I'll have it.'

'Fifteen grand, sir!'

'Fifteen what?'

'Fifteen thousand pounds, sir, and you won't find a nicer example than this.'

We exaggerate, perhaps, but not by much. Such encounters highlight several problems for those who wish to buy good antique furniture. The first is provenance, or where the piece came from and what its life history has been: the fact that the Duke of What's-his-name possessed it 'at some period' doesn't reveal that he only had it in his house just prior to an auction last week and that it had just arrived there from some furniture knacker's yard.

That the table is not in pristine condition is by no means a guarantee of age. In the furniture programme the construction of a magnificent sideboard with beautiful veneered patterns of Grecian urns was shown. It was not a fake, but was called a piece of 'reproduction furniture'. When finished it was an admirable piece of modern craftsmanship, created by a blend of old and new techniques to achieve a truly handsome piece. It was appalling to see what then happened to this perfect product of modern skill. An expert in what the trade correctly calls 'distressing' marched up to it with a hammer and a rock. He proceeded to give it the kind of beating that would evoke sympathy from the most inveterate sadist. He dented it liberally, scarred it around the handles and key-holes, and savaged every edge which might have come into accidental contact with some mythical lackey in its non-existent history. He then coated it with a seemingly impervious layer of black muck and seemed proudly content with his work. We surveyed this disaster and politely shook our heads. We had hoped to film the finished article in a country-house setting to show it off in all its glory, but patently the 'distressor' had gone too far. We had filmed the whole story of this sideboard from its origins from modern veneers and laminated ply-board (which resists warping better than its solid wood precedents) and the whole team was looking forward to seeing the end-product.

The 'distressor' laughed at us, spattered the sideboard with additional flecks and streaks of even darker fluid and began to 'restore' it. Within only minutes it looked quite appealing, and most convincingly older. By the time it had been cleaned, sprayed and wax-polished the piece appeared to be of the age of its original design. The company explained that there was no market for 'perfect' reproductions: 'The public want to buy something that looks old, even though we sell it as brand new. That means we've got to 'distress' it—however lovely you may think our finished work, it won't sell until we've aged it.'

The products of that particular company sell all over the world. They sell them as reproduction furniture. Unfortunately, and not very surprisingly, dealers have been known to pass off their wares as the genuine article. The result is that certain museums in the United States are currently displaying as authentic 'period' furniture, pieces incorporating modern laminates produced as recently as 1970.

The snag with furniture is that if you cut into the object to check the quality or age of the wood, you risk ruining it. There are, however, easier tests. An apocryphal story involving the late Gilbert Harding illustrates the point. He was an enthusiastic connoisseur of antique furniture. It is alleged that even the most self-assured Mayfair salesman would visibly flinch at his approach. If any piece of furniture particularly intrigued him, he would take a screwdriver out of his pocket and carefully remove several screws for close examination. The first machine-made screws were manufactured in 1851: the uniform regularity of their thread makes them relatively easy to differentiate from hand-made varieties. Find one in any piece of furniture supposed to be made before 1851 and you have grounds for suspicion, although it could have been inserted during repairs or restoration. Find several machine-made screws in an 'antique' and you are fully justified in asking some hard questions about the seller's virtue—and Harding, once alerted, would pursue his enquiries with gleeful tenacity. Unfortunately, lest any of our readers should blame us when they are forcibly ejected from a West End furniture gallery after assaulting a genuine Chippendale chair with a screwdriver, we should point out that considerable expertise is needed to guarantee the results of Harding's screw test. As was demonstrated in the furniture programme the forger is just as aware of the 1851 date-line for machine-made screws as the connoisseur. A little judicious distressing with a file and a bit of ageing in acid can give a brand-new screw a very plausible patina and if the precise spiral of its thread is damaged a little it can appear remarkably 'hand-made'.

Often there is no need for such dramatic public assays of authenticity. Apart from when he apes the truly top-quality antique cabinet-makers' craft, the modern faker cannot afford the time-consuming, costly skills which occasionally defy even expert detection. The surprising fact is that such fakers thrive on our laziness. We witnessed buyers in several stores making the most cursory examination of so-called 'antiques', sometimes for prices of well over a thousand pounds. To help in detecting, for example, trickery with what is supposed to be a genuine Sheraton sideboard, a little study of the type of dovetailing and jointing used at the time, and some knowledge about the woods and the way Sheraton cabinet-makers used them, can go a long way towards preventing a costly mistake.

But to realise that an unnamed, 'genuine eighteenth-century' piece is at least partially a fake, all you often have to do is examine the drawers. In one store near Kensington Palace, the drawer of a very pretty break-front bookcase was pulled out. The base looked strangely new; on being turned upside down the name of a much publicised maker of cigars who had only begun trading since Fidel Castro came to power could be seen. No one had even bothered to sand it off: presumably the fakers of middle market 'antique' furniture have a hearty contempt for the knowledge and lack of

curiosity of their clients. The same bookcase had attractive gilt handles, which bore very convincing signs of wear and slight, but appealing patination. Open the drawers, however, and the metal screws from the handles protruded clumsily through rough and obviously recently made metal nuts. The running edges of the 'period' drawers showed hastily roughened treatment meant to imply lengthy use. The back of the bookcase, although stained to look like something listed in the Doomsday Book, was so badly finished and so blatantly made of new wood that it reeked of fresh sap.

Another intriguing sign which rightly horrifies the housewife, and is conversely highly appealing to the novice furniture collector, is woodworm, that little insect that has been associated for a long time with the faker. Many still regard the worm-ridden appearance of any piece of furniture as a guarantee of age. The ways are numerous in which the forger has tried to satisfactorily simulate the holes, the most primitive being jabs with a needle, the most professional coming from skill with the use of dental drills. Stories abound of forgers peppering their wares with buckshot to give a semblance of the active careers of a colony of greedy Georgian wood-worms. Try it, preferably in the security of a rifle-range. The pattern of shot will either be too close together or too uniform, and certainly the 'distressing' will have gone too far and the piece will be so chipped, splintered, and bruised that it will need days of extra work in further 'restoration'. A gentle probing could of course extract the lead from the hole. One deception with fake worm-holes that is practised is to fill them with a tinted wax, either bees' or carnauba. This could be a legitimate thing to do when restoring and if it is done on false holes it can be highly misleading.

Fake worm-holes are not the only indication of roguery in wooden panels—genuine worm-holes in the wrong place are an equally good warning of mischief. Reputable restorers and the better forgers both insist on always using old wood. The restorer would never use wood containing worm-holes, but the bad forger, in the hope of making his work even more deceptive, often does. And equally often, if he does not have some biological understanding of the life-style of wood-worms, he runs the risk of being caught out by being a shade too clever.

The fake Botticelli which Professor Stephen Rees Jones examined for us in the programme about forged paintings was found wrong by him on

93

several counts, but just a quick study of the wood on which it had been painted gave it away without much need for any confirmatory tests. It contained worm-holes; the insect larvae tunnel along the grain of the wood, and, when they turn into insects, emerge on either side of the panel, front or back. Professor Rees Jones pointed to the top edge of the panel and commented, 'Some of these channels come up into thin air. That is quite outside the habits of wood-worms. So this was cut after it had been affected by worm.' Obviously Botticelli himself would not have chosen a wormy piece of wood on which to create a masterpiece, so as the wood painted on was a worm-ridden panel, it had to be a fake.

Similar clues await any painstaking student of furniture. If worm-holes are perceived on any surface cut across the grain it is almost certain the piece was made from already worm-eaten wood. With that knowledge you may draw your own conclusions about its authenticity. Similarly, even with all the holes in a piece coming out of flat surfaces, if only one panel has been attacked, and tapping the wood fails to cause powdered sawdust to show in the holes (a sure sign of recent infestation) the piece must again be regarded with suspicion as the wood-worm is unlikely to have found one panel of a piece made from similar timbers at the same time, uniquely succulent—there should be evidence of worm damage throughout the whole genuine article.

One important tell-tale sign of a fake in not just furniture but virtually every collectable item, can be its price. Only the most brilliant forgeries are priced at around or even sometimes over the market value of the genuine article. Nearly every other fake appears to be marked down to attract the 'bargain hunter'. Therefore, if you have any doubts about the price, be extremely wary and make a careful examination of the object: all the better if you can have someone with you who really knows the subject.

Unfortunately, as anyone who has attempted to build up even the smallest collection of antique furniture will know, many of the best 'finds' change hands at auctions, often held at country-house sales. Such occasions used to be notorious as a venue for 'the ring', a group of dealers who keep the bidding low, except when an outsider innocently tries to outbid them when they club together to defeat him; after the public auction the 'ring' conduct their own private auction among themselves, avoiding the expense of bidding against the general public. Participating in an auction 'ring' is a criminal offence; auctioneers are constantly watching out for suspicious behaviour, but even in the best conducted sale it can be extremely difficult to detect the operation of a 'ring', particularly when it has already decided to buy only a small number of the items on sale.

The furniture director of a leading establishment was asked for his advice on buying, he said:

If you've bought from a reputable dealer and you've discovered that whatever it is is not what he said on the invoice, go and talk to him. Bring witnesses to show that it isn't what he said it was. If he's a dealer worth his salt he will either give you your money back, give you a credit note, or even offer to sell the piece for you. So all's not lost. If you buy at auction, however, I think things are slightly more difficult. Certainly the major London auction houses give you in some cases ten or fifteen days; if, in that time you discover that what you've bought is not as they've catalogued it, you can take it back and there are no questions asked.

He advised that the man in the street should not be preoccupied with fakes.

I don't think you want to go into the shop, an antique shop, and assume that everything in there is a fake, and that all antique dealers are crooks; they're not. The majority are honest, straightforward people making a living. In furniture there aren't that many out and out fakes: more likely pieces have been altered for financial gain, perhaps, for example, with early eighteenth century pieces they may have been reduced in size to make them more attractive.

He added that the big problem with English furniture comes where you have pieces made by the very fine nineteenth-century craftsmen which he regards as often far better made than eighteenth-century furniture, yet made in exactly the same way. Such furniture is today a hundred years old, and has had time to acquire the patination and marks of wear and tear which are the outward signs of antiquity. He considers that the faker usually gives himself away with too much distressing. As he explained, 'You wouldn't normally tie the dog chain around a chair leg.'

As a senior London dealer himself it was not with total disinterest that he encouraged potential buyers to confine purchases to reputable companies. When he was younger he had bought his wife what he thought to be a Victorian ring.

When she took it to be repaired after one of the pearls fell out, it transpired to be a modern copy of a Victorian ring. So I was taken in, by not going to an expert, and paying perhaps a

95

little bit more for expertise. Anybody can open an antique shop. Any bored housewife, failed actor, can rent a shop, put the word 'antiques' over the door, put a copper pan in the window, and suddenly assume all the expertise of an antique dealer. There are no qualifications necessary to become an antique dealer. It's having an eye and a taste and the money that goes with it. This is a big problem.

He warned against one particular, smooth-talking, breed of rogues in the antique trade who, whilst often being considerable experts, prosper by not divulging the extent of their expertise; they are called 'Knockers', and go around knocking on front doors preying on unsuspecting old ladies: for the first thing they see they may offer a very high price, often well above its actual market value. The intrigued listener invites them in and shows them the rest of his or her treasures. The knockers then buy something else, a Sheraton sideboard in the dining-room. They offer four hundred pounds for the sideboard, pay for it in cash, apologise profusely that they have no more cash, and no more room in their van, and are now unable to take the thing they first saw for which they offered so much money. The sideboard they bought is probably worth treble what they paid for it. They never return to buy the first, overvalued object.

Quite apart from the hazard of 'knockers' attempting to relieve you of a genuine article, that expert made one point which every bargain hunter, collector and would-be connoisseur would find useful to remember:

It's vital to buy what you like. Don't just buy for investment. Make sure it's something you really enjoy and always bear in the back of your mind that if it turns out to be a fake, you're stuck with it and you've got to jolly well like it. It's going to be sitting in your home and you're going to look at it for a long time, so be sure that you like it. Don't just rush out, spend a hundred pounds and think that you're going to turn that into five hundred pounds in a year. That's not really the name of the game. Treat it as an added bonus if it happens, but don't go into it with an idea of an investment. Many people do, and I think it shouldn't be the primary reason for buying something.

The antique furniture trade can be highly confusing for the novice: if for example a catalogue lists an object as 'Chippendale', then adds the date at which it was supposed to be made and some details of provenance (who has owned it, when and where), and the piece turns out to be false, the buyer has recourse in law against the seller for misrepresentation. However, the description 'Chippendale type' could mean anything from the piece being made in Chippendale's time from one of his designs to an unashamed modern reproduction, a nineteenth-century fake, or a 'marriage'. By 'marriage' the trade mean a host of alliances, the French call it *l'assemblage*, of parts that may be antique and are put together to form a highly confusing whole. An example of a 'marriage' could be concerned with two Georgian bookcases. The top of one and the base of the other have been accidently damaged beyond reasonable repair. The undamaged top of the latter is matched to the base of the former, thereby sensibly salvaging one good piece from two wrecks. A less reputable alliance is where one antique is carefully taken apart and the bits used as components of several otherwise modern antique copies. In the trade each of these almost wholly new objects might then be catalogued using the description and provenance of the unaltered original, with a let-out clause saying 'heavily restored after a fire' or a similar excuse.

This business of restoration and how far a restorer can go before, in effect, creating a brand-new piece, poses difficult ethical problems for dealer and customer alike. It is largely a matter of conscience that should govern the extremes to which restoration can be carried. The expert had in his office a small pile of broken wood in the corner. When asked: 'Now, say you were given a load of firewood like that, is any restorer clever enough to convert it into something that, because he'd obviously be starting off with genuine old wood, could pass muster as a genuine antique?' He was highly indignant that there was a possible suggestion that he himself would ask anyone to create a fake. The query was rephrased: 'What one is trying to get at is could a really skilled craftsman turn old rubbish like that into a plausible fake and pass it off as "genuine, but heavily restored"?' His anger, it then emerged, was not so much at the questions but at the mistake over the pile of firewood.

He had found the remains of the chair in a country dealer's shop and realised as soon as he got it into the workshop, and started to take the upholstery off that he was in for a long, hard, restoration job. But he believed the chair to be well worth saving. It was made by Thomas Roberts, a late seventeenth-century English chairmaker. He is recorded as having made Queen Anne's Coronation Chair, and supplying chairs for Penshurst Place, a firescreen for Windsor Castle, and more chairs for Hampton Court. He was a court upholsterer, cabinet maker and chair

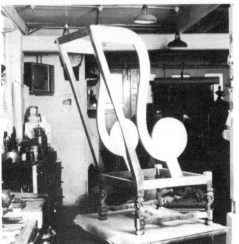

Above: the bare bones of the chair attributed to Thomas Roberts

Opposite: the finished chair upholstered and covered in crewel work

maker. The chair cost four hundred pounds, a good sum by any standards for furniture in that condition. The cost of restoration was estimated to be about a thousand pounds. The specialist went on: 'it depends on how it looks as to how much we can ask for it. There's no great profit in it—it's just a chair that I think is an exciting challenge and worth restoring. Why

reject it now because it's in such a state. We've got the craftsmen to put it back together and make it something for future generations.'

He was asked if he was doing it for the good of his heart or for turning it into a profit at the end.

'A bit of both. I'm passionately interested in that sort of work, in completely restoring something. Obviously at the end of it we hope to make some money—we're a commercial operation. The profit's not going to be tremendous but there's a great deal of satisfaction there, and it's a wonderful story, and it's a wonderful chair.'

He was interrupted, 'But it will be a brand-new chair.'

'No, no—it won't. There was one new piece—underneath the stretcher and one rail was rotten—a rail that you won't even see when it's uphol-stered—that we shall have to replace so there will be two new pieces of wood in the whole of that chair. And they won't be brand-new pieces of wood—we'll use old beech.'

A few months later the chair appeared in the showroom after it had received considerable expert attention. The skill of the restoring craftsman was impressive, how he had produced this perfection from a few bits of worm-riddled, patently useless, derelict wood. It was in fact a lady's chair. The bill from the joiner's workshop alone came to a thousand pounds and in the end, as they'd predicted, only two pieces had to be renewed, the leading rail in the front and the stretcher in the middle underneath. The upholstery was genuine seventeenth-century crewel-work wool embroid-ery, dismounted off its original mounting and then put on to a green linen. The gilding, using traditional methods, simulated the appearance it would have had originally. Who would have thought, looking at that pile of wood we saw earlier, that such a restoration could have been possible. But inevitably it was a very costly business and if you had wanted to buy the chair the figure would have been somewhere around three thousand pounds.

Ironically what makes the detection of genuine antiques more confusing than necessary is not just the custom of 'distressing' modern reproduction pieces, but the practice of re-polishing *bona fide* antiques. After a life of two hundred years, furniture can be expected to have built up a considerable patination, the result of being wax polished and dusted several thousand times, being handled, and suffering all the spillages of wine, beer, tea, coffee and ink that are the natural disasters of every household. Clean off all those signs of age and repolish a piece and it becomes very difficult to be certain about its antiquity, and even more difficult to see if it has been heavily restored, is the product of a skilful marriage, or worst of all, is an outright fake.

There are, however, a few clues which the faker finds extremely difficult to disguise. Two centuries ago well-seasoned timber was in plentiful supply. Cabinet-makers always gave great attention to choosing the ideal wood, and matched it perfectly. Therefore if you see a table, chest of drawers, or chair where the colour of each component is not uniform you have grounds for suspicion. Moreover with large pieces like sideboards they would never have economised by making the top from two or three planks: they always cut them from the solid, so if you detect a join on such a top it is likely to be either Victorian, or later.

Screws have already been mentioned, but even without removing them they can often reveal tell-tale signs about restoration or faking. The genuine screw will have acquired a dark patina that is difficult to reproduce, and the wood around it will also have darkened as a result of slight rusting and a two-centuries build-up of surplus wax and dirt. If the screws have been counter-sunk and their tops covered with a round sliver of wood, the grain and colour of this 'patch' should match the surrounding timber, for the original carpenter would have had access to plenty of surplus matching wood. If the 'patch' is a different colour or grain it must indicate restoration work, for the restorer or faker is unlikely to have a precise match in his store of old timber.

Keyholes and their surrounding brass plates known as escutcheons often provide an easy aid to authentication: if their base is rounded they are likely to be either genuine or modern reproduction, and the reproductions often give themselves away by the lack of discolouration of the brass. If the base of a keyhole is flat and squared off it is almost certainly either seventeenth century or Victorian. The surround of the keyhole can be also be a give-away: if it is small and circular it is almost certainly a Victorian Bramah lock. Open the drawer or door and this suspicion will be confirmed if the retaining plate bears either a patent number or the name of the lock-smith. If the keys still exist, their handles should be thin and describe an elegant bean-shaped outline, and not be just a flattened circle of metal.

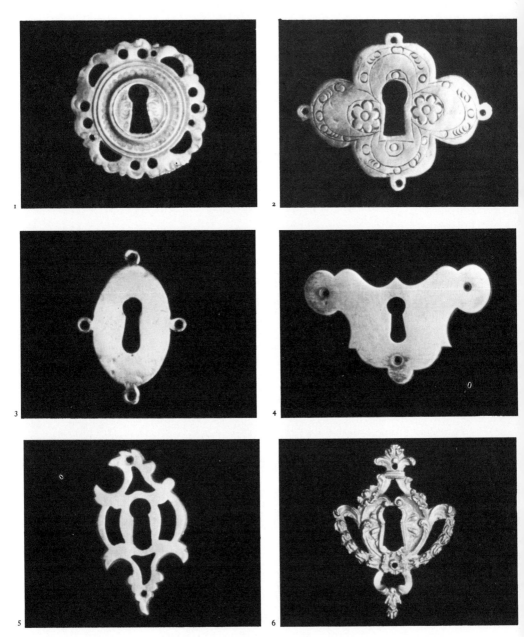

Genuine brass escutcheons: 1. mid-17th century pierced; 2. late-17th century engraved; 3. early-18th century plain oval; 4. early-18th century shaped; 5. mid-18th century pierced and shaped; 6. late-18th century cast in an Adam design incorporating swags

If there is any carving it should be proud, projecting above the surface and not cut into it. Another sign of the genuine is the depth of the carving: it should be bold and strong, and if instead the incisions are relatively shallow, it is a possible sign of the penny-pinching economies of a late Victorian cabinet-maker.

Any forger attempting to 'improve' an old piece of furniture by decorating it with extra details of carving has two alternatives. He can either cut into the wood to gain his effect or glue his carving on the existing surface. If he chooses the latter tactic it is often fairly easy to detect; even with the most modern adhesives it is extremely difficult to achieve a firm, permanent bond if you try to stick pieces on old wood surfaces. The patina of the old surface is almost glue-proof, and the forger has to cut away a thin layer, the exact shape of his carving, to give the glue a sufficiently textured

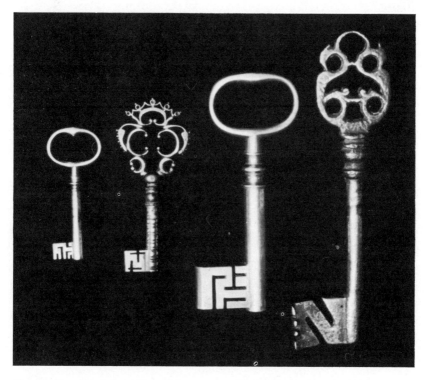

Genuine keys from left to right: 18th-century steel key with oval wire bow; fine Charles I period decorated steel key with engraved barrel; 18th-century steel key with oval wire bow; early 17th-century large steel key with decorated bow

surface for the glue to stick efficiently. Unless the carving fits this shallow trough with exquisite perfection any knowledgeable observer will clearly detect the slight occasional indentation around the side of the carving where it does not firmly abut the edge of the trough. And if the forger attempts to fill this crack, that too is another sign which should alert suspicion. Similarly if the forger attempts to decorate the surface with pierced wooden tracery to simulate an area of caning he encounters even worse problems, and is almost bound to make mistakes which once you realise the extent of his task are even easier to see.

Carved decoration may also be simulated by burning. A cast iron matrix is made to the pattern desired. This is then heated and pressed into the wood in a special manner and after this any excessive charring can be removed with a stiff wire-brush. The finished 'carving' is treated with linseed or teak oil and wax, and can look very antique with the darkening from the iron matrix and the weathered distressed look from the wire-brush. The gentle patina of three or four hundred years can be closely approached by applying benzine in which a little beeswax has been dissolved. Little of this polish should be put on, the rest of the trick relies on plenty of muscle power and a large wool-pad.

A favourite trick where a break or alteration in a leg needs concealing is called 'bandaging', in cabinet-making jargon. The offending scar is hidden by three strips of wood glued horizontally to the front and sides of the leg to make a collar around it. Matching 'bandages' are then attached to all the other legs. The give-away is that the grain and tone of the 'bandage' will never match the leg out of which it was supposed to have been carved; and also if the 'bandage' has not been taken around the back of the leg the join will be easy to see. It is the backs of all sideboards, wardrobes and other pieces of furniture designed to stand against a wall which nearly always provide the clearest evidence of what the trade euphemistically calls 'naughtiness'. Whether a piece has been repolished or not, it is highly improbable that the restorer will have bothered to clean the back. It should be very dark and heavily patinated. If the piece is of recent origin, the result of a marriage, or excessively restored, you will almost certainly find the tell-tale signs on the back.

Finally a return to the subject of provenances and a few further points of caution. First, just because a piece is offered with a detailed provenance to corroborate its authenticity, there is no reason why both the piece itself and its provenance should not themselves both be excellent examples of the forger's art. Secondly, there have often been cases where, although the piece is discovered to be a fake, its provenance was absolutely genuine. If that is a surprise, auction rooms often prepare lavishly illustrated catalogues for their sales, and these contain well-authenticated provenances. Unfortunately there is no possibility of a law which could forbid forgers from acquiring such catalogues and creating copies of the articles described in them. There are laws forbidding forgers to then offer their copies for sale as being genuine, and substantiating that claim by showing the original catalogues as evidence of their piece's last change of ownership, but, as fakes continue to abound, some forgers presumably think it is worth the risk. To all this might be applied the Italian adage: *Fatta la legge trovato l'inganno*, which freely translated means: 'Make a law and the means of evasion are found.'

CHAPTER SEVEN

JEWELLERY

'They're amazing!'

In 1969 Richard Burton paid £416,687 for a 69.42 carats diamond for Elizabeth Taylor. Another stone had joined the catalogue of the rare and publicised gems that have illuminated the history of jewellery. The giant at the top of the list is still Cullinan I which is set in the royal sceptre of Britain and weighs 530.20 carats; second is the Cullinan II at 317.4 carats and this rests in the band of the Imperial State Crown. Among the crown jewels is also the Kohinoor, a stone that has perhaps the most notorious history of any; bloodshed and intrigue and the search for power cloud its past almost from when it was found in 1304. Diamonds seem to create their own particular atmosphere; a compound of breathtaking value – only exceeded by that of rubies – and the legends of violence and romance that follow them. But, for their collectors they often bring considerable anxiety.

Soon after receiving the gift of her diamond Miss Taylor had a copy made. Understandably her insurance people must have suggested that they would be unhappy for her to wear the genuine diamond in public on too many occasions. Yet no expert, even at arm's length, can tell whether she is wearing the genuine or the fake. It might be asked, 'does it matter?' But with diamonds and other gem-stones just as with any other valuable genuine articles it matters enormously because it is no longer a question of the beauty being in the eye of the beholder – the bank manager's eye is perceptive in seeing optical virtues only in terms of tangible assets. However pretty an imitation, however many people it may deceive, its monetary value is all that concerns him. As a result the majority of the finest diamonds and other beautiful gem-stones are entombed in dark bank vaults, perhaps gaining value, but pleasing no one apart from financiers.

Diamonds are not just a girl's best friend, 'they are forever' as De Beers, the world monopolists of the diamond trade, continually remind us in their sales propaganda. Unlike any other gem-stone their price is constantly under review, and De Beers control it as sternly as they are able, lest it should rocket up, or worse plunge down like the occasional alarming fluctuations in the gold market. It was not surprising therefore that when Henri Lemoine of Paris announced in 1905 that he was close to succeeding with his experiments in diamond making, that the world of diamond merchants was considerably ruffled. The hitherto impregnable bastions of the diamond market were, to say the least, startled at the thought of a man who, working in the vein of an alchemist to transform the base into the valuable, might be near success. This time the path led him not amongst bowls of bats' blood, saucers of toads' eyes, and phials of snakes' bile but into an arena that held unthinkable pressures and temperatures that challenged the gut of a volcano, although there was still a mysterious element, a secret paste, a handful of carefully guarded powders.

Henri Lemoine was so seemingly sure of himself that he sought an interview in London with Sir Julius Wernher, the South African financier who founded Wernher, Beit & Co., and who was also a life governor of De Beers Consolidated Mines. Lemoine claimed he could make gem diamonds on a commercial scale. He boasted to Sir Julius he had a secret method that he would exchange for a royalty payment on the diamonds he made if Sir Julius would give him financial backing. He even provided an initial demonstration in a rented laboratory. His recipe was placed in a crucible and heated for about thirty minutes. It was removed, and when cooled from the remains of the ingredients appeared twenty-five small stones which were indubitably diamonds.

Sir Julius was sufficiently convinced to invest forward funds to set up a laboratory in Paris and underwrite three years of work. Sample diamonds were sent to him from time to time by Lemoine. But, when it was pointed out that the man-made stones were exactly similar to those being found in the Jagersfontein mine in the Orange Free State, the culprit was unmasked. The conjurer had secreted natural diamonds in his mixture. He was arrested and received six years for his sleight-of-hand.

Meanwhile others were working honestly along the trail that could lead to almost instant wealth. James Ballantyre Hannay (1855–1931), a Glasgow chemist, did produce some minute stones. Following him came another Frenchman, Henri Moissan (1852–1907) who, inspired by the discovery of small diamonds found in the Canyon Diablo meteorite, thought of the idea of great heat and pressure creating the gems. In England at about the same time some rather devastating attempts were being made by Sir William Crookes, who set about solving the problems of the colossal pressures necessary by exploding cordite in sealed steel tubes.

Then, in 1955, in Schenectady in the United States, the General Electric Company succeeded in making a very small but absolutely perfect diamond by using tremendous pressures and very high temperatures. A few years later they went further and made a diamond big enough to be used in jewellery. With a temperature of 5500 degrees Fahrenheit and a pressure of two and a quarter million pounds per square inch they converted graphite into a one carat stone. Man had truly made his diamond, but it had cost him more than a natural stone mined from the ground.

The story of diamonds dates back nearly two thousand years, when craftsmen in India found that if they rubbed two diamonds together they could develop primitive facets: they had discovered the unique optical properties of diamond which reflects and transmits back more light than any other gem-stone. The primitive craft of diamond cutting gradually became a highly-skilled art, until in 1640 the Dutch devised the forerunner of all the modern cuts, the rose-cut.

Many of the famous diamonds from the past have come from India, and it is from here that some of the fantasies spring: there was Sinbad's 'Valley of the Diamonds' and tales of stones being found in the brains of serpents. One writer suggests that the former legend could have sprung from the sacrificial practices of the Indians against evil spirits when they were opening a new mine; giant birds of prey would carry off the flesh to which stones could have adhered.

As the lure of diamonds became progressively more attractive, so did the fakers' skill in producing simulants. The Romans became adept at making glass copies, and by the Renaissance these vitrified, or 'paste' imitations were backed with painted metal foil to reflect more light and give the extra colour and sparkle that characterises a true diamond. The most famous of these pastes was that produced by James Tassie (1735–99) who worked with Henry Quinn, a physician and a collector of gems. In 1763 they made a vitreous paste that would simulate various gem stones, and they started what almost amounted to mass production. Rudolph Raspe the creator of the celebrated mendacious story-teller Baron Munchausen, catalogued the stones in 1791 and this ran to 15,800 items.

Many people fail, when encountering what might be a 'Tassie', to realise that the easiest test of a diamond set in a ring is not to try to ruin the nearest window by scratching it, but simply to see if the alleged diamond is backed by metal, or set in some kind of cup or mount, which, if it were glass, would enable you to see through it. Diamond, when correctly cut, reflects almost all the light that enters it, and therefore needs no reflecting surface behind it to give it extra 'fire'.

Again, although the deceptive nature of paste diamonds has been the keystone of a century of detective stories, the existence of really excellent diamond simulants was almost a trade secret until quite recently when their commercial potential became irresistible, and companies began to market synthetic simulants like YAG, under trade names like Diagem. YAG on the Mohs hardness scale rates 8.25 against the genuine diamond's 10. This scale was developed by a German mineralogist in 1812, and is based on scratching power of one stone against another.

Advertisements proclaim: 'YAG, the wonder diamond substitute that fools the experts.' There is one, rather blatant, error, YAG may indeed fool an expert specialising in Irish cuckoo clocks, but it will never fool an expert in diamonds provided he is permitted to examine it properly.

Today there are many extremely good diamond simulants, even better than YAG – and YAG itself is marvellously deceptive as was discovered during a BBC Television programme a few years ago about illusion. Members of the studio audience were challenged to tell the difference between a genuine diamond and an imitation. A tray of simulants containing one genuine diamond (which was extremely prominent) was produced and the audience was told that if anyone could spot the real diamond he could keep it. Not unnaturally a lady was the first to jump out of her seat for a try. She was allowed a long, close examination of the tray before insisting that the moment of truth had arrived. She was certain about her choice. The stone she had selected was then studied by an expert, and

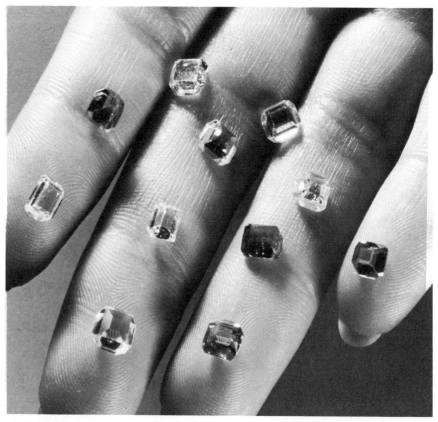

Artificial diamonds created in the laboratory by scientists at the General Electric Research and Development Center in New York

Left: a genuine diamond
Right: a YAG imitation

several million people were grossly disappointed that she picked the wrong one.

A similar test was made during the Jewellery programme of 'The Genuine Article'; could the eye of the viewer spot the genuine diamond amongst the twelve stones displayed in a velvet lined tray? It also provided a chance for viewers, even within the visual limits of ill-adjusted black and white or colour sets, to see the difference between at least half of the dozen stones. As the tray was slightly tilted back from the vertical a kind of window appeared in six of the stones through which one could clearly see the velvet behind them. Some were paste (glass or *diamante*), others synthetic white sapphire or white zircon, a traditional diamond simulant. When cut in, for example, what is called a 'brilliant' cut, light passes into a diamond through the top (or 'table' facets) and almost all of it is reflected back by the facets on the bottom of the stone (the 'pavilion'), hence the vivid sparkle of the true stone. Glass and some other diamond simulants are less efficient at bending light and trapping it than diamond, so at critical angles one can see straight through even the finest cut, paste, imitation diamond. The new modern crystal products are, however, more difficult to identify and jewellers have to resort to quite sophisticated instruments to spot them. With names like lithium niobate, gadalinium-gallium-garnet and ittrium-aluminate, and some seeming to outdo the brilliance and fire of even a diamond to the naked eye, many girls may rightly take a closer look at that ring on their finger and question if they have been taking their best friend too much for granted.

There is one other major pitfall for the collector, and that is the fraudulent coloration of natural diamonds, either by attempting to improve their colour or by giving them a desired tint; all such plans are made to fool an unwary bargain chaser. The methods that were used in the past were often crude; perhaps little more than painting round the girdle (the extreme edge of the stone) with a transparent dye. Some operators would immerse their stones in tinted chemical solutions to deposit a thin veil over the surface. With both the foregoing methods the colour would be removed with alcohol or a proprietary jewel cleaner. A more subtle method for faking colour on a natural stone is by irradiation. The simplest form of this was first made in 1904 by Sir William Crookes, the gentleman who must have come close to blowing himself up in attempts to make synthetic diamonds. His coloured stones could be detected by a geiger counter.

Today the most modern practice is to employ either neutron or electron bombardment. Salerooms in Geneva have had some trouble with yellow diamonds. Genuine off-white poor-quality stones had been treated to give them a highly sought after yellow tint to increase greatly their value. To the true expert's eye this artificially induced colour can cause suspicion. Not long ago a large stone of over 100 carats turned up for auction. It purported to be the famous Deepdene diamond. Bidding rose to nearly £500,000 with the last call coming from one of the best-known jewellers in Europe. Before completing the formalities the stone was tested by an international consortium from London, New York and Switzerland and it was found that irradiation had been used. The stone was not the Deepdene, and the deal was not completed.

In the major diamond marketing centre of the world, just off Hatton Garden in London, is a small laboratory. Here the constant preoccupation of the whole staff is to take neither any diamond nor any other gem-stone for granted. They are all first-class gemmologists and their life's work involves not just microscopes, but refractometers, spectroscopes, X-Rays and fluorescence tests in a constant battle with fakes as they attempt to weed out the genuine from the false.

This graveyard for forged jewels lies deep under the ground, its name-plate in the corridor above is obscure amid a host of other occupants of the

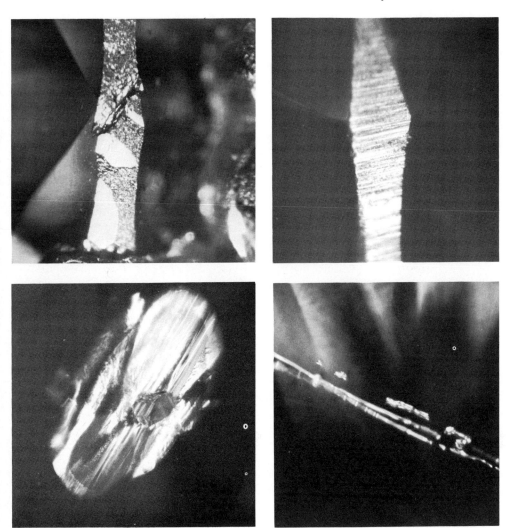

Top left: The girdle edge of diamond, showing the original skin of the diamond crystal

Top right: the girdle edge of a cubic zirconia, showing grinding lines not found on a diamond

Bottom left: diamond inclusion showing a crack caused by stress with a halo surround

Bottom right: inclusions in a cubic zirconia which at first sight appear like a cleavage fracture in diamond, but careful examination under a microscope shows they are extruded glass

building ranging from diamond merchants to manufacturing jewellers. The approach to the laboratory is down a flight of steps, but one is conscious all the time of television surveillance. Only people with prior appointments are admitted, and even then they only gain entry to a small inner-room where they are checked through the grille in yet another strong-room door, the outer door having already locked behind them. The man who originally set up the lab is Basil Anderson who hates the necessity for such precautions, but realises that they are necessary. He is by no means happy at the need for such a laboratory, but as he ruefully explained: 'In jewellery it would be an understatement to say that times have changed – they've changed with a vengeance and I'm often quite glad my age forced me to retire from what used to be a very civilised pursuit.' We suspect that by 'pursuit' Mr Anderson meant 'career', although in his case, with his years of experience in gem detection, he would have been equally justified if he had meant the successful pursuit of fakes and the villains who perpetrated them.

Today Basil Anderson is regarded as one of the top gemmologists in the world. The continual revisions of his classic, definitive work on the subject, *Gem-Testing*, is a vivid illustration of how the jeweller is hard put to keep up with developments in the industry, developments which have become a boon for the forger. The preface of the first edition in 1942 states 'this volume has been written mainly with the ordinary jeweller and dealer in view . . . showing him . . . the easy scientific tests . . . for discriminating with certainty between one stone and another.'

By 1951 the Preface had changed:

In the period which has elapsed . . . . there have been startling developments in the production of synthetic gemstones. Verneuil's flame fusion method . . . has been ingeniously modified to yield a spectacular new gemstone, synthetic rutile, and synthetic star rubies and sapphires. The appearance of the latter is somewhat disturbing, as it represents man's entry into a field in which Nature was thought to be inimitable.

In 1958 the Preface to the Sixth edition revealed,

There have been several important developments . . . since the last edition of this book. A new gem species, 'sinhalite', has been added to the list . . . it has already been accepted as stones belonging to other species . . . The arrival of strontium titanate, ... less easy to distinguish at sight from diamond than any other natural or artificial product. The synthetic emerald . . . . causing perturbation among those who deal in emeralds.

By the Seventh Edition in 1964 there had been a major increase in 'perturbation' among emerald dealers, making 'the critical study of all emeralds more than ever necessary'.

The Eighth Edition in 1971 warns that the trade 'is now faced . . . with a bewildering number of man-made stones – not to mention new methods of treating and 'faking' natural stones to improve their appearance'.

Because of his unique position in the history of modern gemmology, Mr Anderson has built up an almost unrivalled expertise, and few can be more conscious of the problems of fake detection. He explains:

Up till the beginning of this century the chief problems the jeweller had to contend with were either imitation stones, mainly made of coloured glass, or doublets, which consist of real stones cemented to a glass base. The jeweller with his very good eye, knowledge of stones, and with rather crude tests using a hardened file which would score a mark on glass quite easily but wouldn't touch natural gemstone, was able to cope fairly well with such fakes.

Then, late in the nineteenth century an extraordinary process for making synthetic gems was invented. By synthetic I mean a stone which has the same properties and the same crystal structure as the natural stone. The invention by Professor Verneuil in France meant that for the first time large quantities of synthetic stones could be made.

In nature a natural ruby can take a thousand years to form and is very rare. The Verneuil process takes two hours, and the jeweller's file is no longer any good to him to differentiate between a natural and a Verneuil ruby. The jeweller had to begin to learn the principles of science and use instruments like the microscope. The basis for the so-called corundum gems like ruby and sapphire is very pure aluminium oxide. Verneuil passed this in a fine powder through an extremely hot flame of oxyhydrogen. At over 2000 degrees centigrade the alumina melts, falling in a shower of droplets on a little pedestal to form a kind of stalagmite of ruby. As the synthetic ruby grows into a tiny dome, each droplet crystallises into a very fine layer. In section the layers can be clearly seen under a microscope as a thin series of gently curving parallel lines. With practice these lines can be seen with an ordinary ten times magnifying lens. In a natural ruby any parallel lines that are visible are straight because they are parallel to the faces of original natural crystal. Further almost all natural stones contain little particles of other crystals which have grown alongside the mineral in nature and are angular in shape and altogether different from the little bubbles which you often see in a Verneuil synthetic. But the task which Mr Anderson was first asked to tackle in 1925 concerned not stones, but pearls.

In the early 1920s the Japanese devised a method by which pearls could be grown like natural pearls in oysters by inserting into the body of the oyster a bead of mother of pearl. These oysters were cultivated in farms in the sheltered bays off the coast of Japan. The bead was wrapped in a bit of the skin of the oyster called the mantle, the pearl-secreting organism of the oyster. This was inserted into the soft body of living oysters which were kept in cages suspended from rafts in the bays. After two or three years a sufficient coating of natural pearl had been made by the oyster to create what appeared from the outside to be a perfectly good natural pearl.

As Mr Anderson explained,

It's difficult today to visualise the situation at that time and how important pearls were on the London and Paris markets. The best natural pearls were fished in the waters of the Persian Gulf and also off the coast of Ceylon. They were sent to Bombay for cleaning and drilling. The natives needed astonishing skill to drill as small a hole as possible to conserve the weight. Then the pearls were carefully matched for size and colour and assembled into bunches, all finished with silver tassels; a very beautiful sight indeed!

The great shock to the pearl trade was when they found that some of the pearls in those bunches, which were the fundamental source of all fine pearl jewellery, were being substituted by the new cultured pearls. It's rather mysterious how it happened because it certainly wouldn't have been worth the while for the Arab merchants to ruin their trade by such things. I suppose it was a great temptation for some of the people handling the pearls because they had very small wages. It was a real shock because you must understand there's a tremendous chain of confidence in this trade, the whole thing depends on confidence. In Hatton Garden in the days when I first came into it you could see this confidence working: there would be small dealers and brokers with parcels of diamonds in doorways and they would exchange these parcels without even a note of hand. You must have an absolutely sacrosanct source otherwise the whole of the trade becomes sullied by the incursion of false materials. Well in 1925, things had got to the point where these bunches could no longer be trusted, and the diamond, pearl and precious stone section of the London Chamber of Commerce decided on a rather bold step of establishing a laboratory which would be independent of any particular firm and which could, by scientific testing, make reports as to whether pearls were genuine or otherwise. I was asked to take the job, and though this was an entirely new field for me, I thought I'd have a go.

I was sent over to Paris to learn what they'd been doing in the way of testing, came back with inadequate apparatus, and had a miserable time to start with because I didn't really know anything about pearls. Eventually we had a very ingenious apparatus, the endoscope; it incorporates a thin hollow needle, like a hypodermic needle, in which were inserted two little mirrors. A strong beam of light was sent into the drill-hole of the pearls, and by this means you could see the effects of the light through the pearl and tell whether it was natural or cultured.

After the Second World War there was the sudden realisation among merchants importing stones from Rangoon, rubies from the mines of Burma, and sapphires from the East, that, to their horror, a proportion of these were synthetic. Basil Anderson said,

Some of the stones had already been mounted in eternity rings, bar brooches, and bracelets and were found to be synthetic. It was a tremendous shock and caused a lot of trouble because the importer assumes he has got a genuine stone coming in, and it goes to the manufacturing jeweller who makes it up in good faith to find its way to the retailer. It could cause a tremendous blow to the prestige of the jeweller who was a perfectly honest person. All these stones had to be winkled out of their settings and replaced by natural stones.

In the laboratory Anderson's team examined all the parcels imported from the east, and tested every stone to guarantee it as natural. He took on many more staff and obtained more microscopes, and in just the first year after being hit by this problem, the team had to individually test over one hundred thousand stones.

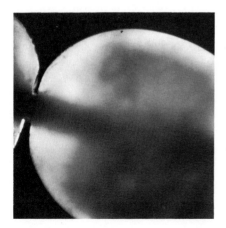 

Natural pearl (left): in contrast to a cultured pearl there is no nucleus or parallel shadow path. Cultured pearl (right): the hazy curved swathes show its layered structure

Considering the recent explosion in the number and quality of synthetic stones now readily available, Mr Anderson was asked to give a frank appraisal of the current situation facing the average High Street jeweller. He paused for several seconds, then shook his head rather sadly:

It really is very confusing, certainly for the ordinary jeweller unless he's been trained. There seems to be a definite purpose behind the production of these imitation or synthetic materials, with an attempt not merely to represent the stone in a palatable way, to make a stone which is equally good to the eye as the natural one but very much cheaper, but also there's this tendency to want to deceive not only the public but the gemmologist. A great deal of ingenuity has gone into making composite stones like doublets, part natural and part synthetic: in a setting they can be quite confusing and difficult. Scientists now have a tremendous knowledge about growing crystals of all kinds, not necessarily primarily with the idea of making synthetic gem-stones, but for electronic purposes and lasers and that kind of thing. The knowledge of how to grow crystals of all kinds has increased and where the stones they produce are attractive to the eye, it's tempting to use them as imitation gem-stones. That's particularly so with diamond, the supreme gem-stone. In the old days one never had to worry about imitations of diamond because they were so different. Above all the jeweller knew his diamonds, their appearance, their sharpness of facets and of the edges of the facets, the perfection of the reflections – everything about the stone said to him 'diamond!' Anything that wasn't diamond he would reckon to recognise with just a pocket lens without much trouble. But sometimes, even so, he could be deceived by a confidence trickster: you don't see the same thing when you're being conned.

As an instance of this, Mr Anderson recounts one interesting case early in the lab's history in which a very clever, persuasive rogue called Rice, a tall distinguished man with white hair and a black patch over his eye, established confidence with a pawnbroker. He handed in a gold watch which he said he would redeem a little later. When he returned for the redemption he would show the jeweller what was apparently a five-stone diamond ring in which one stone was missing. The stones were not diamond but white zircons which in rather poor light – and he always chose the time late in the day when the light was poor – can easily be mistaken for diamonds. Rice would then ask the jeweller how much it would cost to replace the stone without even mentioning the word 'diamond', and the jeweller would perhaps say 'about sixty pounds'. Then Rice would say, 'Well, I must get that done sometime, but I'm a bit short of cash at the moment, so perhaps you wouldn't mind lending me something on the ring.' And he would leave the ring with the jeweller and the jeweller would put it in his safe. He gave a very good address, but a false one, and next morning the jeweller would open his safe, look at this ring away from the influence of this persuasive Mr Rice, and see to his horror that the stones obviously weren't diamond.

Rice had rings supplied from Clerkenwell, from a man who made them up specially. He succeeded about twenty times with this fairly simple trick. Then one day he made the mistake of going into a shop which, though it had a different name from the ones he had been in before, was owned by the same proprietor, and he had already warned his branch that this was liable to happen. So when Rice left his ring the man quietly got in touch with the police, and that was the end of the trickster's career.

Mr Anderson was called in as an expert witness.

It's very difficult to explain to the layman or a jury the exact difference between diamonds and imitations. But one spectacular difference between diamond and all other minerals, since it's composed of pure carbon, is that it's very transparent to X-Rays. If a ring containing stones is exposed to X-Rays and photographed, the diamond is so transparent to the rays that it shows as though the stone were not there at all. The zircon rings which Mr Rice was trying to pawn were completely opaque except for the one apparent gap where there was no stone at all. It was the first time this kind of exhibit had been put in as forensic evidence and proved a very easy way of explaining to the jury that the stones were different from true diamond.

Today not only juries but even jewellers themselves have problems identifying the best, most recent gem simulants. An eminent gemmologist is Alan Hodgkinson with his own gem-lab on the outskirts of Glasgow; here he runs brief 'refresher' courses for jewellers to keep them up-to-date with all the new developments which perplex the market today.

This is a fairly formidable task because there are always advances in science, and no less in gemmology, and also with the tricksters who follow the trade. There is the phenomenon of new crystals being grown almost every month, and these crystals – whether they're for scientific use in industry or for gemmology, may soon seem to find their way into the trade in one way or another!

One of Hodgkinson's students, an experienced practising jeweller, admitted his own particular worry of the moment.

What I consider will be a big problem in the next few years is a 'synthetic cubic zirconia' (a form of zirconia), a diamond simulant very, very similar to diamond – it has a good brilliance and 'fire', there are small flaws in the stone which make it very difficult to tell from diamond. If you're not experienced, and you've not seen the stones, it's very difficult if someone brings one into the shop to think it could be anything other than diamond, especially if it's flawed.

Another student jumped in to confess similar problems which he had encountered: 'Synthetic opals look very, very convincing, and give a play of fire which the retail jeweller, not knowing they were synthetic, would immediately say "real opal".'

With all the foregoing, just what is the chance of an ordinary person being able to be certain of the genuine article? The advice given was:

Deal with an honest jeweller. All jewellers of any reputation at all are honest – they've got to be or they wouldn't be in business. The real danger comes when the public think there's a bargain going: they're shown a diamond in a public house, and offered it at what seems a bargain price. There are no such things as bargains for the general public in stones. Either the stone is not what it's supposed to be, or it's stolen property. Steer clear of any purchases not made in a reputable shop, that's the only really safe way.

Another thing the public should be warned about is making the mistake that they can get bargains in bazaar shops out east. Because it's sold to them near where the jewels are produced they think they may get a bargain and that is a very dangerous practice indeed. There are more synthetics sold in such places than in the whole of Britain.

CHAPTER EIGHT

PAINTINGS, DRAWINGS AND PRINTS I

In no field of art forgery has the guerrilla warfare between collectors, dealers and forgers been more determined and long-standing than in that of paintings, drawings and prints. Faking of paintings apparently started somewhere around the beginning of the fifteenth century. Before that there had been a fair amount of copying and imitation, and obviously many of these early efforts have over the centuries become valuable properties as genuine articles.

The forger of paintings has probably used more ingenuity and skill with his craft than fakers working in other fields. He knows that he has a formidable task ahead of him if he is going to have any hope at all of fooling the professionals. The expert that concerns him most is the thorough art historian whose well-trained eye will pick up any slip, but the modern forger is also concerned that having once been picked up, he should have a second chance of getting away with it, if he can fool the scientist.

Most of the principal efforts of the forgers of paintings have been in the medium of oils. Working in this field, they are first of all confronted with the need to get a support fitting for the period. Thus, if they are working to imitate a seventeenth-century painter, it is no use their using a machine-woven canvas, as prior to the early part of the nineteenth century all canvas was handwoven, and this can be easily recognised by the slightly uneven texture and the obvious different weaves; so most forgers going for the early masters will regrettably get hold of pictures of the right period by minor hands and then ruthlessly remove the paint with solvents right down to the canvas itself. This is essential, because if they should leave any trace of the previous image either in underpainting or in the priming or ground on the canvas, X-rays would show it up and even possibly infra-red examination would too. For the forger setting out to ape a work on a wood panel it is perhaps a little simpler. A wooden support of the right type and age can often be picked up when buildings are being demolished or by a surreptitious visit to a scrap or timber yard, and all should be well if the forger knows his history of techniques and methods. He must be careful, however, not to use a modern plane or saw – an easy giveaway; the back, if it has to be shaped, must be treated in the traditional manner with a form of adze. If the wood is not quite right for age, the appearance of extra years can be added by a judicious treatment with dilute nitric acid, potassium permanganate crystals, coffee, tea, or even liquorice and other similar stains, although these will make the risk of discovery greater.

Having prepared his support, the deceiver then comes to a difficult field, that of the colours which would have been used at the particular time. Many a forger has been detected for using pigments that were not available at the time. Traces of French ultramarine are a complete give-away with pictures purporting to be prior to 1800; the colour was only made viable in 1838 by a Frenchman, Monsieur Guimet. Cadmium yellows and reds, chrome yellows and greens come in at the beginning of the nineteenth century, and Prussian blue at the beginning of the eighteenth century. Having worked out his palette of colours, the next problem for the trickster is what vehicle or liquid to put with the pigments so that they not only will conform to the kind of brush marks or impasto of the painter he is faking, but also will harden out in a reasonable time. A normal oil painting, if applied with heavy impasto by someone like Van Gogh or another of the modern school, will take anything up to ten years plus before the paint will harden out right through.

There was an instance a few years ago where an art historian was asked to visit a certain house where the owner said that he had a fine Coello, an early Spanish master. When he arrived at the house which was deep in the country, and up a long drive shrouded in trees, he was greeted by the owner who ushered him in to a fine entrance hall and said:

'There, what do you think of it?'

The historian looked around and couldn't see any picture that looked anything like a Coello. Then his host said: 'Here,' and pointed to a portrait which was very smudgy and woolly in outline, quite unlike the crisp, detailed work of the Spanish painter. The historian examined it and felt it looked remarkably recent. The patina of several hundred years was not in evidence and there was little about the work to suggest that it was by Coello. The paint, apart from anything else, appeared far too thick in some areas and pointing to this he turned to the owner and said,

'That worries me.'

The man replied, 'It's been in my family for a long, long time.'

The historian said, 'Well, have you a needle?'

The owner, somewhat mystified, went off and got a needle, and he was asked,

'Do you mind if I very gently prick this piece of thick paint which is very close to the frame? It will make hardly any sign at all.'

The owner said he didn't mind, and when the paint was pricked it was quite clear that the picture must have been painted not a hundred years ago, not five, but possibly in the previous twelve months. The paint underneath the skin was quite moist. The owner expressed horror and misunderstanding and said,

'I don't know what's happened. My restorer had the picture about a year and a half ago and brought it back last month. It is so colourful now; before it went I could hardly see any colour at all.'

After the historian had left, he wasn't quite sure as to what the business was about. Had he been asked down there by the owner in collusion with the restorer, in the hope that he would give a certificate, or some form of opinion in writing as to the authenticity of the so-called Coello? Or had the owner, in all innocence, been done, by the restorer, who had played the old trick of having a very dirty painting in for treatment, and keeping it for an abnormally long time during which a copy is painted and this is then returned to the owner?

Among the convincing features that are a give-away in old oil paintings are the particular types of cracks that go across the paint. There are many varieties of craquelure, and the forger, if he is going to hope to succeed, has to be able to master these. There are four principal ways in which he can do it. Having painted his picture on a canvas, he can roll it backwards and forwards over a dowel rod about one inch to one and a half inches in circumference. This has to be done with care; but if it is carried out slowly it can produce a quite convincing craquelure which will go not only through the varnished top layer but right through the paint and the ground underneath, so that if it is examined by magnification it could look authentic. The second method of producing a craquelure, both on canvas or a wood panel, is the laborious method of painting on the cracks, using a little dilute raw umber or some suchlike dead colour, diluted with a little varnish and turpentine substitute, or turpentine. This is done with a very small brush or the flight feather from a teal or widgeon. Painting on the cracks will hardly ever fool an expert. At a distance it may look quite convincing, but as soon as any form of magnification is brought to bear, the trick will be quickly discovered.

The third method, again for a panel or a canvas, is to scratch on the cracks. This is done after the varnishing has been completed; the forger works away with a fine needle in an old brush-handle, drawing in a system of cracks of the right period, and when he has finished he will rub some dirt off the studio floor into the marks he has made. Again, this is not a satisfactory method, as a quite low-power magnification will give it away. It is easy to show up by taking a small piece of cotton wool, slightly moistened with white spirit, and applying this gently to the suspected area when the ruse will be apparent. A fourth method for pictures on canvas is, when the paint is thoroughly dried out, the picture can be put into an extremely slow oven for half an hour or an hour, or longer, depending on the particular canvas, ground or paint, and this can produce a quite convincing overall craquelure. There is a fifth way of achieving a surface crack. This is done when the varnish is almost dry, the faker brushes over the whole surface with a fairly strong glue. The glue and the varnish layers will dry at different speeds and bring up a system of rather coarse cracking. The best glue to use here is a hoof variety which will have plenty of pull as it dries out.

But by far the most successful method as far as the forger is concerned, is to put something with the pigment, before he paints, which will, as it dries, crack of its own accord. One of the commonest liquids suitable for this purpose is egg white. The egg needs to be fresh, and after the yolk has been separated from the white it is ground into the pigments chosen, and the combination is painted into the picture in the normal way; if left in an ordinary dry atmosphere over two or three days this will dry out and the forger will have a fine and very convincing cracking right through his paint. Should he want to accelerate the process, he can use a hair drier, which will probably bring the drying time down to about half an hour; but by doing that he may cause the adhesion of the paint to the canvas or panel to loosen.

This business of cracks through the paint can be of some assistance when shopping in a down-market area. Often paintings of the eighteenth and seventeenth centuries may be seen in dealers' windows or on display at auction sales that are apparently quite perfect with literally no sign of cracking at all. What has happened here, almost certainly, is that the pictures are modern fakes or have been grossly overpainted by a hack restorer. One flash from a portable ultra-violet lamp will show up the deceit at once, as it is likely that practically the whole of the picture surface will fluoresce.

If the forger has been unable to obtain the necessary old canvas, there is one way he can get round this, and that is by painting on to a modern canvas and then relining this on to another new canvas; an action which would not necessarily give rise to suspicion, as most paintings, certainly of a hundred years or more old, would have been relined because an old canvas tends to weaken and rot and this relining would be done as a conserving measure. Probably, the most satisfactory way for the faker to do it would be to fit the forgery, on its own new canvas, on to the relining canvas, not with a wax and resin adhesive, as that could be lifted at the edges with a little heat without causing any damage, but rather with a very strong water adhesive glue which would be very difficult indeed to dislodge. He would need to treat the edges of the canvas by either slightly scorching with a taper flame or by brushing on nitric acid or a caustic substance, and in this case the stretchers could be modern, as again this would not be suspect because such would be used with a relining by a restorer.

It is likely that the final act of a forger in many cases, if he is painting a picture of some age, is to give it a convincing finish. Most of the early varnishes used were natural resins such as mastic, damar and particularly copal. Over the centuries several coats have been applied at intervals to many pictures, which gives them a very unprepossessing darkish yellow brown appearance and this tends to obscure much of the detail. It is the kind of look that was popular in the nineteenth century when even John Constable's beautiful, fresh, atmospheric landscapes were apparently brushed over with a dark obliterating coach-varnish by dealers, because such a delightful, fresh naturalistic look was not popular, not the fashion. But for the forger this type of varnishing is a bonus; not only does it perhaps obscure not over-adept brushwork and detail, but, sadly, even today, a number of collectors are convinced that if they see a dark old picture in which just vague ghost-like figures and details can be made out, it must be authentic. If, for the forger, the varnish alone does not give a satisfactory result, the effect can be deepened by wiping over the picture a greasy soot which has come from an oil lamp or from tallow smoke, and finally brushing it smooth – making sure that there is no glitter left, not even a sheen, perhaps leaving it leaning against a wall face up for a month or two. There is nothing like a bit of dusty-attic atmosphere to produce a convincing image of great age.

As paintings of quality and works by the masters are being bought up more and more by museums and galleries, and investment companies are purchasing them to be stored away as securities, so the trade is having literally to scrape around the walls to find enough stock. Wrecks, perhaps from acts of iconoclasm or because of fire, are called into service, and there have been examples where restorers have taken small fragments, in some cases as little as maybe ten per cent in area, and with skill and cunning have built up a convincing whole. The word pastiche which has been mentioned earlier, is particularly applicable to pictures which are being fraudulently composed. Not long ago there came to light in a small country town in Ireland a real puzzle. Looked at one way, it appeared to be by Lucas Cranach, the early German painter. From another angle it appeared to have elements of Albrecht Dürer. It took quite a little unravelling. In most pastiches, the forger was content to build it up by sections: the left-hand corner Dürer, the right-hand corner Cranach, etc. But here, what he had done was to intertwine the two styles so that they did not readily become recognisable. There was a typical example of Cranach style treatment, with a hard-eyed woman and crisp gold chain and piles of coins, mixed up with the simulated mysticism and delicate handling of Dürer. To make matters worse, from the condition of the canvas and the appearance of the stretchers, it was a contemporary pastiche; that is made in the sixteenth century, which made the problem of identifying it more difficult.

Today, with some people moving from great houses to smaller homes, a need can arise for a very large picture to be cut down. This can be a perfectly *bona fide* operation, although in no way desirable if the painting is a good one. But this practice can also be put to use by a disreputable character who may see good profit to be made if three or four or more separate pictures are cut out of a large one; for one thing, they will be of a much more ready-saleable size. The process is a very simple one. Having worked out a satisfactory composition or set of compositions in certain areas of a canvas, the various parts can be speedily cut out, relined on to new canvas, framed and placed in the showroom.

It is surprising the ruses that have been attempted, not only in this century but also in earlier times. Some twenty years or so ago a restorer went to a house where there had been a fire, which fortunately had been extinguished before any great material damage could be done, although large quantities of smoke had been produced and this had very much darkened some fine paintings in one of the big salons. With most of the pictures it was a comparatively simple method to remove this tarry smoke until one portrait came along which had every evidence, from a superficial look, of being of an ancestor somewhere around the beginning of this century. But when gentle tests were applied near the edge of the picture something very extraordinary happened, because not only did the tarry smoke come away, but the dark varnish and what appeared to be dyes and pigments also came away. Very soon the cause was apparent and the restorer had to tell the owner that this particular portrait was not at all what it seemed. It was, in fact, a large photograph which had been stuck on the canvas and then painted over with transparent colours and dyes, after which it had been heavily varnished. It was supposed to have been by a good hand and maybe someone in the family had been a little short of ready cash and had had recourse to a little realising of assets.

This practice of sticking photographs and reproductions on a canvas, certainly in the lower levels of the market, is not at all unknown. The most skilful way to do it is to have a black and white print or even a good colour reproduction. If the paper is thick it needs to be skinned down as far as possible without breaking through on to the surface of the picture. Then it is stuck on to a fairly coarse-grained canvas, generally with a water-soluble glue; it needs to be well kneaded into the grain of the canvas so that the texture shows up through it. The reproduction can then be touched up as necessary; given a little *sfumato* from smoky tallow tapers, and lastly varnished. Many of these squalid little deceits have shamelessly been passed on to unsuspecting customers. It is often very difficult for a restorer to convince a client that they have been deceived. A flower painting, which gave every evidence of being by one of the leading Dutch seventeenth-century painters, had hung in the home of an elderly retired teacher and she had obviously regarded it as a security for the future. Undoubtedly it had been done skilfully; whilst in the frame there didn't seem to be any give-away at all, the texture and lumpiness of the canvas were very convincing and it had been relined. The paint itself had a fairly shallow impasto that would be expected, and it wasn't until the canvas was taken out of the frame that the edges of the paper could be seen and the sad news broken.

There is another approach the skilful forger may fall back on and this is damage. He will be quite well aware that a painting, say from the early Flemish period, fifteenth century or thereabouts, is very unlikely to have escaped completely unscathed. Apart from the cracking on the surface, it is possible there will be areas that have been damaged by abrasion and by unwise cleaning; therefore the forger, having completed his fake, will deliberately abrade certain areas, using possibly an agate burnisher dipped into a little fine abrasive powder such as tripoli or crocus, something that won't give an obvious scratch as would a glass paper. This trick can often be picked up if the picture in question is closely examined to see just where these abrasive or paint losses occur. If such defacements are genuine, the damage obviously may be anywhere. If the picture in question is a fake, the damage will be very carefully placed and certainly would not be over a vital feature such as a face, a hand, or some piece of elaborate jewellery.

The forger can grow rich because too many collectors or other people going after pictures look at the wrong things. Instead of being concerned with style and on the watch for anachronisms, the viewer, all too often, is taken in by simple things, such as that restoration means authenticity; and even that old fly spots can be considered as a pointer to quality. It's no difficult matter for the faker to mix up some paint of the right consistency and spot around the picture, using a very small miniature brush or the tip of a wild-fowl feather. If he is in a mass-production mood he can mix the paint a little thinner and dip a hog brush in it and spatter it across the canvas or panel by running his finger through the bristles. He can then follow up the 'fly spots' by putting on his dark varnish and, as a certain refinement, once the varnish has dried, giving it a kind of uneven appearance which old dried varnish often has: this can be done with a piece of cotton wool in a weak solvent such as white spirit, dabbing it here and there to produce the effect required. It is possible to achieve a kind of bloom which again many associate with old paintings, rather like the misty look on black grapes. Before the varnish is put on, certain areas can be very slightly moistened with water and then a fairly thick mastic varnish can be used before the moisture dries, which will often bring the convincing dull, cloudy look needed.

Having done all in his power to simulate age by getting a convincing support and the rest, the forger will possibly turn to signatures. In the past, certainly prior to 1800, many painters seldom signed their pictures, but this will not necessarily deter the faker. Indeed this is a fact that forgers can't always seem to appreciate, and they will quite often literally plaster early forgeries with names which the masters themselves would never have put on. It might be thought here that the large multi-volume painting dictionaries can be of assistance to the collector, particularly if they have specimen signatures against some of the artists' names, but these unfortunately are not always taken from pictures and may be from documents and so may differ. They can doubtless be helpful to an honest individual in some instances, but they can also assist the forger, who can copy from these very same sources, and fraudulent use of signatures may not necessarily only be done by the faker; it is not unknown for unscrupulous dealers who want to up-grade certain pictures to add an illustrious name to a rather second-grade work. Yet again, John Public, ever eager for a bargain and convinced that he is going to get one, falls for it.

A so-called 'floating' signature is one which the deceiver doesn't even bother to put underneath the varnish. It is simply painted on the top. It can quite often be seen by the naked eye, particularly if a light is held to one side to show up the brush strokes in relief. The more difficult signatures to pick up are those where the varnish has been removed and a genuine signature has been taken out and a new one put in place, and then the picture has been revarnished.

The idea has been put forward for modern painters to protect their work with an adaptation of the Bertillon fingerprint system. In one corner close to the edge of the frame whilst the paint is still quite tacky the artist could press in a thumb or fingerprint, although this would not necessarily by any means be a hundred per cent protection. It would not be difficult to erase. In the past a number of collectors have tried to protect matters by affixing seals with their crest or coat of arms on the back of canvasses or panels. This does give some protection, but of course it is not unknown for the forger to find them rather useful. It is not a very difficult matter to remove them and then place them on to the back of a fake to provide part of that convincing certificate.

American collectors and particularly directors of their galleries and museums cast a doubtful eye at the practice of some of their European cousins who casually at times, it seems, issue certificates for paintings which, at the least, will advance the price and at the worst be part and parcel of an outright and expensive fraud. Often the language is very clever. It goes round and round in academic phrases until it has so enmeshed the truth that it is almost impossible to uncover. Many painters today and in the past have been and are well aware of this traffic in names: this is a deplorable chink in the armour of some collectors, when they disregard completely the artistic content of a picture, its whole aesthetic appeal. They just go for the name, and so inevitably in the end are going to catch a rotten one. There was an instance where a millionaire collector would actually visit an exhibition with his agent and sit down in a corner and buy up to a dozen or more pictures, just from the catalogue, by name and subject. Then he was off again without even seeing what he had bought until it landed up in some marble temple to the arts.

One painter who tried to safeguard his work was the Frenchman Claude, noted for his exquisite landscapes and mythological scenes that are filled with a wonderful golden light. Claude produced his *Liber Veritatis*, a folio of engravings of his works. But here again there is not total protection. In fact, engravings taken from paintings can be yet another aid to the forger. It might be thought that a contemporary engraving of a painting, where the original artist's name is on one side at the bottom and the engraver's at the other, could be a proof that the painting is genuine or that it did actually exist. Regrettably this is far from the truth. There have been many instances where a particularly striking composition has been given a rough handling by the unscrupulous. There is the case of a Van Dyck mounted portrait of Charles I which insensitive characters have copied and changed the head of Charles I, and, somewhat ironically, produced mounted portraits of Cromwell and Louis XIV.

The picture market can suffer considerable confusion with works that have come from the picture factory studios, particularly from the seventeenth century. One of the most famous of these establishments was that of Sir Peter Paul Rubens in Antwerp where he employed at different times artists of the quality of Van Dyck, Teniers, Jordaens, Frans Snyders, Jan Breughel, and many others. Generally the practice would be that an artist who was particularly good at a subject, for example animals, like Snyders, would attend to that part of the composition: flowers could be Jan Breughel, and so on. Rubens adopted this mass production because he himself with all his energy was unable to keep pace with the tremendous number of commissions he received. Apart from being an artist of great quality and talent, he was a diplomat, welcomed at the many Courts of Europe, and as he travelled round, royalty and noblemen heaped orders for paintings upon him. Thus there are a great many pictures which have that feeling of Rubens, that touch. Perhaps the Master put in a few of his famous long swirling strokes, others may be entirely the product of his assistants.

There was also Sir Peter Lely, a contemporary of Rubens, who was born in Westphalia and came to London in 1641, and there, despite native opposition, more or less cornered the portrait market. His studio was filled with apprentices, minor artists, who would in some cases paint practically the whole canvas with the exception of the face and possibly the hands. It has been said that Lely might, when he had an important sitter, have three or four unfinished canvasses of this sort brought in, with different robes and different costumes, and let the sitter choose; and then he would very speedily put in the face and missing features. He must, apart from anything else, have had considerable tact, because he was in favour with Charles I, then Oliver Cromwell, and then back to the Royalists with Charles II. He is supposed by some to have been a little dishonest when he painted copies of many of the pictures in the Royal collection, and it is not completely certain what happened to them or the originals.

Another of the conveyor-belt production specialists around the same time was Sir Godfrey Kneller, also a German, who came across to England in 1674 and found himself in great demand by Charles II and also his Court. He apparently could paint at tremendous speed and it is said that at one time the King, to save himself sitting time, ordered that he should be painted simultaneously by Kneller and Lely and that Kneller completed his picture while Lely was still at the underpainting stage. All this kind of factory production causes much burrowing around to ferret out a genuine canvas. Both Lely and Kneller were notable artists in their own right. Yet if a picture by either of them is on offer it needs a great deal of research to make sure whether it is entirely original by one of them or not; whether it is mostly done by some of their hacks or is an outright forgery.

Families of painters can cause further trouble and disillusionment when attempts are made to find out just who painted what. At the same time they offer much opportunity for the forger. He can paint in the manner of a certain artist with a complicated family tree and fairly simply insert his fake under the name of one of the others. One of the most confusing examples of the proliferation of family endeavour is the household of the De Vos and their descendants. There are a number of painters with this name, nearly all of them working and living in the seventeenth century; moreover to add to the general fog and misattribution, painters with this name have continued in Holland right through to this century. Most of the De Vos's come from a variety of branches of the family or allied families of the same name. Most of them, to confuse matters, paint the same subjects, landscapes, portraits and animals. Let us start the story with Cornelis de Vos who was born at Hulst in Holland about 1585. Early in the seventeenth century there is another Cornelis de Vos who was no relation to the first one. Lambertus de Vos from Mechlin was working in the sixteenth century and a little earlier in the same century Marten de Vos from Antwerp was the son of a Pieter who had been elected a member of the Antwerp Academy in 1519. Marten had a son whom he helpfully christened Marten; he became a painter who was also born in Antwerp; and father Marten had a brother Pieter de Vos, who had a son called Willem. Then there is Paulus, the brother of the first Cornelis. In the seventeenth century there was Jan de Vos, and to complete this gathering there is Simon de Vos, born Antwerp 1603 – he gets more entangled still by studying in Rubens' atelier, to such effect that apparently some of his altar pieces were mistaken for those of Rubens. The De Vos's are not quite finished with yet, because there are on record a possible further Pieter, and Hendrik and Willem, as well as there being a distinct possibility that there could be even more under this surname.

In the eighteenth and nineteenth centuries in England there was another artistic family who, since their time, have caused a lot of trouble for collectors particularly of horse pictures. These were the Alkens. This tribe started off with Sefferin (1717–1782) and carried right through until Henry Gordon Alken died in 1894. Between these two there are Samuel, son of the original Sefferin, and four of his sons Sam, George, Sefferin and Henry. This Henry then had two sons whom, to help matters along, he christened Henry and Sefferin. All the Alkens painted in the same manner; all were horse painters; and all signed their work S. or H. Alken. Not quite all, because the last Alken was christened Samuel Henry but was called Henry Gordon and used to sign his work at times H. Alken Jnr; at other times he left out the Junior, when he was a bit short of cash and was trying to pass off his work as that of his father. Today paintings by Henry Alken can be comfortably up into four figures.

This same name, or near same name business, can lay a devastating labyrinth for the scholar or the collector trying to pull out the genuine from all the rest. Somewhere round about 1619 at either Utrecht in Holland or Schoonhoven there was born one Hendrik Naeuwincx (or Naiwinck).

This painter was a contemporary of the famous Jan Asselyn, who at times would help out by putting animals and figures into the landscapes of Naeuwincx – useful for the bent dealer, as Asselyn's paintings are worth considerably more than the lesser artist. In the seventeenth century there also lived in Hamburg a landscape painter, Nauinx (or Navinx), whose work at times was very close to that of Naeuwincx, and even then you can't quite nail it, because Nauinx or Navinx had his side-kick who put in the figures for him, one J. M. Weyer. This kind of name confusion is repeated far too often in the history of art for the comfort of the collector but assuredly not enough for that of the faker, as it offers him marvellous camouflage.

To further complicate the position, fashion, prudery, and bigotry can enter the field. For example, in the late eighteenth century the voluptuously-bosomed females beloved of Lely and other painters who excelled in painting the fleshy flesh were too much for some owners who had them disguised, either with carefully constructed bodices or lace frontals, or with long luxurious curling locks of hair. Religious paintings have been altered to suit a particular purchaser. Small points such as gestures of hands have been changed; the direction of eyes has been altered. Then too there are the artists who have painted over whole areas of canvas to totally transform the composition. There is the well-known example of the portrait of Mrs Payne and her two daughters by Sir Joshua Reynolds. At some time early in its life someone must have thought it would be better without the mother, and had her completely obliterated and replaced by a bit more vegetation and cloud.

The Doerner Institute in Munich has an excellent example of a modern forgery of El Greco which has been partially cleaned off over a small area which reveals that it has been painted on top of probably an early nineteenth-century portrait.

Sadly quite celebrated painters have sometimes joined in a fraud business. One such was Luca Giordano who was born in Naples in 1632, the son of Antonio Giordano, an obscure painter, whom apparently he surpassed in skill when he was only eight years old. By the time he was thirteen, according to contemporary comment, he had acquired great invention and readiness of hand; he copied the works of Raphael and Michelangelo. His father, not finding great demand for his own work, followed Luca when he

Sir Joshua Reynolds'
painting of Mrs Payne
and her two daughters,
after the removal of
over-painting

The same portrait with
Mrs Payne painted out

This forgery of an El Greco was revealed by cleaning a small portion of the painting

went to Rome and saw that there was such a demand for his son's brilliant sketches that apparently he would cry out to him 'Luca, make haste'. The son got himself into trouble over a painting 'Christ healing the Cripple', which had been purchased by one of his clients as an authentic Dürer. The picture apparently bore the well-known monogram of Dürer, and the client thought that he had an original, but then Luca indicated his own signature, which was apparently along the bottom of the painting which turned out to be a pastiche of various areas from several of Dürer's prints. The annoyed client tried a lawsuit, but according to contemporary records the magistrate cleared Luca and he continued on his merry way, producing paintings by the dozen and more. He made twelve different copies of a Raphael painting in the Vatican, twenty drawings after the Battle of Constantine by Giulio Romano besides numerous copies of Michelangelo, and Caravaggio. He imitated the style of practically every leading and distinguished painter both of his time and earlier, and seemed to be able to insert himself into the personality of the particular painter and to reproduce their brush strokes, control and whole feeling. The writer Bellori compared Luca Giordano with a bee that collects honey from the sweets of every flower; he said it would have been better for the painter's fame if he had established a character of his own and if imitation were not so apparent in all his productions. As with others of his time an exact list of his works cannot be compiled and it is no comfort to collectors to know that apparently he was more prolific than even Tintoretto and other artists.

In Venice at the same time lived the supreme imitator of many of the great painters of the Venetian school, Pietro della Vecchia, who was born in Venice in 1605. Although he showed a good deal of talent in the handling of paint, he never seemed to form an individual style of his own; but applied himself to imitating the work of, amongst others, Giorgione and Titian. His powers were quite considerable, particularly when aping Giorgione. So much so that many of his pictures have been mistaken for the production of this master.

In France in the seventeenth century two other painters who had the ability to produce these dangerously deceptive imitations were Sébastien Bourdon and Jean Michelin. Bourdon was a dab brush with some of the Italians, especially Annibale Carracci; whilst Michelin made fakes pertaining to be by the brothers Le Nain, his target. There were three of these brothers: Antoine, Louis and Mathieu and to further stir the pot all three were known to have worked on each others' pictures.

As the history of art is scanned, the inescapable conclusion is that a great many of the painters were 'at it' under one guise or another. Frans Hals had a gifted son, Frans Hals the Younger. He painted still life and portraits and sometimes copied the works of his father and at other times imitated him. Reynier Hals, also the son of Frans the Elder, may have been a somewhat mediocre hand at his small genre compositions, but it is quite possible that a number of his works have over the years been displayed under the name of his uncle Dirk.

Back in Italy again there is an unusual case: Andrea D'Agnolo, better known as Andrea del Sarto, who was born in Florence in 1486. In some records he is wrongly named Vannuchi and went under the mouthful of a full name as Andrea d'Agnolo di Francesco di Luca di Paolo del Migliore, which probably accounts for the fact that when he did sign his pictures he used a monogram. Del Sarto, an artist of decided quality and talent in his own right, was also a highly skilled imitator in the style and manner of other painters. The art historian of the lives of the painters of the Renaissance time, Vasari, records a quite extraordinary incident that he himself actually witnessed. Raphael had painted for the Cardinal Giulio de' Medici, who was afterwards Pope Clement VII, the portrait of Leo X. The background and drapery were put in by Giulio Romano who seems to have been mixed up with many incidents. Apparently Federigo II, Duke of Mantua, was going through Florence on his way to Rome when he saw the picture and asked Clement VII to make him a present of it. The Pope gave directions to Ottaviano de' Medici to send the portrait to Mantua. Ottaviano was unwilling to deprive Florence of such a fine work of art and he got Andrea del Sarto to paint an exact copy of it. This copy was sent on to the Duke of Mantua at a time when the painter Giulio Romano was still in his service. No one suspected the deception, even Giulio himself was completely deceived. It wasn't until Vasari met Romano and told him what had happened and showed him the private mark of Andrea del Sarto that he was convinced. Vasari, also a painter himself, had an apt comment on restorers of his time when he remarked, 'It would be far better for a masterpiece to remain ruined by time than to have it ruined by retouching by an inferior hand.'

The Mona Lisa by Leonardo in the Louvre has caused more than her share of confusion in the art world. Few paintings can have been copied and imitated as much. Today there is a Signor Antonio Bin, a Venetian, who has painted three hundred or more copies, and scattered around the world there are many hundreds more. Some of the owners undoubtedly believe that they have the real Mona Lisa. In fact there is a gentleman in Massachusetts, America, who claims that the genuine Mona Lisa has hung in his family residence since the end of the eighteenth century.

The Mona Lisa features in one of the more startling fake stories. Before the First World War a gang of rogues had the nerve to set up in Paris and during bouts of lavish entertainment intimate to the gullible that they could acquire various famous works from the Louvre. Copies of some of the great treasures from this museum were sold to those who can only have been witless buyers. They gave their orders, the prices were agreed and

Above: one of the Tours Museum's fake Mona Lisas
Right: the original in the Louvre

Left: another version from Tours and (above) a
sixteenth-century copy from the Walters Art
Gallery, Baltimore

not very long afterwards they found the objects delivered to them, nearly always outside of France. They would arrive impressively packaged and with plentiful supplies of provenance, some of it written on Louvre-headed notepaper; there would be seals and notes and the rest that put a cast-iron 'certainty' on the object's authenticity. They always included a small letter for 'the eyes of the new owner only' which said briefly that his particular treasure had disappeared from the museum and that an imitation had been put temporarily in the gallery whilst investigations were proceeding to stop speculation and comment by the public. Surprisingly these bright gentlemen got away with their guilty ruse for three years and then they were asked to do the ultimate. An American wanted the Mona Lisa. After their initial surprise and some consternation, they delivered the 'Mona Lisa' across the Atlantic in June 1910. Some time after the collector had it, either through careless talk or because of vanity, the story leaked out and a journalist claimed that the Mona Lisa in the Louvre was just a copy. An immense amount of expert opinion flashed to and fro and in the end the lady in the Louvre was authenticated. It took a lot of talking from the gang but eventually they persuaded their American that he did have the original.

Many excellent copies of this smiling lady are around. There are two in the Tours Museum. There is one by a pupil of Leonardo in the Mulhouse Museum. The Prado, Madrid, has one, thought to be by a pupil of Leonardo's. The Walters Art Gallery, Baltimore, has a sixteenth-century version. The William D. Vernon Collection, New York, has one and a value of two and a half million dollars has been placed on it. They claim that it was from Marie Antoinette's personal collection and was given by the Queen in 1793 to a young American. The Lord Brownlow Collection of Grantham, England, has a version which is held secure from the public eye. There are even a couple of nude versions of the lady: one apparently painted by a student of Leonardo's, in the Lord Spencer Collection, Northampton, England, and another in a collection in Rome, which is claimed to be an authentic Leonardo.

A rather novel approach to forging pictures, in fact works of art as a whole, came up in the first half of the nineteenth century. It is an idea which could have been pushed a lot further than it has been. Peter Thompson was apparently a budding architect living in Regent's Park,

London, and undoubtedly must have had some skill, as he sent in a set of drawings for the competition for the new Houses of Parliament. As a sideline Peter Thompson became a faker, but it was not quite so straightforward as that, because he also invented the artist whose work he was faking. Thompson's imaginary painter was one Captain John Eyre who was 'born' in Bakewell, Derbyshire, on 6 October 1604 and was reputed to be a descendant of Simon Eyre, a shoemaker who also had been Lord Mayor of London. This part was roughly true, as a branch of this family was known to have lived in the Bakewell area. The fabrication claimed that the said John Eyre received a good education, studying at Oxford, and then travelled with Prince Charles, later to be Charles I. Next in the 'biography' came details of Captain John Eyre's service with the Royalist cause until the trial of John Hampden, after which he switched to the Roundhead side. Apparently he had 'met' and 'painted' Cromwell. He was also 'wounded' while leading a charge with his regiment at the Battle of Marston Moor. After he 'died' at Bakewell on 23 July 1644 some three hundred of his charming works appeared mysteriously and providentially in his 'house'.

Thompson made his fictitious painter produce a series of sensitive and accurate architectural drawings. They were very much in the style and quality of Wenceslaus Hollar, and many of them showed fortifications of London carried out largely in pen and ink on old paper that had been treated to simulate age. There were also a series of monuments from London churches and some of the drawings carried comments in a rather strange attempt at seventeenth-century script. Those that had figures were the weakest and a portrait, so-called, of the playwright Ben Jonson was nothing but a weak copy from a mural in Shakespeare's house at Southwark. Peter Thompson set out to launch his 'artist' in 1852 by bringing out an edition of etched facsimiles of the fortification drawings, which were priced at five and ten shillings. The subscribers' list was long and it was headed by Prince Albert. It is still quite possible that Eyre's drawings can be moving around, in folios or carefully mounted and framed; in fact a drawing of 'Southwark Fair' has twice been brought to the British Museum for authentication as a genuine seventeenth-century work.

The early German painters of the fifteenth century have drawn their

The portrait on the left is a pastiche of the two original Holbeins shown above. The head, slightly altered, is taken from the right-hand portrait; while the fur collar and the hands are from the left-hand portrait. The position of the rings has been changed

share from the faker's palette. Holbein the Younger had a familiar, Bartholomäus Sarburgh, one of whose productions is probably the 'Jacob Meyer Madonna' in the Dresden Gallery. There has been much argument over this painting; but for some time now the version which is in Darmstadt has been credited as being genuine. The Dresden version has had a varied life and was probably made in about 1621 by Sarburgh; it then travelled across to France to Mary Medici; later it went to Venice, travelling by a dog-leg via Amsterdam; and finally to Augustus III of Saxony through his agent Count Francesco who bought it from an Italian family the Delfinos, in 1746.

Another early German painter who has always proved attractive to the forger, perhaps because of his rather strange and naïve manner that lacks subtlety but makes up for this with a strange grotesque quality, is Lucas Cranach the Elder. He had two familiars, Hans Leonhard Schäufelein and Franz Wolfgang Rohrich, both active at the beginning of the nineteenth century. The latter, a German-Swiss, turned out fine Cranachs literally by the score. Amongst others he is known to have painted at least forty copies of a Saxon Duchess, probably Sophie, with her young son Johann Friedrich, and these have found their way into notable public collections and probably there are a number still hanging as prized Cranachs in many private galleries.

In the field of proliferation of copies, imitations, fakes, pastiches of his works, Jean Baptiste Camille Corot (1796–1875) leaves the rest a long way behind. He was born in Paris and studied with Michallon and then Victor Bertin. His method of work on his own account was to sketch out of doors in the spring, summer and early autumn, and then in the winter work up his sketches in his studio. His particular misty, romantic landscapes achieved tremendous popularity not only in his own time but right through to the present day. He was a likeable person, generous, remembering his own poverty when young, and giving large sums of money to poor artists during the Siege of 1870. At his height his studio resembled something approaching that of Rubens. He must have been a happy-go-lucky character because he had one very strange quirk and that was to quite often sign pictures that were by his students with his own name and even others' works that might be brought to him. He might put a few strokes in and then sign them Corot. When he died his studio was closed and this was the signal for the commencement of a veritable industry, the production in

A fake Corot, from the British Museum

numerous workshops of Corot forgeries in not only France but Germany, Switzerland and elsewhere. Alfred Robaut compiled what was considered to be a complete catalogue of genuine works by Corot but in the end this work was never truly completed as the scene became more and more clogged with not just hundreds but thousands of false Corots.

Here comes someone on to the stage who might be the supreme sucker of all time – Dr Jousseaume, a French doctor, who after his death was known to have collected not less than 2,414 spurious Corots, both paintings and drawings. Apparently during his lifetime, Dr Jousseaume had boasted that he had this huge number of works by the master and had never paid more than a hundred and ten francs for any of them. The barefaced deceivers had got round the awkward fact that this large number of spurious works were not in Robaut's catalogue by telling the unfortunate doctor that they had come across a secret hoard of Corot's work.

In actual fact there are only about seven hundred paintings and drawings that are without dispute credited to Corot to which some wit added that of these eight thousand were in America, but even he was a long way out because a responsible opinion has said that in the last two decades it is likely that comfortably over a hundred thousand Corots have appeared on walls throughout the United States alone.

There is another French painter of the same period, Jean-François Millet, who has suffered the attentions of a rather more intimate forger. Millet who, with his gentle unpretentious landscape scenes of peasants working in the fields, drew considerable public support, died in 1875, and in this century during the 'thirties, forgeries of his paintings started to appear on both sides of the Channel. It came to light at first that these were being produced by Paul Cazot and good they must have been, for he is supposed to have been paid a hundred and fifty thousand francs for one fake alone. In 1935, in France, matters got as far as the Law Courts and there the extraordinary revelation came out that the principal faker was not Cazot but the grandson of Jean-François Millet who had been running a Millet factory with the help of Cazot. He had done extremely well with his family name and, the connection with his grandfather being quite authentic, he issued certificates gratuitously with a very large number of forgeries to American, English and French collectors. One gentleman in London had fallen for the bait and bought sixty for about three million francs.

It does seem that many of the leading members of the French school of the latter part of the nineteenth century and into this century attracted the forger, even the primitive naïve pictures of Rousseau *Le Douanier* were forged and found a ready market at around twenty-five thousand francs. There was Madame Claude Latour who was convicted in 1947 for being concerned with the mass-production of Picassos and Utrillos. She uttered her work with the help of a twenty-two-year-old bright dealer, Jacques Marisse, who cheerfully paid her between a hundred and a thousand francs and then round the corner was selling the fakes as originals for up to seventy thousand. It is recorded that Madame Latour must have had remarkable skill, because when Utrillo was shown some of her work he was unable to point out the fake and the original in each case. This lady, who went under the nickname of 'Zezi du Montparnasse', left behind her quite a trail of argument and distress. Utrillo's works with their soft, chalky texture and simplified form lend themselves to skilled forging and they can be very deceptive.

CHAPTER NINE

PAINTINGS, DRAWINGS AND PRINTS II

During the 1920s there were other assaults on the credulity of collectors and dealers. In 1924 Otto Wacker, aged twenty-six, who had already been a failure as a taxi-cab owner and night-club dancer, opened a picture gallery in Victoriastrasse in Berlin. Much of the work he offered was of low-grade quality but astoundingly a flush of new Van Goghs appeared here before the public gaze. This at once attracted the interest of the experts, and when Wacker was cross-examined as to where he got these from, he said:

'I am sorry, I have been sworn to secrecy. It is from a gentleman who is now living in Switzerland and at times in Egypt, a Russian, and I have given him my word I will not reveal his name as he could get into severe trouble for bringing these treasures out of post-Revolution Russia.'

146

At the time the Dutch expert J. Baart de la Faille was in the process of putting together his definitive catalogue of the works of Vincent Van Gogh and, like many another art historian engaged on a similar task, advertised for help from anyone who had previously owned Van Goghs or had any information or records of the painter. This advertisement was answered by Wacker, and when it came out in 1928 the large catalogue, entitled *L'Oeuvre de Vincent Van Gogh: Catalogue Raisonné*, contained details of the thirty Van Goghs in Wacker's possession and thus as far as the art world was concerned the paintings were totally and incontrovertibly authenticated. Wacker, not content with this, went further and paid a small fee to other known Van Gogh experts for further certification. These included Leo Blumenreich, Hans Rosenhagen and Julius Meier-Graefe. To give some idea of how much an expert will commit himself when authenticating a painting on paper, De La Faille backed up the picture 'Self-portrait at the Easel' that was sold to Chester Dale in New York by stating:

The undersigned declares that he has examined the painting reproduced on the other side measuring 58 cm in height and 46.5 cm in width painted on canvas. He considers it as an authentic and characteristic work of Vincent Van Gogh, painted in 1888 during his sojourn in Arles. It will be described and reproduced in his catalogue raisonné on the work of the master. Berlin July 20th 1927.

Signed J.B.de la Faille

In the same street and nearly opposite Wacker's gallery was the long-standing establishment of Paul Cassirer who, encouraged by this display of knowledgeable back-up for the newly discovered Van Goghs, joined in their display. The Van Goghs began to be dispersed through a number of Germany's leading dealers: Thannhäuser in Munich, Kommeter in Hamburg, and also as far afield as Hodebert in Paris; and from thence to the big collectors, not only on this side of the Atlantic but also in America. All was going well until Wacker sent four of his Van Goghs to Grete Ring, another dealer, who took a look at them and was suspicious. She consulted an expert, who joined her in the opinion that they were fraudulent. They were sent back to Wacker with a comment to this effect, but he turned down out of hand the judgement, pointing to the certification he had and to the fact that the pictures were included in the De la Faille catalogue.

The usual contest between the experts now started to grow, and not long after the issue of his catalogue raisonné, De la Faille issued a disclaimer stating that the thirty Van Goghs were forgeries.

The Wacker Van Goghs, seen by themselves are to a degree convincing, whether they were painted by him or by some experienced assistant in the background: and yet they fail, perhaps because they do not have the restraint Van Gogh himself used, and if anything they outdo his explosive style. The hounds started to close in on the young deceiver; and it was very soon found that on police questioning none of the doubtful paintings could be traced any further back than Otto Wacker himself, and it was likely that there was no Russian émigré who had brought them out of the Soviet Union and was now living in Switzerland and Egypt. But Wacker was of a tenacious nature: he swore there was a Russian, but he said he regretted that he was quite sure that under no conditions would the Russian consent to meet the police. He also tried to prevent the amendment of the De la Faille catalogue. The evidence became extremely difficult to gather and was further obstructed by the fusillade of words between opposing sides of expert opinion. Eventually, in April 1932, the trial of Otto Wacker and his brother Leonard, presumably the principal assistant, began in the Central Lay Assessors Court in Berlin. One of the principal witnesses at the prosecution, personally known to the author, was Vincent Van Gogh's nephew, Vincent Wilhelm, who stated that after his uncle's death his pictures had been dispersed but most of them were accurately placed and it was only during a shortish so-called Brabant period that there was evidence of some missing paintings. For the rest, the trial proved to be a feast for those interested in gathering artistic invective. One of the pithier statements came from a Van Gogh expert, the art critic of the *Frankfurter Zeitung*, Meier-Graefe who claimed: 'Anyone who buys pictures and pays enormous prices for them on the strength of expert opinion alone deserves to meet with disaster.'

X-ray photographs were produced by Helmuth Ruhemann, who at that time was chemist for the Prussian State Museum, and later worked in the National Gallery, London, and these showed the contrast between an original Van Gogh 'Reaper in a Cornfield' and Wacker's fake Van Gogh of the same subject; how much weaker the forgery was. Vincent Van Gogh built up his pictures to a set plan and at all stages the picture is unquestionably a Van Gogh right through; whereas the underpainting of the Wacker specimen was woolly and showed little sign of planning. Van Gogh applied his paints directly from the tube without any medium to dilute them; Wacker forgeries apparently had been built up with layers of some type of plaster and this was then painted over to simulate the heavy impasto of Van Gogh.

Other eminent people of the art world who were called to attend the trial included Professor Justi and the unfortunate Dr de la Faille, a Director of the New York branch of the firm of art dealers Wildenstein & Co, a painter, Von Koenig, and many others. At the end of a positive artistic furore, on 19 April Otto Wacker was sentenced to a year's imprisonment for persistent fraud, 'partially coincident to the grave and persistent falsification of documents'. Wacker appealed against this sentence and a new hearing was held in Berlin's supreme court. Next time he didn't do quite so well – he had forfeiture of his civil rights for a period of three years; he was fined thirty thousand marks; and given a nineteen months' prison sentence. There was at the end a little gratification for Wacker, for such was the general mystification and confusion by the highly contradictory statements of the learned witnesses that some of the forgeries somehow again entered the fine-art channel for distribution.

Moving now to the field of mural painting, a large-scale forgery was uncovered in 1952 at Lübeck in Western Germany. The Marienkirche there had been heavily damaged by an RAF raid in the war and restoration was not undertaken until 1948. During this time the guts of the building lay open to the weather: apart from the bombing and the subsequent fire, the interior had been further damaged by the attentions of the Fire Brigade with their hoses. It had been known that there were some frescoes that originally decorated part of the interior of the church and that these had been covered over with whitewash by iconoclasts in the fifteenth century. Some of the whitewash was peeling away and revealed traces of medieval frescoes about sixty feet above ground level. The work of restoration was handed to a well-known and respected restorer, Dietrich Fey, and he was assisted by a young painter of considerable skill, Lothar Malskat, who had also had some training as a restorer. Ample finances were available and to a degree the dignitaries of the church and others were to blame for what was to happen because they gave permission for a greater degree of restoration than was necessary, and this in the end really amounted to large areas of total repainting.

Scaffolding was erected inside the church and canvas screens were spread to hide what was going on from the public gaze. It was Malskat who carried out the actual work and in many cases the walls were cleaned bare of traces of the old medieval work and completely new pictures were laid down.

September 1951 was the seven hundredth anniversary of the founding of the Marienkirche and the building was once again thrown open to the public and the opening ceremony was attended not only by top art experts but also by Chancellor Adenauer. Fey received honours, including special stamps being issued by the Post Office showing the details of the restoration, and no less than a hundred and fifty thousand marks were allocated for further necessary work. Poor Lothar Malskat got no praise nor apparently was Fey forthcoming with the fee owing to him.

The meanness on the part of Dietrich Fey was to cost him dear. Malskat lived out his bitterness during the winter but by the following spring he could hold his feelings no longer, and on 9 May 1952 he made a confession to the authorities that the frescoes in the Marienkirche were not restorations at all but were forgeries, partly by himself and partly by Fey. The Press joined the sneering laughter of the art historians, and accusations were thrown against Malskat that he was seeking self-aggrandisement. Fey himself turned on his valuable assistant, accusing him of slander and defamatory remarks. Those who knew that the partnership of Fey and Malskat had split up saw this as a ruse by Malskat to hurt Fey. Once again the Greek chorus of expert opinion began to pontificate. The respected Swede Dr Berthil Berthelsson found the new frescoes to be 'entirely unique; they are to be found nowhere else in the world', a statement more apt than he probably intended. The frescoes were lauded as early Gothic masterpieces in a paper published by the Institute of Art History at Kiel University. The careful and dedicated restoration work was commented on in a treatise published in Switzerland in 1952 by Hans Jurgen Hansen entitled *The Rural Paintings in St Mary's Church, Lübeck*.

Malskat was forced to provide evidence to back up his statement as to the authorship of the frescoes. He obliged. He showed details that had been copied from Bernath's *History of Fresco Painting*, also portraits of

Coptic Saints in the Kaiser Friedrich Museum in Berlin. Other models which he had used included the face of a well-known German film actress, members of the church staff, his father, Genghis Khan, and in one place he even included the head of Rasputin with a halo. In August of 1952 Malskat came further out in the open when he admitted he had also forged medieval paintings during restoration work in Schleswig and Ratzeburg Cathedrals. In the former he had made a classic mistake of the forger: he had put in an anachronism, and on a fine scale; because at the bottom of one of the works was a frieze of medallions containing animals, some imaginary, some real, and the real included turkeys. The frescoes in Schleswig were thought to be painted in early Gothic times and in fact they were well authenticated as being from that period; how then could the early German artist of that time have painted in turkeys which hadn't been brought back from America until about 1550? The confessions, however, of Malskat were still not complete. He now admitted to the forging of some six hundred paintings in the manner of such as Breughel, Cézanne, Chagall, Corot, Cranach, Degas, Delacroix, Dürer, Gauguin, Hodler, Klee, Kokoschka, Manet, Monet, Picasso, Pissarro, Rembrandt, Renoir, Tintoretto, Toulouse-Lautrec, Turner, Utrillo, Van Gogh, Vlaminck and Watteau.

For a time before his arrest Malskat achieved some popularity with the general public. He gave press and radio interviews and became the hero, as the little man who had defeated the experts. But he was arrested on 23 January 1953. Fey had previously been arrested, and when his house was searched drawings and paintings had been discovered. The gathering of evidence took some time and the main court case did not begin until 9 August 1954 and then went on for sixty-six days. It was not until the following 25 January that Malskat and Fey were sentenced; Fey to twenty months and Malskat to eighteen months. After the trial one expert stated that it was likely if Malskat had not confessed, his better works would still be acclaimed as original and be fooling the art world.

Malskat was released from prison in August 1957, his sentence being shortened by remission, and he then took up a career as an artist. The fact that he committed artistic crime upon crime had in no way lessened his popularity with clients and he found himself with a full order book from people who wanted pictures in the early Gothic manner. Amongst other places, he decorated the walls of Tre Kronor Restaurant at Stockholm. He brought back his celebrated turkey as a decoration for the entrance doors of the Royal Tennis Courts in the Swedish capital, proving that if an artist does sell his soul to Mephistopheles, he will reap a harvest for a period.

The vagaries of art prices at times are a mystery. Some artists' value climbs steadily; others go up and down in a switchback; and others remain seemingly undiscovered for long periods; such a one was Jan Vermeer. Today he is one of the most highly-valued painters: in fact, it is hard to suggest a figure he would fetch if a painting by him came into the open sale room. Yet in the seventeenth century Vermeer found it necessary, in order to get a reasonable figure for his paintings, to add different names instead of his own. Nicholas Maes was one artist whose name he used, and there was another painting, to which had been added fraudulently the name of Pieter de Hooch. Sales figures in his early years back up this action: 1696 – twenty-one pictures were sold at prices between £2.10s. and £15; 1719, in Amsterdam, the 'Woman with the Pitcher' fetched £10.10s.; in 1907 the value had appreciated, she was sold to the Rijksmuseum for a price thought to be £50,000. In 1810 the 'Singing Lesson', which is now in the Frick Foundation, fetched only £51. The nearest recorded sale to the present day, 1959, 'Girl's Head', measuring only 18" × 16", was sold to Charles Wrightsman, New York, for an estimated figure of £400,000, the same picture being sold in 1816 for just three florins. For many, there is a complete excellence about Vermeer's work, an exquisite perfection in his subtle handling of light, colour relationship and composition, which put him almost beyond the reach of a forger. This painter's painter was to be the target in the 1930s and 1940s for one of the most successful assaults on the art world, the knowledge of the experts, the understanding of the dealers, and the cheque books of galleries, museums and collectors.

On 29 May 1945 two Dutch police officers called at the Amsterdam studio, No. 321 Keizersgracht, of Han Van Meegeren. The War was barely three weeks over and it had left the face of Europe torn open by chaos: there was hardly a city of any size that was not severely devastated with bombing and house-to-house fighting. The roads were clogged with masses of displaced people trying to stagger their way to wherever their home was. During the six years of war there had been looting and transfer of works of art on a vast scale, headed by that arch-grabber Herman Göring. There was muddle and confusion as hidden hoards of treasures turned up in salt mines, and forgotten mountain hideouts. It hardly seemed possible that it could all be sorted out and the treasures that had not been destroyed, lost, burned or re-stolen by looters would eventually come back to their original homes. Then, from this wide-spread array of incalculable worth, the scattered artistic wealth of centuries, started to come the most extraordinary story of art forgery. The Dutch Commissioners who were in charge of finding the stolen and removed art treasures of the Netherlands came upon a very strange picture. It was one of those from the collection of Göring who must have rivalled any other predator of the arts throughout history, not only for the sheer volume but also for the quality of the objects which he had stolen with the aid of the Nazis. The investigators were confronted with a painting entitled 'The Woman taken in Adultery' which in their opinion was unmistakably by Vermeer. But when they consulted the records of the galleries and museums they found that what they had stumbled on was a completely unknown Vermeer. How had it got into the collection of one of their enemies? They assumed that this exquisite Vermeer must have been in some little-known private collection and Göring had acquired it in an illegal manner, as all the works of Vermeer were protected by law and it was a serious offence to export any work of such artistic importance. In fact any person who had done this and allowed it to go to an enemy was a collaborator.

The enquiries were thorough and thus when the Dutch police went along to the studio of Van Meegeren they carried warrants with them for his arrest on a charge of 'collaboration with the enemy', for they had found that it was he who had been principally responsible for the sale of this national treasure to Göring and the crime, if it was proved, would bring him a very heavy prison sentence indeed. When first confronted with the charge, Van Meegeren furiously denied it. His claim was that he had not known that Göring was to be the ultimate buyer, as he said that he had dealt in his usual way through an agent and the price had been settled with no indication as to whom the buyer would be. His story was not believed and he was arrested and taken to prison. Here for several weeks he lapsed into silence, resisting questioning and refusing to answer the charge or to offer any information at all.

But six weeks later he changed and faced his questioners.

'Fools,' he shouted. 'You are fools like the rest of them! I sold no great national treasure – I painted it myself!'

He went on to list as his own a number of paintings that had already been claimed by experts, art historians and the rest as more masterpieces by Vermeer, and others at the same time claimed to be by Pieter de Hooch and Frans Hals. He signed a confession stating that he had faked fourteen paintings by Dutch masters. But as in other cases of a forger's confession the experts didn't believe him, or perhaps didn't want to believe him. The theory was that he was trying to avoid the serious punishment for collaboration with the enemy by telling a vain and ridiculous lie.

Who was this rather slight, wizened, grey-haired figure that was claiming to be the equal of one of Holland's greatest painters? Han Van Meegeren was born in 1889 at Deventer in Holland: his father, Henricus, a local schoolmaster, was a puritanical and strict man. Henricus was forty when he married and Han was his second son. When he was grown up Han admitted that he could remember that in his early life he was not even allowed to speak in his father's presence unless he was first spoken to. At school Han was taught drawing and painting by Bartus Korteling, a teacher and an artist in his own right, who was to become a lifelong friend. The boy showed talent and even quite early on began to win awards, although his father did everything he could to thwart this aspect of his son's career. It is recorded that on one occasion, when he found a bundle of drawings by Han, he tore them up and burnt them in the fire, because he felt that these had something to do with his son's lack of progress in other subjects.

Perhaps this was the first disturbing experience for Van Meegeren which began to alter his mental outlook. From that time there seemed to be a built-in resistance and a rejection of authority. There is the story of when he was passing his local police station and he apparently noticed the key in the lock of the outside door. He turned, crept back unobserved, pushed the door to and locked it and threw the key away. No one had seen him. He retreated to an observation place where he could see without being observed, and then waited to see what would happen. He was rewarded by the sight of uniformed policemen forcing their way out of the windows of the locked building, endeavouring to open the door, and finally having to break it down. Han was having his first private treat of a victory over authority and bureaucracy.

His family life was now in a state of almost perpetual unhappiness and discord but at school he worked on under the kind and generous guidance of Korteling. In 1907, when he was eighteen, his father was at last forced to see that his son had talent and he was allowed to go to Delft where he studied architecture at the Institute of Technology. Here he was the one person on the outside. Weak and introspective by nature he had no desire to play games, join in a group, or to form any attachment with the girl students. What he did was to saturate himself in the knowledge that was around him. His interest in painting grew so that whilst studying architecture he set out to win the Gold Medal that was awarded every five years for the best painting from a student at the Institute of Technology. This he did and by 1913 he began to sell his own work. In fact one water colour of this period sold for almost five hundred dollars, a worthy figure even for an established painter. Well before this he had met Anna der Voogt, a girl with a similar nature to his, the daughter of a Dutchman and a Sumatran. They married early in 1912 and for a time their home at Rijswyk was a centre where he could paint happily, even if they were many times in dire need. In 1914 he moved to the Hague, where his drawings, water colours and portraits drew the patronage of the social set. On the day that Britain declared war on Germany in 1914, Han received a degree from the Hague Academy of Art.

At this stage Han was to receive another mental buffet; when conscription started he was found totally unfit for military service and his sense of physical inferiority turned him more and more inwards to a soul that was pickling in its own bitterness.

He was offered a Professorship at the Academy, but he turned it down. Strangely enough his own work was making good progress and there were favourable notices from critics and he found himself in demand for painting. One of his most famous pictures, Deer, is reported to have been reproduced more than any other in Holland. He had done it as a demonstration during one of his classes. An exhibition of his paintings brought him considerable success. The orders were coming in from many sources and dealers were after his work. In 1920 he met Jo van Walraven, an actress and an art critic's wife of mixed Spanish and Dutch ancestry. In

1921 a second exhibition was again a complete success. The critics were unanimous, or nearly so. Just one critic didn't even give a review. Han knew the man, and added this slight to his core of bitterness. In 1923 he divorced Anna but was not to marry Jo until 1929. In the intervening years he was living with her, lowering his health by excesses, making considerable money but letting it run to waste. He had to provide for Anna and also for the expensive tastes of Jo. He turned to portraits, commercial art, advertising. He came to England and again made good money with portraits, but the praise of the critics was dropping away despite his material success, and the adulation from their pens was what he needed. The lack of it further soured him. In 1930 he and Jo left Holland and moved to the Riviera, settling finally in Nice. On his own admission he had managed to build up a capital of some £15,000 at this time from the portraits of rich American and British tourists.

Van Meegeren apparently had a meeting one night over a bottle with the connoisseur, Theo van Wijngaarden, and their talk turned to fakes and genuine old paintings, and it came up that Dr Abraham Bredius, the doyen of the Dutch art critics who studied old masters, had insisted to Wijngaarden that a certain genuine Frans Hals was faked. Wijngaarden told Van Meegeren how he had reacted to this comment. Over the next few weeks he had persuaded an old artist friend of his to forge a Rembrandt, and when he showed it to Bredius, the learned man at once gave a certificate of its complete authenticity: whereupon Wijngaarden had apparently ripped up the painting in front of Bredius to show what he thought of such a man. To the embittered Van Meegeren this information brought inspiration. He sneered at the whole art world: he despised it and all of the dealers, historians, collectors, gallery directors – the lot: and he, Han van Meegeren, would trap them.

For a time he produced quite excellent fakes of Hals, De Hooch, Terborch; but the target wasn't quite big enough for his vanity. He suddenly decided that he would fake the genius himself, Jan Vermeer. Han was nothing less than a hard and dedicated worker when he started on a course. First of all he researched into the whole art scene, and he realised that art historians were expecting that paintings with an overall religious content by Vermeer might be found. They felt that Vermeer could have travelled to Italy and would have absorbed the influence of the Italian painters, notably the dramatic use of chiaroscuro of the great Caravaggio. At Roquebrune near Nice he found an isolated house in which to work and produce his masterpiece.

Han's work on pigments was painstaking, he found details in a book by A. M. de Wild called *Vermeer's Technique* as to vehicles and colours that had been used and he knew that no modern artificial colours would pass even the most casual chemical analysis. Vermeer's famous blue was genuine ultramarine, a lovely tint that is extracted from the semi-precious stone Lapis Lazuli. Later in a statement to the police he told them how in the early part of 1931 he had obtained supplies from Winsor and Newton and the firm said that four separate orders for this valuable colour, totalling twelve and a half ounces, had been made. It had been assumed that Van Meegeren was the customer on each occasion, although his name did not appear on the firm's records. It is really rather strange that after having gone to the expense of securing the real ultramarine, in two of his later paintings he was stupid enough to include cobalt blue, a pigment not discovered until 1802. He tried various vehicles and binding agents for his colours, searching through recipes of past centuries. He tried baking processes in a large specially made kiln, but none seemed to be satisfactory. Too often the paint film was scorched and the dried film was not at all convincing, apart from anything else all the oil and resin vehicles for the colours took a very long time to dry out. Then he hit on the idea of mixing the pigment with phenol and formaldehyde, the two chemicals which were used in the production of Bakelite, a hard synthetic material which had been developed in the United States in 1908. He found by experimenting and adjusting the amounts of these two chemicals and by adding a little synthetic lilac oil that he could get the exact consistency of paint he wanted, and also that this same paint when heated up to about 100 °C for a short period would produce a paint film that was very hard and resistant to solvents and appeared consistent with the paint film of an original Vermeer.

The subject which Van Meegeren chose for his first Vermeer was the 'Supper at Emmaus'. The first step was to obtain a seventeenth-century picture, preferably by a Dutch artist, so that he would have canvas comparable to that which had been used by Vermeer. He then set to work with solvents and cleaning agents, such as soda, to remove all signs of the original painting, paying particular attention that there were no traces of white lead left as these would show up very quickly by radiography. Part of the ground would be left, because it would contain the ancient craquelure which could be of value in the final painting.

Then with his pigments mixed with the artificial resin of phenol formaldehyde, he created his 'Supper at Emmaus', reflecting the style he felt the expert would recognise as belonging to the lost period of Vermeer's output. It strongly reflected the theatrical lighting of Caravaggio. When the paint had been dried out and baked he applied the first coat of varnish which was then cracked by rolling the canvas, paint surface outwards, around a wooden rod or similar object, and after this he covered the surface of the cracked varnish with ink so that it penetrated into the cracks. When this had dried the excess ink was wiped off the surface of the varnish with a cloth and then the last coat of varnish, which was slightly tinted brown, was added to give that essential old master look.

For some time Van Meegeren could have been subject to doubt that his master fake could survive the ordeal of expert examination when he uttered it, but as the days passed he became more and more confident that his work would dupe the art world which he so despised. The picture was finished in the summer of 1937 and now he set out to find a buyer. Obviously he couldn't do it himself: he must have a middleman, and he remembered a lawyer, an old friend, a Mr X, who Van Meegeren knew was open to a little monetary encouragement. Mr X may or may not have known that the picture was a forgery, but anyhow he accepted the role of agent. To Mr X Van Meegeren came up with the supposition that the 'Supper at Emmaus' was by Vermeer and it had been for two or three generations in a castle in South-West Holland. The family were well-to-do and had a fine showing of paintings, including others by Rembrandt, Hals, El Greco and Holbein; they had settled in the South of France with their collection. The pictures apparently belonged in part to the lady of the house and in part to her daughter. He further went on that the daughter had a house near Strasbourg and the lady had now moved close to Lake Como in Italy. He romanticised further claiming that the lady of the house had a deep affection for him and had asked him if he could realise some money for her on a commission basis of course, by the sale of one of her pictures.

'Supper at Emmaus' by Han Van Meegeren

159

Mr X wrote to Abraham Bredius telling him of his discovery of this picture, which he felt could be a work of one of the greatest Dutch masters. A few days later the critic joined Mr X at Monaco, not far from Roquebrune. He saw the painting and was at once enthusiastic about it and asked to have it photographed. Very soon after this Bredius wrote to Mr X with a certificate of guarantee on the back of the photographic print testifying that he considered the picture to be a genuine Vermeer. At the same time Bredius informed Mr X that he would reserve the rights of his discovery for himself; in fact, he did announce this in the *Burlington Magazine* in November 1937 on page 211 and he made what was afterwards to be a pretty damning statement by a critic of his eminence. In part this read:

It is a wonderful moment in the life of a lover of art when he finds himself suddenly confronted with a hitherto unknown painting by a great master, untouched, on the original canvas, and without any restorative, just as it left the painter's studio! And what a picture! Neither the beautiful signature 'I.V.Meer' nor the pointille on the bread which Christ is blessing, is necessary to convince us that we have here a – I am inclined to say – *the* masterpiece of Johannes Vermeer of Delft, and moreover, one of his largest works, quite different from all his other paintings and yet every inch a Vermeer. . . .

Before he had so committed himself he had taken four tests which he considered would be proof of authenticity. The first was the resistance of the paint to alcohol and other solvents, second, evidence of white lead in the white portions, third, X-ray examination of the substrata, and microscopic and spectroscopic examination of the principal pigments. None of these produced evidence to cast a doubt on the authenticity of the picture. Further, the judgement by Bredius was supported straightaway by other Dutch experts, including Professor Martin and Dr Schneider of the Mauritshuis, F. Schmidt-Dengerer of the Rijksmuseum and Dr Hannema of the Boymans.

Bredius was determined that this 'masterpiece' which he had discovered must not fall into hands other than the Dutch and the result was that in December of 1937 the 'Supper at Emmaus' was bought for the Boymans Museum in Rotterdam for fifty-eight thousand pounds, the cost being shared between the Rembrant Society and the State.

The scene can be imagined as the unique discovery was put on show in the presence of Bredius and the other peers of the art world of Holland and

Europe, and somewhere in the shades Han Van Meegeren was rubbing his hands with secret pleasure as he saw his dearest wish come true. In his own eyes he had the art world humbled at his feet. Praise was lavished on the picture and it seems that at that time only one person had seen through it in October 1937; the Paris representative of Duveen Brothers, the art dealers in New York, had been sent a request by his bosses to inspect the picture. He had done so and replied with the following cable:

'SEEN TODAY AT BANK LARGE VERMEER ABOUT FOUR FEET BY THREE CHRIST'S SUPPER AT EMMAUS SUPPOSED BELONG PRIVATE FAMILY CERTIFIED BY BREDIUS WHO WRITING ARTICLE BURLINGTON MAGAZINE NOVEMBER STOP PRICE POUNDS NINETY THOUSAND STOP PICTURE ROTTEN FAKE'

On this success Van Meegeren rested for three or four years then he continued to produce fake Vermeers. There came in 1941 a study of 'Christ's Head', bought for sixty-one thousand pounds by D. G. van Beuningen and traded in to Hoogendjuk, an art dealer, in part payment for the 'Last Supper'. The same year the 'Last Supper', again bought for one hundred and seventy-eight thousand pounds by D. G. van Beuningen of Rotterdam. This was followed in 1942 by 'Isaac blessing Jacob', for a hundred and forty-one thousand pounds which went to W. van der Vorm of Rotterdam. In 1942 'The Woman Taken in Adultery', at one hundred and eighty-three thousand pounds, was bought by Göring which was to be the forger's undoing. And another Vermeer, 'The Washing of Christ's Feet', in 1943 was acquired by the Dutch State for one hundred and forty-four thousand pounds. Van Meegeren spread his shot and included Pieter de Hooch, 'The Card Players', bought by D. G. van Beuningen for thirty-two thousand pounds about 1939, and 'A Drinking Party' bought for twenty-four thousand pounds by W. van der Vorm in 1940. In all his take was eight hundred and twenty-one thousand pounds.

At his trial the prosecution had an unprecedented array of professional expertise from the art world. It was headed by Dr Paul Coremans, Director of the Central Laboratory of the Belgian Museums in Brussels, and certainly one of the finest authorities on restoration and painting techniques, and one who did most to uncover the truth. Others included Dr A. van Schendel, Director of the Department of Painting at the Rijksmuseum; Professor R. J. Gettens of the Fogg Museum, Harvard

'Portrait of a Man' in the manner of Gerard ter Borch by Han Van Meegeren

'Woman reading a Letter' by Han Van Meegeren

University; Dr J. C. A. Kappelmeier, Director of Sikkens Varnishes, Sassenheim, Holland; and Professor P. Terpstra of the State University, Groningen. Under the cross-fire of the indisputable evidence that this team could now produce, inevitably Han was found guilty and bearing in mind the state of his health, the judge relented on the full four years he could have had for his swindle, so he was sentenced to one year's imprisonment. He was not to emerge from this, as he fell ill and was transferred to the Valerius Clinic where he died at the age of fifty-eight on 30 December 1947.

An interesting point – at the end of the trial after the sentence he was asked by the judge if he had any statement to make on the work of the scientists who had investigated him and his forgeries. With a bitter tone in his voice he replied, 'I find this work excellent. Indeed it is phenomenal. It will never be possible to get away with forgery again. To me such work seems much more clever than – for example – the painting of "Christ's Supper at Emmaus".'

But, despite the forecast of Han Van Meegeren of the dim future for forgers of paintings at the hands of ruthless scientists, the story goes on; and it is very unlikely that while art appreciation is expressed to a degree in ever-leap-frogging prices, the forger will pack up his brushes and paints.

February 1959 and there was consternation in Oslo. Two unknown and alleged masterpieces by the great Norwegian painter Edvard Munch turned up. One was bought by the Oslo Modern Art Gallery for seventeen thousand kronen and a leading collector bought the other for forty-seven thousand kronen. Gossip started and from this grew suspicion and then yet another forger came forth and confessed. This time Caspar Caspersen, a skilled cabinet-maker, told the startled and incredulous experts that he was the mysterious Munch faker. Yet again the story repeats itself of disbelief and mocking laughter, but Caspar continued in his affirmation and managed to convince experts that he had done it.

In fact, in a prison cell, Caspar produced in less than three hours an easily recognisable 'Summer Landscape' in the brave expressionist manner of Edvard Munch.

The techniques and methods of many of the great names of the twentieth century have unfortunately lent themselves to numerous forays by forgers, particularly if the works are in water colour, pastel, charcoal, pencil or other drawing method, where the support is paper. This is because it is still comparatively easy to get hold of a paper fairly similar to that which would have been used by a master of this period. A watchful faker can keep an eye on sales from old artists' studios and can often pick up a supply that has been salted away by the elderly painter. On this matter of papers, until the early part of the nineteenth century the paper used by artists would have been made from rags and of a high quality. An expert on paper needs only a very small piece to be able to tell him its history when it is examined under a microscope and by simple chemical tests.

One of the first of the forgers to give modern art a real working over was Jean Pierre Schecroun who was born in Madagascar in 1929. He arrived in Paris in 1949 and showed a good deal of promise at the École des Beaux Arts. For a time he worked in the studio of Fernand Léger and made a particular study of the styles and methods of a number of famous and successful painters. Then he found, like many another bright student, that what seemed to be embryo talent was perhaps just a scintillating sparkle which was not enough to earn a living for a painter in his own right. But he very soon found his true *métier* when he befriended a small group of people who saw in the young Schecroun a commodity that could be marketed. Together with this bunch of confidence tricksters Schecroun moved off on what might be termed an art tour of Europe. Not bothering to waste the time with oils, with all the long-term preparation and lengthy periods of drying, he worked with water colours, pastels, and different drawing techniques and scattered in his trail fraudulent examples of work by such artists as Braque, Hartung, Kandinsky, Léger, Lhote, Miró, Picasso and others, earning some two hundred thousand dollars for his gang. When he was finally arrested and put in the box he based his defence on the theme 'My trial will be that of a picture dealer', which is one way of further confusing matters.

Another gentleman who cut out a healthy fortune from collectors' desire for the modern was David Stein. He was born in Egypt and studied at the Sorbonne and early in his twenties he had a fascination for Picasso, reading about him, studying his works and trying in every way to take on the atmosphere and the mind of Picasso. Quite soon he tried to copy one of Picasso's works of the 1930s and, more out of interest than of anything else, took it to an art dealer who immediately bought it for five thousand dollars as a genuine Picasso. The temptation was too great and the young Stein set to work really hard. Not only Picasso came off his brush, but Braque, Chagall, Matisse, Dufy, Van Dongen, Miró, Derain. Eventually the law caught up with him, partly because they had been alerted by the fact that Chagall himself when in America had been shown a number of 'Chagalls' by Stein. He had condemned them outright as very poor fakes. On 23 January 1959 Stein was fined six thousand dollars and sentenced from two and a half to five years in Sing Sing. When inside he continued to paint but this time his Braques, Chagalls and Matisses clearly bore the signature of Stein; in the same manner that the more recent works by a similar master imitator, Elmyr Hory, have done, his fakes are clearly signed with his signature but still find ready bidders.

With the faking of drawings of whatever period, apart from the actual copying or imitating of original examples, a pet trick of the faker is to take

'Lady Reclining on Chaise Longue' in the manner of Matisse by De Hory. It was sold under his own name for £700 in 1977

what is called a counter-proof from an original work. This is a comparatively simple matter and what the forger does is first to damp very lightly the surface of the drawing to be copied. This is done with a fine atomising spray; next he damps a sheet of similar quality paper, puts this on top of the damp drawing and then gives it a fairly thorough going over with a rubber roller or puts it through an etching press. This will cause a reverse impression to be implanted on to the clean sheet of paper on top. The impression will be the wrong way round and it may need some working on, but to the casual, not very well-initiated eye, an acceptable and quite saleable item is easily produced. The same kind of method can be employed with a little more skill on the part of the faker with engravings and etchings, although here he is up against the snag of the so-called plate-mark which shows with this type of print making. To a degree this plate-mark can be forged by the use of a hot iron prior to the counter-proofing, or with a small electric spatula afterwards. With some of the prints, he might first of all have slightly to moisten the ink with a light spray of white spirit, alcohol or chloroform. Fake prints by this method are never very satisfactory and would only deceive those with little knowledge of print-making methods. They will of course also be reversed.

Paper can be given fairly convincing ageing by damping it, placing it between sheets of blotting-paper, and then putting it (still in the blotting-paper) on the floor and just walking about on it. It can be stained with weak tea and coffee, and concentrated coffee can also be spotted on to produce very satisfactory 'foxing' marks. Even water marks are not beyond the reach of the faker and with care he can produce quite good examples by using either weak acid or one or other of the concentrated toilet and drain cleaners.

As far as is known, one of the earliest forgers of drawings was a Dutchman, Denys Calvaert (1540–1619), who lived in Bologna. He made a speciality of producing variations of Michelangelo's work and Raphael's. Often these variations were built up from details of their frescoes. As an intermediary to get rid of the drawings he was in league with a gentleman by the name of Pomponio, who apparently gave them a light smoking before selling them to collectors, among whom was included the Cardinal d'Este. On the whole, fakers of drawings have not been so successful as those concentrating on paintings or other media. A line drawing lays bare obviously and clearly any deficiencies in the forger's armoury and calls for a directness and purity most forgers would shun. Try as he may, he can't quite capture that freshness of the original artist and his stroke inevitably has to be made in a halting manner, which is particularly evident in comparison with an original.

One of the most plagued of all artists in history certainly must have been the German Albrecht Dürer. Not only were his paintings subjected to extensive alterations, but his water colours and drawings were faked, and in particular his prints. The expert Heller lists no less than three hundred people who worked after or in the manner of the Nuremberg genius. The list included such as Virgil Solis, who signed his copies V.S.; Hieronymus Wierx, who had some success with his version of the Dürer engraving of the 'Knight, Death and the Devil'. Also there were J. C. Vischer, Ulrich Kraus, Martin Rota, Lambert Hopfer and Erhard Schön. But the best known of Dürer's plagiarists was the Italian Marc Antonio Raimondi. Amongst other titles and series he copied or faked of Dürer's were the 'Little Passion' and the 'Life of the Virgin'; both produced within quite a short time of the publication of the original by Dürer himself. In the case of the 'Little Passion' Raimondi did not affix the Dürer monogram AD, but he did for the 'Life of the Virgin'. Also with 'Adam and Eve', in 1504, he inserted the famous tablet with the Dürer monogram exactly as the master would have done. Raimondi was an odd one, because he was an artist of no little talent and when it is possible to compare his fake Dürers with the original thing, it can be seen how he has brought freehand detail of his own invention into the prints, which may make them to some more attractive, but at the same time makes them less faithful copies than others.

Poor Dürer, he even had the indignity in 1512 of hearing that one bright deceiver had the gall to be trying to sell fake prints complete with the AD monogram right outside the Town Hall in Nuremberg. He appealed to his patron, the Emperor Maximillian, who forbade anybody to make copies or imitations of Dürer's work. Stiff punishments were announced and the edict had some effect.

After Dürer's death one of his principal fakers was Hans Hoffman who was openly patronised by Rudolf II of Prague, who, amongst other works, commissioned a copy of Dürer's famous 'Hare', from Hoffman. By the seventeenth century the craze for Dürer was greater than ever. Practically every major collector of his prints was plagued with fakes. The Archduke Leopold Wilhelm of Austria apparently had more than sixty. The first Elector of Bavaria, Maximilian I, didn't help matters. He thought very highly of Dürer but couldn't get any original works by him and so commissioned a whole series of pictures in the manner of Dürer from his court painters.

The danger of print collecting is epitomised with what has happened with the work of Dürer: so many expert hands, different plates, and states taken during the artist's time, and prints that have been taken and are being taken from printing blocks or plates that have been photographically copied and produced. Here only experience and knowledge can be the real safeguard. The engraved line should be slightly standing up from the paper: it can be picked up sometimes by touch, or by examination with a strong raking light, whereas modern flat printing methods lack the crispness or sharpness. Again it comes back to this: be careful.

Whatever type of painting, drawing or print is sought, if there is any smell of the word 'bargain' or other suspect feature, hold off. Floating around at the moment there are some quite convincing reproductions of pencil drawings by artists like Augustus John, Sir William Nicholson and Wilson Steer. These are generally done on cartridge paper and may even bear a pencil number up in one corner suggesting that they could have been torn from a sketch book. On examination with a reasonably powerful magnifying glass the deception becomes quite clear. They are printed by a very fine screen process and the magnification shows up the tiny dots, which although they are black on white paper, when viewed from about two or three feet the eye is deceived into thinking the line is grey, rather in the same manner that the pointillist colour theory works.

Pictures are considered by many to be one of the so-called 'safest' hedges against inflation. In fact even such bodies as British Rail pension fund have invested over twenty-three million pounds in works of art, which they will leave to appreciate for a twenty-year period before possibly re-selling, with a hoped-for guarantee of capital growth.

Albrecht Dürer must be smiling down on the art scene today when he notices such items as a chalk portrait by Wolf Huber which has had his monogram added to it and which fetches a price of a hundred and five thousand pounds. At the same time a small water colour by Dürer himself of a little bit of a hill and one or two buildings fetches six hundred and forty thousand pounds. Perhaps from where he is he can see who is really pulling the strings on this extraordinary and tightly-knit brotherhood of exchange. Today much of the real money muscle power comes from the directors of galleries and museums around the world who often have not only vast endowments but in some cases the promise of large national funds at their disposal.

These people walk across the artistic landscape gathering in the treasures, the works of genius and the rest as they come from private collections. The link man in between is the dealer, who to a very large extent controls the market and introduces new fashions. There is no doubt that the art market, particularly where pictures are concerned, is pulling in money like no other magnet. Few could have predicted twenty-five years ago the bonanza that was coming. Old masters have increased in value by up to eight times, British paintings between nine and ten, Impressionists between sixteen and twenty, old-master drawings between twenty and twenty-five times, and at the top of the golden mountain old-master prints with a multiple ahead of thirty times. Small wonder this field draws the copyist, the imitator and the faker.

CHAPTER TEN

SCIENTIFIC
INSTRUMENTS

One of the ugliest aspects of forgery is the chain of innocent people it can embarrass not only financially, but also in terms of prestige and reputation. Neither collectors nor dealers like to admit that they have been fooled: such mistakes inevitably cast doubts on their connoisseurship. As a result the proportion of publicly-exposed cases of faking is small compared with the large number of discreetly hushed up cases where expensive acquisitions have proved not quite right. In 1975 sinister rumours suggested that certain renowned collectors of scientific instruments had been duped by a superb craftsman who had infiltrated into the market some exquisite fake antique sun-dials and astrolabes. Some of the leading dealers in the world were also said to have been unwittingly involved.

Skilled deceivers have the advantage of surprise. By watching market trends, sensing dwindling supplies of the genuine, they can prepare their deceits and launch them at a time of their own choosing. Eager collectors of scientific instruments are more often enthusiasts about the history of science and technology than experts in antiques and are therefore occasionally very liable to be deceived.

Unfortunately for the collector the forging of scientific instruments has been going on for centuries, although today it is receiving an impetus from the current trend to collect antiques as a hedge against inflation. There seems to be an almost inexhaustible supply of buyers, prepared to part with enormous sums for objects that may have only the vaguest provenance. Innumerable sets of 'early' Nuremberg weights have been sold, often so badly made that they will not nest properly. In the last century forgers in Birmingham made comfortable profits by churning out 'water clocks' on a massive scale. Fakes of instruments may be not only badly made but can also be 'double deceits' as the object they purport to be a replica of may not even exist except as a figment in the mind of the forger.

The field becomes more complicated as from the end of the seventeenth century onwards scientists, craftsmen and collectors became fascinated with strange experimental devices. Early in the eighteenth century it became the vogue to commission almost perversely weird instruments which not only demonstrated scientific principles but at the same time were objects of entertainment – like today's executive toys. One of the leading collectors of such extravagances was the Rev. J. T. Desaguliers (1683–1744) who brought them together for the edification of the Royal children. Today this hoard is known as the George III Collection: it includes a model of Archimedes' hydraulic screw for water raising made by George Adams in about 1760, and Smeaton's variation on the exhausting pump. The latter was a great favourite with the specialist collector of the period as with it he could demonstrate the phenomena of objects falling in a vacuum and the subsequent non-transmission of sound.

In a more macabre vein, our ancestors experimented with the effects of reduced and increased atmospheric pressures on living creatures. Thomas Hornsby (1763–1810), a Reader in Experimental Philosophy at Oxford, had one particularly unpleasant party trick. He would place a cat in a glass chamber to which was attached an exhausting pump. As he drew out the air he would remark: 'You will observe, gentlemen, that the animal exhibits symptoms of uneasiness . . . The animal seems to be considerably incommoded.' At one time he became so immersed in his research that it is recorded that it was only by the timely intrusion of his servant that a certain lady's pet was saved from extinction.

Around 1800 the so-called 'Temple of Vesta' was made, which was an example of an instant chemical fire machine. Vesta was the Roman goddess associated with the hearth; a flame was kept continually burning, jealously guarded in her temple by the Vestal Virgins. The small temple 'machine' was a work of art and considerable craftsmanship, designed with architectural elegance. Inside hydrogen was generated and by pressing a button it was released through the mouth of a miniature lion and at the same time ignited by a small spark from a concealed electrostatic device.

From these and more ordinary scientific instruments there is a wide choice not only for the collector but also the faker. Such examples are heavily competed for in the saleroom.

The three main divisions for many collectors are instruments concerned with astronomy, navigation and measurement. Although those for magnification, surgery, dentistry, drawing and surveying are also popular.

One of the most treasured instruments of the early astronomers was the astrolabe, a device used for taking the altitude of the sun, moon and stars. The earliest forms were 'armillae' and spherical. Hipparchus was one of the leading astronomers who played a part in developing the idea. The astrolabe was widely used throughout the fifteenth, sixteenth and seventeenth centuries. Although there were some large models, most were quite small, compact and portable. Ptolemy mentioned them in AD 140, Arab and Persian astronomers improved them, and by the tenth century they were familiar to most of the intelligentsia of Western civilisation. Astrolabes were used, before the advent of clocks, during the day as portable sundials and at night as star charts. For Muslims they told both the direction of Mecca and the appropriate time for prayers, and for would-be surveyors they became the first theodolites.

Most astrolabes comprise a series of flat metal plates which revolve within the same diameter, some pierced to permit the viewer to register several measures at the same moment – rather like putting two transparent protractors on top of one another. The key plate is called the 'rete': it is a star chart as viewed by an observer looking back at our known universe from outer space.

The best astrolabes are the epitome of elegance and accuracy, and are highly prized because they embody both the finest aesthetic craftsmanship and an expert knowledge of astronomy. And it is nearly always the lack of the latter that gives away the forgery: the most common fault in fake astrolabes is that they simply don't work!

Other astronomical instruments that are likely to have found their way into collectors' cabinets and therefore have attracted the attention of the faker include celestial globes, dating back as far as 350 BC. In the Naples Museum is the earliest known existing globe of this type, called the 'Atlante Farnese', dating from 200 BC. There are lunar dials that tell the hour of the night by a shadow cast by a gnomon in moonlight. The Orrery, a complicated instrument, shows the principal movements of the solar system. The original one was made by John Rowley of London in 1713 and the name arose when a Rowley copy came into the possession of Charles Boyle, fourth Earl of Orrery. The orrery was not a sudden invention but rather a development from earlier experiments.

Instruments for navigation which are favourites with mariner-collectors include the Back Staff, a device similar to a cross staff, used for taking the altitudes of the heavenly bodies, the Nocturnal for finding the time at night by the position of the stars and also for determining latitude, and the Octant for measuring angles which was similar to the sextant invented in 1730 by John Hadley.

Measuring instruments are diverse, including the abacus for mathematical calculations, used by the ancient world and still in use in some countries now. Napier's bones were a set of wooden blocks used for multiplying and dividing. Then there was the Groma for giving right angles which was used by the early Egyptians and early Romans.

There have been a number of celebrated instrument makers; among the early recorded was Bernhard Walter of Nuremberg. He included amongst his clients the famous Regiomontanus for whom he supplied a set of instruments that would today be worth a fortune. Apparently when Walter died his heirs threw his manuscripts into the rubbish bin and gave the contents of his workshop to a scrap man. The same fate awaited the exquisite instruments of Tycho Brahe and the superb collection of clocks of the Emperor Charles V. As these treasures have never been re-assembled, nobody knows whether they have been destroyed or accurately copied, married or otherwise become a part of the underworld trade in illicit articles.

At the end of March 1976 Sotheby's issued a very significant statement which sent a tremor of fear and suspicion through the world of antique dealers. Sotheby's intention was to reassure its own clients, but in so doing did they sound an alarm? Perhaps the whispered rumours were based on fact. Sotheby's declaration went as follows:

From time to time in the history of the art market a master forger has emerged. Amongst them have been Bastianini, Van Meegeren and Thomas Wise. It is alleged that a forger of scientific instruments may have successfully hoodwinked collectors, dealers and auctioneers. Sotheby's, as the only auctioneers in Great Britain who provide a five year guarantee against forgery, naturally stand behind their conditions of sale and will not only make restitution to any purchaser who has in fact been damaged as a result of the alleged fraud but in this particular case, will also make restitution to such purchasers of instruments from this source purchased before the implementation of this five year guarantee period, provided that forgery is established to Sotheby's complete satisfaction.

Scotland Yard's Art and Antiques Squad were called in to investigate the authenticity of a brass astrolabe, dated at around 1710. It had been auctioned to a Swiss dealer for £3400. The Head of the Art and Antiques Squad was telephoned but he was unable to provide us with any information as the case had now become *sub judice*.

But in the way of such things information came in from another direction. In the September 1974 edition of the French magazine, *Art et Curiosité*, an article appeared on the subject of authenticating astrolabes. Its author was the Paris dealer Alain Brieux, who had made astrolabes a special study for over twenty years, but explained that he too had been caught out by possibly the very same English forger whom Scotland Yard were now attempting to trace. He had written his article in the hope of alerting others to the deceptive nature of the man's work.

A regular purchaser of books about antique scientific instruments from M. Brieux's establishment had visited him with another Englishman who sold him an allegedly eighteenth-century ring-dial. It appealed to M. Brieux because it incorporated seemingly unique features: it was the first

Top: an authentic astrolabe signed by Muhammad Muqim al-Yezdi. Bottom: a false astrolabe also supposedly signed by Muhammad Muqim al-Yezdi; note its lack of elegance and the imprecise notation of the degrees

Top: a genuine astrolabe signed by Muhammed Muqim al-Yezdi
Below: a fake again betrayed by its clumsy workmanship

combined astrolabe and astronomical ring he had ever come across. Unfortunately it was not long before he came across several very similar objects, all recently bought by other French dealers. The forger had presumably learnt about astrolabes from the books sold to him by M. Brieux prior to succeeding in fooling this Frenchman and his friends with his new, misapplied knowledge.

M. Brieux decided to make a detailed comparison of all the newly acquired ring-dials. If genuine the brass in them would have been beaten to a uniform thickness by hand. But although this uniformity might look perfectly flat and regular to the naked eye, if several sample measurements of the thickness of the brass were taken, they would reveal the slight variations inevitable in genuine early handwork of this kind. M. Brieux measured each ring-dial at several points: the thickness was always a precise 1.65 mm. He concluded they must all be made from modern brass sheet. He made another discovery which confirmed his findings. Although the dials were signed by various French and German craftsmen, they all contained one stylistic similarity which made it almost impossible for each of them to have been created by a different hand. The forger had made the classic mistake of being a trifle too clever. To give his numerals an archaic appearance he decorated every '5' he engraved with a characteristic squiggle. He used similar squiggles to embellish both ends of the letter 'S'. They are the kind of clues which even the most perceptive of experts can search for, and stare at blindly for hours before they suddenly become transparently obvious, and from that moment a child's guide to authentication.

Unfortunately for this forger he made one more mistake. He returned to M. Brieux's premises and this time tried to sell an even rarer kind of instrument. M. Brieux examined it that evening and, as he expected, found it was made of 1.65 mm brass. Next day, when faced with the fact that he was trying to sell a modern fake, the forger protested vehemently and threatened M. Brieux with both the police and the British Embassy. However he knew his bluff had been called and, forgetting to take his 'priceless sixteenth-century treasure' with him, left, not as the saying goes 'never to return', but to reappear some time later in the dock of the Old Bailey.

In the first film of the series we had shown some very genuine and some highly suspicious scientific instruments. We had also featured fake astrolabes, but because legal action was still pending, were unable to mention the strong probability of a master forger currently operating in this area. In June 1978 we were finishing the last programme of the series: it lacked a really topical and appropriate ending. Then Scotland Yard's Art and Antiques Squad came up trumps. They allowed us to film a representative collection of these current and very clever fakes: astrolabes, universal equinoctual ring-dials and a nautical hemisphere. The last is indeed rare. There is no known example of one ever being actually made, although there is an illustration of a design for one in a book published in the seventeenth century by Michel Coignet. The fake nautical hemisphere was offered to M. Brieux at twenty thousand francs. Rather naturally it aroused his suspicions.

The craftsman, a twentieth-century master metal-smith, had secreted his workshop away in Slough, Buckinghamshire. Apart from the errors just mentioned his productions showed considerable skill, and the impressive antique finish had been achieved by putting his finished instruments in a box with old nuts, bolts and jagged pieces of iron and giving it a thorough and prolonged shaking. The result of this was to cause the objects to have a passable covering of moss-scratches and patination was added by dipping them in weak nitric acid. The faker's reward for all this expertise was a period in prison.

During the research for the programme about fake scientific instruments we came across some of the finest, most plausible, but ungenuine articles ever created. Original examples in good condition of antique microscopes, telescopes, astrolabes and compasses are extremely rare. This rarity makes it virtually impossible for any student of their history to be given the opportunity of actually handling them. Museum curators and collectors of antiques are often enthusiastic about showing off their wares behind the secure custody of locked glass cabinets, but mostly blanch at the prospect of their treasures actually being used for the very purpose they were originally made. When you are responsible for the priceless, insurance companies tend to insist on a very stern 'hands off' policy.

One answer to this educational dilemma, and to the collectors' greed for the unobtainable, is the replica. In the field of microscopes it used to be the custom for the American pharmaceutical industry to give such articles to the otherwise largely incorruptible general practitioner. Financial

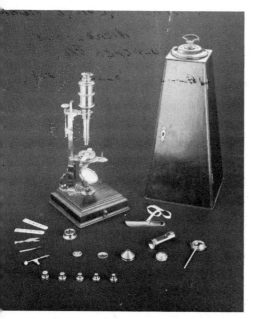

Top left: an authentic Edinburgh Wilson microscope. Right: a copy
Bottom left: an original John Cuff side pillar microscope. Right: a copy

restraints and inflation have temporarily ruined that particular market for replica microscopes, but they are beginning to achieve big sales as prestige display items with Japanese doctors.

Using real ivory to make the pre-prepared microscope slides originally required by eighteenth-century dilettantes, and the skin of sting-rays to produce the authentic shagreen which cloaked the barrels of the finest instruments, the end-products of this replica industry can be highly deceptive. An example of an early microscope designed by John Cuff was filmed and it showed how even the most infinitesimally small detail was perfect. It was in pristine condition, so pristine in fact that it was not so much too good to be true, as too new. A sadly dilapidated, but very similar, microscope was put beside the replica. It was a genuine John Cuff, and, despite its condition, worth well over a thousand pounds, twice the price you would have been asked for the glossy replica. A sobering thought is that an unscrupulous person with a brush, cotton wool, some weak nitric acid and a few hours to spare could age the brass replica by two hundred years and make a considerable profit on its sale.

As a precaution against the resale of their replicas as genuine antiques the makers conceal a nasty surprise for anyone tempted to pass off their reproductions as the real thing. A genuine Cuff microscope is a hundred per cent brass. Their replica is almost a hundred per cent brass, but not quite. Totally invisible, and embedded deep inside the brass of the microscope arm, is a small steel magnet, which anyone with only a simple pocket compass can easily detect.

How old do scientific instruments have to be before they will attract first the collector and then his attendant faker? Instruments in use in the First World War and in the twenties and thirties are now much in demand and, from the forger's point of view, are simpler as he does not have to worry about such items as handbeaten sheets; he can safely use machine-rolled plate and in many cases factory produced parts.

Let us only hope that, as in the case of paintings, ceramics and jewellery, science itself will soon find irrefutable methods of differentiating the false from the genuine. Thereby allowing us to study the history of Science without being confused by the anachronisms often caused by fake scientific instruments.

CHAPTER ELEVEN

SCULPTURE, CARVING AND MODELLING

The Renaissance in Italy, the overflowing riches of the great banker families in Rome and Florence and other centres, brought an unprecedented impetus to all the creative arts, and also to the uncreative arts. At this time, parallel to the master works of genius, came a wave of counterfeiting and forgery and fraudulent use of copies that has only been matched by the activities that intertwine the art world now. Today there is a heady sense of unreality associated with much of the disposal of great works of art. The auctioneer's voice counting the rising multi-thousand-pound bids drones on with the mesmeric measure of a metronome; the ears of the dealer measure and weigh the market, the softly spoken, swollen prices; this is the barter-babel through which the works of art must pass.

Even from the hands of one so gifted as Michelangelo a deceit could grow. The tale of a life-sized 'Sleeping Cupid' that he worked in the Classic manner perhaps casts a merited suspicion on the collectors of the Renaissance who could have been duped on a greater scale than the somewhat sparse records on this subject suggest.

Michelangelo imitated the antique so well that the figure was greatly admired by Lorenzo the Magnificent, and although Lorenzo did not wish to purchase the work, he suggested it could be given an antique appearance, perhaps by some carefully applied colouring or by burying in sour ground. The sleeping figure, when it had acquired a convincing aged look, was taken to Rome and apparently reburied in a vineyard and then 'discovered'. With an introduction from Lorenzo, Michelangelo took it to the art dealer Baldassare de Milanese. He in turn offered the piece to Cardinal Riario San Georgio who was delighted with this charming little 'ancient' figure and paid Baldassare two hundred gold ducats. All Michelangelo got from the dealer was thirty ducats. Seemingly not long after the sale the Cardinal found out that he had been fooled; he returned the sculpture and made Baldassare return his money. There is some suggestion that the unfortunate Cupid was then given a little knocking about by Baldassare to give it the expected 'bits missing look' and was then yet again buried and the 'discovery' trick played once more. Condivi records how a short time later, in some weird way, the Cupid passed into the hands of the Duke Valentino, and then became the property of the Marchioness of Mantua. Then the little figure disappears into the shadows. Towards the end of the sixteenth century another 'Sleeping Cupid' came on the scene; this may have been the model from which Michelangelo worked, or it may have been a copy from his forgery, or a copy of a copy of that forgery.

Collectors of the sixteenth century would have needed to be quite as alert as collectors should be today. The tricks the forgers, imitators and dealers could use were numerous. There was, for instance, a fashion amongst these deceivers when preparing the 'antique pieces', which they intended to sell to their customers, to mutilate the clay model of a figure before it was cast, breaking off limbs and fragments of the features before the molten bronze was poured. There is an example of a genuine antique bronze which was 'restored' being somewhat spoiled as the faker restorer was careless and the metal of the arm replacing one that was broken off was

A Renaissance Florentine relief showing the inside of a sculptor's workshop

of a different alloy to the main part of the figure. The dealers of Florence at this period would have had on display numbers of bronze statuettes to satisfy the demand of amateur collectors who would know little and could easily be deceived. Andrea del Verrocchio, the master of Leonardo, is reported by Vasari as casting numerous small figures in bronze because he saw how greedy the public were for little antique statuettes. Evidently he also ran a rewarding line in fragments of statues which found a ready market. Another craftsman was Vellano, who went even further back than the Greek and made fraudulent imitations of early Egyptian work. One more character in this field was Andrea Briesco, who rather overdid matters, because with his little statuettes he overdressed them and they appeared at times in full suits of consular armour, embroidered togas; grandiose apparel in contrast to the somewhat crude violent expressions Briesco gave to the faces.

Fired clay reliefs offered the faker an excellent opportunity; for example, if a madonna was being worked on, the procedure would be roughly this: a plaster mould would be made from a good original and then a clay replica would be formed from this mould; whilst this clay was still slightly moist the faker could make small changes which, when the piece was finished, to the inexperienced eye could give the appearance of a genuine and original object. He might change the pose of the madonna; the clay being cut with a wire behind the head and neck, and then with a little careful manipulation the face being given a fresh direction, to look to right or left or down. The same treatment could be given to the arms and hands. Finally the relief could be treated and finished in the normal way. The colouring and patination of fired clay is not difficult for a skilled operator. The pigments can be put on as tempera and a very convincing age patina can be applied with water that has been coloured, or by rubbing on tobacco ash or soot with the fingers. Claywork has a considerable attraction for the faker. There is not the expense of marble for carving or of bronze casting.

Even from the early Roman times certain craftsmen were causing consternation amongst collectors of bronzes by their skill in applying the different patinations to the alloy. This method of deception has gone on through the history of collecting, and especially with examples from the sixteenth, seventeenth and eighteenth centuries it makes the acquisition of bronzes a dangerous hobby.

There are numerous ways, quite apart from burying, of ageing marble and stone. Here, as with bronze, the pastiche raises its confusing head; the forger at times copying different parts of two or three or more originals, often using a mechanical device called a pointing machine which helps him to transform the proportions and form of the original model to either a smaller figure such as a maquette or a full-size figure; this instrument is somewhat similar to a pantograph which an artist can use to enlarge a drawing or make it smaller. One of the commonest methods used by some of the fakers in history to give the antique look to marble or stone was to wash the piece with water containing a little green vitriol. The advantage of this is the liquid will penetrate quite deeply and the colour will not wash off if it is applied soon after the figure has been carved. Nitrate of silver has also been used. To avoid leaving an overall even look the faker will have several bowls of different dilutions to get that slightly blotched appearance of true age. Italians, experts in the art of ageing, have used such colours as cochineal, gamboge, dragon's blood, logwood and verdigris.

Wood carvings can be given their share of the years by treatment with an alkali, permanganate of potash and other substances. Where gilding has been applied over gesso, once it has set, part can be abraded away and then a veiling can be washed over it containing liquorice juice or ground-up burnt paper.

Ivory has always been a popular collectors' item and as with bronzes it can be one of the trickiest spheres for the neophyte. The characteristic cracks of old ivory are apparently produced quite simply by the somewhat brutal method of plunging the object into boiling water, pulling it out and drying it quickly before a hot fire and repeating as necessary. A little tobacco juice rubbed in is effective, as is also the smoke from waxed tapers. It is not unknown for freshly-cut ivory forgeries to have been placed in a piece of damp hay or manure which is fermenting, and then left until they have taken on the subtle warm patina so beloved of the expert collector.

The practice by some fakers of making after-casts can be a snare for the unwary. Here, only practice and experience and thorough examination can be a protection. The original cast of a bronze is almost always worked over by the sculptor and chased smooth, having small details refined; it is this attention which gives the life and the charm to a bronze cast; whereas an after-cast will generally be left more or less as it is, or if it is worked up by the faker, his finishing will be done in a manner that is ignorant of the intention of the original artist, and this does show.

Since the eighteenth century there has been brisk demand by collectors who have set themselves up with fine houses with lakes and well-laid-out gardens for ornaments, and many must have been the load of marble baroque benches, urns and seventeenth-century French lead figures that found themselves scattered around the great gardens of the country. The supply of the genuine must have got a little thin or perhaps the asking figure for the original became too high, and so along came gentlemen who worked in what is politely called reconstituted stone, and they supplied the needs of landscape gardeners by producing baroque and romanesque objects using a mixture of ground-down stone, a little cement with water as a basis, and into this would be mixed some rust and other colours. The mixture would then be packed into moulds and when set would be given further surface treatment with acids or alkalis to produce that semblance of slightly crumbling age in line with Portland stone and sandstone. This reconstituted stone helps the deceiver as it will age or mellow quite quickly, the surface is porous, and lichen and algae can grow.

Most periods have produced their star performers in the production of fakery, but the greatest deceivers in sculpture seem to have come forward in the nineteenth and twentieth centuries. Giovanni Bastianini

(1830–1868) worked rather in the manner of Van Meegeren, in that he created his own free invented figures and these were in the style and manner of the greats of the Renaissance. His procedure caused one of the most contentious forgery scandals. From his workshop came a life-size bust of a friend and follower of Savonarola, Girolamo Benivieni. This work had the most astonishing realism; every detail of the face was clearly indicated; the bone structure was convincing; and the upper part of the torso was shown as dressed in a recognisable typical Renaissance garment, the headgear also being of the same period.

The bust of Benivieni started on its way to notoriety via the Florentine dealer Antonio Freppa, who apparently paid Bastianini three hundred and fifty francs for it. Freppa sold it to Count Novilos, a connoisseur who travelled in Italy in search of finds, for seven hundred francs. The Count passed it on again, this time to another Count, Nieuwekirke, for thirteen thousand francs. This Count was a protégé of Princess Mathilde Bonaparte and it was she who was largely responsible for its acquisition by the Louvre at a figure of fourteen thousand francs.

The main factor that had duped these various gentlemen and the princess was that, unlike many of the other Renaissance fakers and imitators, Bastianini had the ability to transpose himself back into the creative spirit of the fifteenth century. He liked to work straight from nature and the model chosen in this case was an old man, a worker in a cigar factory called Guiseppe Bonaiuti. All would have been well but for greed. Count Novilos apparently had had an understanding that he would split the profits he made with Antonio Freppa, but when it came to dividing the gains, he refused and the Florentine dealer, naturally being enraged and bitter, started a campaign to reveal the true story. Word was passed around that this piece, which was supposed to have originated in the fifteenth century, and which was attributed to the school of some of the greatest masters of the Renaissance, which included such as Donatello and Verrocchio, was nothing more than a forgery that had been made by Giovanni Bastianini in the year 1864.

When Count Novilos showed Bastianini's work in 1867 as a specimen of Renaissance culture at the Retrospective Art Show of the Palais Champs Élysées one critic wrote:

'We have not known Benivieni, but are prepared to swear that this portrait must have been extremely like him. Who is the artist that modelled it? We are almost tempted to label the work with a string of names from the glorious period of Florentine art.'

As the rumours grew that the bust was a forgery, Bastianini followed the procedure of many other forgers; he owned up. This brought the usual response from experts that the man must be a braggart. The sculptor Lequense came out strongly and said that Bastianini was a liar and that anybody who had the skill to model the clay with the genius shown here was no longer with us, their talents had disappeared; and he challenged Bastianini to demonstrate his skill.

It is of interest that stylistically the clear realism of the bust was out of character with the more free manner of the Renaissance and more in keeping with the realism of the early Roman. The cross-fire between Bastianini and Lequense continued for some time, at moments dropping almost to the petty, when Lequense suggested that a piece had been replaced by the pressure of a finger leaving the print behind.

Bastianini replied, 'Aren't fingers always used for modelling?'

Lequense followed up with 'The clay differs from that used in Italy today, it has become porous with age.'

Bastianini continued, 'What makes you say that? I will send you a specimen of the clay ordinarily used.'

Lequense then accused him of applying the patina with tobacco smoke, to which Bastianini retorted that if he had guessed his method there were no secrets to be given away. A number of other leading historians and experts joined in. The usual educated papers were written from both sides, and it is evident that initially Bastianini himself intended the work to be a forgery and to be issued as such. To refute the accusation that he hadn't made it, he produced the first plaster cast of the head, which he had kept, and also witnesses who had seen him at work. He had done an earlier bust of Savonarola, the Dominican preacher, which had been shown at the Palazzo Riccardi in Florence. This had been bought by Vincenzo Capponi, a Florentine dealer, who got it for six hundred and forty francs and promptly sold it for ten thousand francs. The Victoria and Albert Museum in London purchased a second bust of Savonarola in 1896. This museum also purchased other works in the same manner. In 1857 eighty pounds had been paid for a marble relief of the Madonna and Child which at first carried an attribution to Antonio Rossellino, in 1861 a terracotta bust, and two years later a second terracotta.

A further work of Bastianini's which caused considerable argument amongst the experts was 'La Chanteuse Florentine'. It showed a lady in the days of the Renaissance in a brocade frock done with traces of gilding and polychrome. She was made of terracotta, and the piece passed into a leading collection in Paris where it was catalogued as an important work of the Italian Renaissance. No one can be quite certain what other Bastianinis there are around the place, and in fact there could have been a great many more, if the brilliant deceiver had not died at the early age of thirty-eight.

Another nineteenth-century gentleman who specialised in the early Renaissance was Ferrante Zampini. He worked primarily in terracotta either left plain or coloured. One of his early successes was a head which had a close relationship to the portrait of Colleoni, the ex-condottiere general of the Venetian Republic, and this found an eager buyer as a genuine Verrocchio. He produced a large lunette with the subject of The Pietà. This was one of a group of his works which took in the Munich art authorities, but before it got to them it had first gone from Zampini's studio to that of Bonafedi, who was an expert in applying colouring and giving patina to clay. From him it had been sold for twelve thousand francs as a modern work to Paolini, a violinist, who then sold it, still as a modern, to a German, and so it went through a number of collectors and finally landed in Munich as a Renaissance piece for which they paid out fourteen thousand francs.

Zampini, like Bastianini, had a remarkable talent for getting into the spirit of the early Renaissance. A French collector bought from a dealer a genuine piece of Renaissance work and a piece done by Zampini. After arriving in Paris the collector examined the two pieces carefully and sent back the real statue to the dealer, saying it was a fake, but kept the Zampini. Zampini, however, clever as he was with his imitations, slipped up several times with his choice of clay. There was a Professor A. of Florence whose credentials as an art expert were second to none who bought a terracotta figure by Zampini, certain that it was a work from the fourteenth century. A little while after the piece was put in his collection it began to show a scaling of the surface known as *sbullettare*; this implies a kind of pitting of the surface of the terracotta rather like a type of woodworm infestation. The word actually is derived from *bulletta* meaning a tack or nail, as it gives the impression that nails have been driven in and pulled out. The reason for this was that Zampini had often used *impruneta* clay, similar to that used by the Della Robbias, but for all his expertise he apparently did not know that this particular clay exhibited a rather strange characteristic which could appear several months after it had been in the kiln; it was this scaling, this *sbullettare*. The way to have prevented this would have been to damp the object as soon as it had been fired. It was unfortunate for Zampini that Professor A. did know that early terracotta antique busts should not suffer from this kind of disease. A similar purchase was made by another erudite gentleman, Professor B., when he bought a bust attributed to Verrochio, a short time afterwards. This too started this unsightly scaling. The suspicions of these two gentlemen were aroused and the uncovering of Zampini was set in motion. In his own way he was a specialist with this particular art form. Many of his pieces sold for large sums, but again it was not the forger who made most out of it but intermediary agents.

During the First World War the art world was in a state of confusion and was to a high degree glutted as many owners, hit by inflation or the movement back and forth of armies in various countries, sought to recoup their losses by the sale of their collections. In 1918 a number of quite out-of-the-ordinary pieces of sculpture started to appear in a Paris saleroom. Excellent examples of Greek, Roman, Gothic and Renaissance periods. There was intense speculation as to just where these could have come from. Rumours spread around that one of the greatest private collections in Italy was being split up, other whispers suggested that the Vatican, needing more capital, was putting some of its unique treasures on the market. But it was none of these things. It was the first conquest by someone who, for many, holds still the top position as a forger of sculpture. Someone who was to have a long run, as it was not until 1928 that he was uncovered.

This was Alceo Dossena (1878–1937), and as with some of the other imitators turned forgers, Dossena at the beginning certainly did not set out as a forger and many believe that he was more or less duped by a dealer throughout his working life, and that it was the dealer who made forgeries of the innocent imitative productions of this skilled man. He was a simple, shy character who worked in a small studio alongside the river Tiber in Rome. There are no records that he ever did claim that what he produced was the work of anybody else but himself. His philosophy, he explained to someone, as:

'I was born in our time, but with the soul, taste and perception of other ages.'

Having been recruited into the army, it is known that in 1916 on Christmas Eve, on leave in Rome, Dossena went into a small café for a glass of wine. He hoped, by perhaps selling to the landlord the small wooden figure of the Madonna which he had carved, and which was wrapped up in paper under his arm, to have some money for his Christmas shopping. When he received his glass of wine he undid the parcel and offered it to the man behind the bar. The fellow was not interested, but felt it looked quite good and sent round for a dealer he knew by the name of Alfredo Fasoli. On coming to the café and seeing the figure, Fasoli was secretly pleased with the quality he recognised, and he asked Dossena where he had got it from. Dossena replied that he was selling it for a friend. Without more ado Fasoli gave him a hundred lire, which delighted the simple Dossena. When Fasoli returned to his shop he examined the Madonna carefully and realised that it was a fine example of carving, at the same time he saw that it was modern. He was also struck with the thought that anybody who could achieve such quality could probably, with a little help, put on the all-important display of ageing.

After his release from military service, Dossena met Fasoli again, quite by accident. The latter probably put the query to Dossena as to whether he knew if his friend had any more pieces like the one he had bought earlier. Having found out that it was actually Dossena who had done the carving, Fasoli possibly proposed that Alceo should produce more of this work as he felt sure that he would be able to sell it for him. So Dossena, in his workshop in Rome, commenced making sculpture for Alfredo Fasoli. Their partnership started with the production of a medieval figure. Fasoli, pleased with it, sold it for three thousand lire of which he passed two hundred lire to Dossena.

Alceo Dossena was a kind of reincarnation of many talents of the Renaissance greats. He could work with equal confidence in stone, wood and terracotta, and, on top of that, he could imitate not just the styles of

Madonna and Child' by Alceo Dossena

the Renaissance, but those of medieval times and the earlier periods. As matters progressed, Fasoli, in 1921, gave Dossena an order for an ambitious 'Early Renaissance' tomb in the style of the great sculptor Mino da Fiesole, known as the 'Tomb of the Savelli'. This was also backed up by a nice piece of provenance in the form of a receipt signed by Mino da Fiesole for money paid for work by the Savelli. Dossena, for this high Gothic excellence, received twenty-five thousand lire. The tomb, after it had gone through a number of hands including those of not only Fasoli, but also Romano Palesi, was sold in New York for six million lire.

Another masterpiece by Dossena was his figure of Athene which was ordered to be in the Classic style, a period some fifteen hundred years prior to the cultural period of his Savelli Tomb. But again this remarkable craftsman got into his time machine and produced an exquisite figure about 5′6″ tall and of a quality that could be compared to a number of the early figures of the period he was imitating. The goddess was shown accoutred for battle with breast-plate and helmet and a small circular shield on the left arm. She, after various passages through different hands, was bought by Jakob Hirsch, the New York dealer, for thirty million lire.

The convincing aged look which Dossena achieved with his pieces and which left them with an authentic-looking patina was carried out in his workshop. Here he had a bath sunk in the floor in which would be various solutions of acids and alkalis, the composition of which he kept as a secret to himself. The statue or piece to be treated was lowered into the bath, being dipped again and again in various solutions until the white Carrara marble took on that particular glowing dark creamy look so convincing to the eye of the collector who is already almost certain the piece is authentic.

In the intervening years from the end of the First World War until the time when Dossena's activities were uncovered, certain dealers initiated by Alfredo Fasoli, middlemen and other jackals who follow such a trail must have had the feeling they had found a rich lode and they made the best of it. Not only did they commission pieces from this wonderman, but also thought up extravagant provenances; they invented collections from which the treasures were supposed to have come, and all the time the poor man who was making all this for them was, it appears, an innocent who was receiving a miserable pittance for his skill.

Eventually, however, he did hear stories of the vast figures that people were prepared to pay for his work. He was also, about this time, a little short of ready money and he approached Fasoli, saying could he not perhaps increase the payment that was given him for each piece, or could he not perhaps let him have an advance on the next orders. Very foolishly Fasoli and his dealers turned this down out of hand, and so Dossena decided to come out in the open.

Experts in the field sneered at the thought that this simple stonemason beside the Tiber could possibly have produced such masterpieces. Had not museum directors, gallery directors, connoisseurs and critics all authenticated the pieces? How could a large section of the art world suddenly own up to the fact that they had been completely taken in. Viciously, many thought up every idea they could to disgrace Dossena; some claimed that perhaps, if he had done them, he had only copied them; but they couldn't back this up by producing the pieces he was supposed to have copied them from.

To try and establish what he said was the truth, Dossena even allowed himself to be filmed whilst actually modelling. Later one of the film crew said: 'Dossena worked so hard, and his results were always so unexpected that the camera could hardly keep up with him – half an hour later he had modelled in clay the figure of a goddess, some sixty cm. high, in the Attic style. . . .'

Some experts tried to stay in a neutral field, saying that certain pieces had always worried them and they had noticed stylistic queries. But his talent was too great to be believed and he found himself rejected. His last years were spent in troublesome waters; he tried to bring an action for fraud against Fasoli and other dealers, but he found himself attacked by Fasoli for, of all things, being a political agitator. The final irony was that Dossena, after making fortunes for others, died in a paupers' hospital in Rome.

In 1909 Wilhelm Bode, the General Manager of the Prussian art collections, bought for the Berlin Museum a wax bust of 'Flora', which he considered to be an original work by Leonardo da Vinci. This lit the fuse on one of the most baffling cases and started a train of arguments that has still not ceased. Is she, or is she not, a forgery? It also showed the difficulty of authenticating wax sculpture. The case provided more publicity and conflict by the experts than even that of Van Meegeren which was to follow some forty odd years later.

*'Flora' in the manner of
Leonardo da Vinci*

The bust itself showed the goddess Flora, life-size, and the back was left in a rough, unfinished state, probably as she had been intended for display in a niche. She was tinted and had also been damaged, both forearms being broken away. Seemingly, as far as the story could be traced, from Bode's account, she had been found in a shop in King Street, London, by a dealer, a Mr Marks. She had been apparently sold off at a London auction in 1907 for a very small figure and thence through the usual passage of middlemen the German firm of Durlacher had acquired her for a hundred and fifty pounds; but when Bode made his purchase the figure had risen to a hundred and fifty thousand marks. As a possible crumb of further authenticity for Bode, part of her missing right hand turned up in the museum in the same year of purchase. But no sooner had Dr Bode got his prime exhibit in position than nasty rumours reached his ears from England that 'Flora' was not what she was supposed to be and was actually a forgery.

Some experts claim this bust of Flora was the work of the nineteenth-century sculptor, Richard Cockle Lucas, who possibly based it on the bust opposite. Others said it was an original Leonardo

The teams for and against supporting the director of the museum lined up. On one side there were Wilhelm Bode himself, Edmund Hildebrandt and the art critic of the *Berliner Tageblatt* Adolf Donach. Leading the pack who were crying 'fake' on the other side was Gustav Pauli of the Kunsthalle, Hamburg, who quite simply stated that he felt stylistically the bust was completely wrong and in his opinion resembled some of the figures modelled of Queen Victoria.

On 23 October 1909 *The Times* published a letter from a Charles Cooksey, an auctioneer in Southampton, and this gentleman suggested that 'Flora' had been made by a minor English sculptor, Richard Cockle Lucas, and further, that Lucas's son, A. D. Lucas, could come forward and state that he had assisted his father with the bust, and that the model had been made from a painting of the Leonardo school which a dealer had brought to his father's workshop asking that a copy be made from it. The

195

son, whose name was Albert Dürer Lucas, by this time was eighty-one years old. The statement in the letter was backed up by other letters from a Mr Thomas Whitburn who had been a friend of A. D. Lucas; these appeared on 29 October in the *Daily Mail* and on 11 November in *The Times*. The writer said that he remembered quite well meeting Richard Cockle Lucas when he was working on a wax bust in his studio after a painting supposed to be by Leonardo.

The following year, 1910, further confusion was created when the English art historian, Mr V. Lucas, wrote about the bust saying that it was the work of his namesake sculptor. Fourteen years later he withdrew the statement and came up with the opinion in a letter to *The Times* that he was absolutely sure that 'Flora' was the authentic work of Da Vinci.

Scientists tested small fragments of paint by microchemical analysis and these came up with the result showing archil was present, a dye that comes from lichen. Although this was used in the time of Leonardo, it was not proof in any way at all because a forger could quite easily make up this colour. Attention to this point was drawn by another expert, Theodore von Frimmel.

Matters now seemed to get more complicated still. A German sculptor, Martin Schauss, was asked by Bode to examine the bust and said in his opinion he felt Bastianini could have had something to do with it. Gustav Pauli continued his assault, claiming that the wax pointed to a modern production which was unlike that of other Renaissance-proved originals and he felt the so-called appearance of age was simulation by a forger. Other loose suggestions included the fact that perhaps after all the bust was an original which at one time had been used by children as a plaything, been damaged, and then restored by Richard Cockle Lucas.

Then the world of the dealers entered in on the scene when Augusto Jandolo announced that another 'Flora' had turned up; this time in marble. It had been bought by an art dealer, Alfredo Barsanti, for fifty lire, who had then found a ready buyer, the Museum of Fine Arts in Boston, who had paid forty-eight thousand lire for it. In this museum it reposed in splendour, being given the accolade by L. D. Caskey, that it was one of the great treasures of the collection, although there was still some doubt about its authenticity. Barsanti must have fallen over himself with excitement when he found yet another 'Flora' in Florence. This one was apparently by

Verrocchio who had been the master of Leonardo. Barsanti had paid two thousand lire for the bust, but now strangely enough he found himself in a position of not being able to re-sell it. The word was passed round that this latest 'Flora' was an obvious fake. But the dealer was equally convinced that this was a genuine piece in front of him, and with some knowledge gleaned from reading of the patination methods of the trade, he somewhat perhaps unwisely started cleaning this 'Flora'. But luck was with him, and he must have restored the bust near to its original state and was able to get the blessing of one of the leading Italian art historians, Ruddioro Schiff, who declared that it was indeed a genuine Verrocchio. Shortly after this Barsanti was able to sell this 'Flora' to Lord Duveen, although there were many doubts about its true creation. But the poor wax 'Flora' is rather like the little Greek horse at the Met. in New York, she also is not quite sure who was her father.

In 1959, in February, another example of a dealer using the work of a simple craftsman for his own ends came to light. Living in the small village of St Ulrich in the Southern Tyrol was one Joseph Rifesser, a wood-carver with considerable skill and flourish in the way that he copied examples of Gothic sculpture. It is said these imitations of Gothic Madonnas were done by the young sculptor without any intention of fraudulent intent, although this does appear a little odd as he mastered the technique of chemically ageing his pieces very effectively. His imitations were intended for the tourist trade, and his carved figures could find eager buyers.

In the previous November the catalogue of one of the Christmas sales which was to be held in the famous Dorotheum saleroom in Vienna listed as one of the principal lots:

'Gothic statue of the Madonna in a pronounced S-shaped posture, with crown and wimple'.

The catalogue further added that it was considered to be a work of a Burgundian sculptor about 1380 and the thought was also added that it was likely to be related in craftsmanship to a slightly similar figure that had been sold in their 539th sale as lot No. 351. That earlier figure had fetched sixty thousand Austrian schillings. As usual, experts examined and expressed their opinion and the consensus was that this piece, as with the other, was genuine.

Notice of this sale and the illustration was seen by Rifesser when he was travelling in Germany and he could hardly credit that what he recognised as his own work was there labelled as fourteenth-century Gothic Burgundian etc., He went to Vienna and viewed his statue in the Dorotheum. It was one of five that he had copied from old genuine Gothic models several years previously. In 1957 he had sold all these copies to a dealer Josef Auer, of Bischofshofen, for prices between three and four hundred marks. Rifesser was extremely troubled and asked the advice of a leading Munich lawyer, Dr Benhard Hauser, who as soon as he heard the story reported the matter to the Dorotheum at once. At the same time other dealers in Vienna were becoming suspicious about the piece and one of them reported the object to the police. On the Continent, in some countries, they take a much more serious view of forgery of works of art and this information from the dealer and subsequent rather speedy investigation resulted in the arrest of Josef Auer and at his trial he was sent to prison for a year.

When looking at Rifesser's Madonna with the after knowledge that it is a forgery it is rather like now looking at the 'Supper at Emmaus' by Van Meegeren; the mind does wonder how these two pieces got through.

But examples of forgery from a new unknown source, if they are of some standard, have a fair chance of getting past the guard of the art historian, the expert and police, because they have the advantage of surprise. It is only when the forger or, as in Rifesser's case, the dealer, starts trying to unload too much that suspicion is aroused and the uncovering of the faker can be near. Holding in mind the virility and power of some of the early Germanic carvers such as Tilman Riemenschneider and those who came before him, this small madonna becomes further exposed. She lacks strength and decision, but most of all she lacks what can only be called a genuine sincerity of a religious carving of the period.

Each example of the forger's work hammers home again and again that to the collector two things really matter. Know as much about your subject as possible and with that train the eye. Picking up a forgery can at times be rather like meeting a person. The first impression may arouse doubts. With the second impression the doubts may be suppressed, but continued association will confirm them.

CHAPTER TWELVE

STAMPS

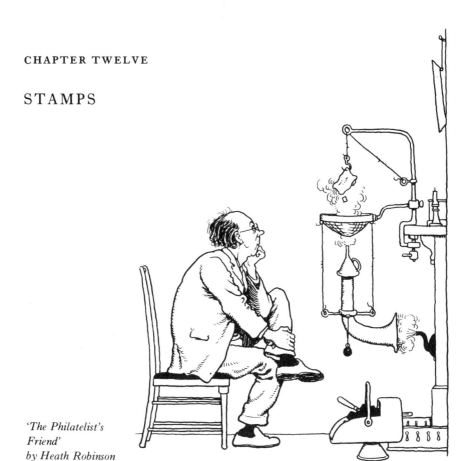

'The Philatelist's Friend' by Heath Robinson

When, in 1840, Rowland Hill nationalised payments for sending letters in Britain he unwittingly opened another door for the forger. Out went that first Penny Post and in came the skilled engraver and artist who could sense that here was a ready market for fraud.

Within remarkably few years the friends of every forger, the collectors, were searching for rare stamps, unique postmarks and cancellations and the forgers had begun to fill the gaps where supply failed to meet demand. Compared with convictions for counterfeiting currency the penalties were, and are, much less, but the large rewards made the faking of stamps, and particularly rare ones, well worth the effort. Today the multicoloured complexity of modern postage stamps largely defies even the best-equipped, and most adept forger. But that still leaves a big gap. From

Rowland Hill until even the Second World War many stamps were produced by relatively basic techniques, presenting the forger with a difficult but by no means insurmountable challenge.

To many, stamp-collecting is just a transient hobby which temporarily satisfies the magpie in every little boy or girl. However, for an amazingly large number of mature, rational adults philately represents not only contact with thousands of far-away places with strange sounding names, but a possible economic investment, a sound hedge against inflation, and all the spin-off advantages of a potentially lucrative pastime which involves insights into geography, history, art, printing techniques, literature and even psychology. Another less advertised attraction of collecting fine stamps is that they take up very little space and are easily transported from country to country with little fear of detection by either customs or tax revenue officials. With current taxes on profit, wealth taxes, corporation taxes, value added taxes etcetera, stamps give the half-honest an enviable entry to a tax haven.

Nothing whets a collector's appetite more than rarity and even the most humble philatelist believes that if he buys first-day covers they are almost certain to increase in value as the years go by. The Coronation of George VI provided collectors with a superb opportunity to buy a host of first-day cancellations of Coronation Day covers from every corner of the British Empire. Two English stamp dealers in Birmingham and Smethwick, George Whitehurst and John Harris, were quick to cash in on the demand. They offered 12 May covers from such far-flung colonies as the British Solomon Islands, St Helena, Broken Hill, Northern Rhodesia, Accra, The Gold Coast, Belize, the British Honduras and the Gilbert and Ellice Islands. Their customers were later horrified to read an article in *The Philatelist* which exposed the stamps as fakes. The pair of dealers had copied genuine cancellations using dies specially made in Leeds and forged enough markings to gain themselves at least ten thousand pounds. After the publication of the article they were tried and sentenced to prison, Whitehurst to eighteen months, Harris to nine.

Today the author of that perceptive article is one of the most respected experts in the world of philately. He heads the renowned international company of stamp dealers which bears his name, Robson Lowe. Considering the fact that, as a dealer, he has paid a heavy price for his experience of a lifetime's battle with stamp-forgers, he harbours them remarkably little malice. Indeed he talks of some of them with a mischievous twinkle in his eye, seeming barely to conceal a sneaking admiration for their technique:

I've never approached a forger by saying you are a criminal. I say, 'Well, I do like the way you did that, I think it's marvellous, you got me fooled for two or three days before I found out. However did you do it?' And he tells you how he did it! Most forgers forge because they have an artistic desire for copying to perfection. The best forgers get an enormous satisfaction out of fooling somebody who calls himself an expert. If they can possibly get a certificate of genuineness, well that's made their week, their month, their life – that they've produced something that somebody has said is genuine. And if you go to the forgery school that used to be kept at Maidstone jail and talk to the forgers it's really most interesting. They're invariably good husbands, good fathers, good family men, craftsmen with a terrific sense of humour who pull one another's legs and tell one another where they went wrong.

Some tales of stamp forgery are, however, by no means so light-hearted. During the research for the television programme Robson Lowe related the most tragic of all, concerning a rice grower in China in the 1920s.

A Chinese Post Office inspector had noticed that in one village more circulars with three cent stamps on them were being posted than they were selling three cent stamps at the Post Office. The village post master reported that the man posting almost all the circulars was a rice grower. He asked him where he had obtained his three cent stamps, then worth about three farthings. The rice grower explained that since the postage had gone up from one cent to three cents he could no longer make a living advertising his rice. He therefore had been forced to make his own three cent stamps by getting lots of used stamps which were valueless, cutting out the bits that weren't cancelled, patching them together, and painting in by hand those parts which were left bare. Just think of the amount of labour that went into making each single three farthing stamp, and by a man who was already struggling to make the equivalent of only twenty pounds a year to support his wife and family. On the spot the magistrate had his right hand amputated so that he didn't go in for this any more. He was removed to Peking, where, on conviction he was executed.

Lest the budding stamp collector think, however, that fake stamps are merely a matter of history, as recently as 1962 an important collection of Mexican stamps gathered by a Professor Hohner Lizama was scheduled for sale in London. The four hundred and ninety-five lots were mainly the creations of a notorious Belgian forger, Raoul de Thuin, who was born in 1890. Even the expert auctioneers failed to detect the forgeries, and it was only after a specialist suggested certain grounds for suspicion that the sale was stopped. As for quantity, one authority, Dr Varro Tyler, reckons that the creations of one single forger, Wada Kotaro, outnumber genuine copies of classic Japanese stamps found in general collections by a ratio of ten to one. A Paris dealer apparently bought fifty thousand sets at the time of the great exhibition in 1900. Wada's forgeries were printed by Yamanaka from small copper plates with hand-drawn etched designs.

As Dr Tyler points out in his fascinating studies of philatelic forgeries, even some of the most famous names in the stamp world are not wholly without blemish. During a lengthy career, the man who has been considered the pioneer British stamp dealer, Stanley Gibbons, was at one time working on rather questionable philatelic practices, not now considered completely reputable, although they were at the time. In 1871 he bought the lithographic stone of a five-cent value of the 1862 issue of Argentina from a South American printer Robert Lange. Armed with this, he produced a large number of unofficial reprints of the five-cent stamp, further he had some of the figures of the value changed to ten cents and fifteen cents so that he could have imitations of the complete set.

The nefarious activities of the twilight world where fraudulently conceived objects are passed off as the genuine article are aptly named 'Shady deals'. Rudolf 'Greasy Dick' Thomas, an American stamp dealer, was notorious for having the worst-lit store in Chicago. Another Chicago dealer, Harry Steinberg, boasted that he was probably the only customer ever to see Thomas' stamps reasonably well before buying them: he made his visits armed with a flash-light.

In the London shop of Alfred Benjamin and Julian Hippolite Sarpy, they had a small handwritten sign posted underneath a gas-jet at the far end of the back counter where it was not visible to those entering. It read as follows:

'Special notice. I will not be answerable for the genuineness of any stamps bought at this establishment unless I give a written guarantee at the time of purchase. By order of A. Benjamin.'

To obscure the notice further from the vision of unwary customers, it was partly covered by a large card hanging from the gas jet, 'THIS IS MY BUSY DAY.' Benjamin's bowler hat also habitually hung from the unlit jet. (Tolcher, H. H., *Stanley Gibbons Monthly Journal*, 1892.)

To the trade, however, these partners were markedly less covert about the nature of their wares. Their business card read, 'Dealers in all kinds of fac-similes, faked surcharges, and fiscal postals, 1 Cullum Street, London. Fakes of all kinds on the shortest notice.'

As a boy Robson Lowe was highly intrigued by Mr Benjamin; he recounts:

He was rather a sort of Potash and Pearlmutter type. The shop was uncleaned and dirty and I regret to say that dear old Ben was pretty much the same. One did see him in a clean shirt once a month, and I don't quite know about any other personal hygiene; I was ten, and to me he was a fascinating character because he'd been in jail for selling a forgery. And then he'd come out and advertised the stamp that he'd been in jail for as the famous stamp for which he'd been sent to prison, the penny Sydney view, and he doubled the price and all the collectors bought it as a forgery now, at twice the price they'd been paying for it when they'd been buying it as genuine. And out of the proceeds he bought himself a little villa in the old Kent Road which he called 'Sydney View'! He was a fascinating old character and I have in my collection stamps I bought from him. But when I said, 'Ben, I would like that,' he clouted me, and said 'You little fool, I told you I made it!' and I said, 'But Ben, that's why I want it.' He didn't understand that he fascinated me as a juvenile collector of somebody who made things.

The irony of the stamp world is that, due to their extreme rarity, collectors often prize more highly stamps which contain errors than their perfect originals. A Japanese stamp dealer, Jonoski Takuma, exemplifies the kind of extremes in skilled craftsmanship which some fakers achieve. Before he turned his hand to stamps, he made a living through his exquisite ability at carving emu eggs. One particularly rare Australian stamp is the three penny of 1856 which lacks perforations and has an error in the watermark of two instead of three. As Dr Tyler reports: 'Takuma carefully thinned down an ordinary three penny stamp and glued on it the back of a genuine two penny stamp of the same issue. Since the paper of these stamps was fairly thick, the watermark was mostly impressed on the reverse side, and when carefully done, the laminated fakes were extremely deceptive.'

Probably Takuma's most successful effort was the postal forgery of the 1888 two penny Emu stamp of New South Wales which he prepared in 1895. It was so well done that from 1916 to 1963 it was catalogued as a genuine stamp. This was a forgery made to deceive the Post Office, not philatelists.

The Bournemouth Forgeries

Africa

Used in Niger Coast Protectorate
"FORCADOS RIVER A — OC 3 — 01"

Genuine.

Forgery.

Niger Coast and Southern Nigeria Combination
"SAPELE - A - JY 20 — 04"

Forgery

Genuine

Forgery

Forged date stamps compared with the genuine

204

In philately there is a distinct difference between faking and forgery. Forgery involves making a facsimile stamp and attempting to pass it off as genuine. Faking, however, means altering a stamp so that it looks a much rarer variety than it was in real life. A good example is the 1864 imperforate of Great Britain. Because these stamps were normally perforated, the ones lacking perforations are exceedingly rare, and, whereas the perforated are worth about five new pence, the imperforates can fetch two hundred pounds. To pocket a £199.95 profit the faker chops off the perforations and adds false margins. Fortunately for the trade this process is not quite as easy as it sounds, and the reader will have to forgive us if we refrain from giving any further helpful do-it-yourself hints.

To complicate matters for the stamp collector the legal situation regarding both the sale and possession of forged and fake stamps varies from country to country. Fakes and forgeries are widely collected – as Robson Lowe himself said:

I've got a marvellous collection which I call 'forgeries that have fooled me', and I mount them up, and I preserve their history and why they fooled me in the hopes that some of my younger colleagues, who rather love finding where the old man was caught out, will learn from it. You learn from your mistakes very quickly, and if you're a professional, and have to pay for them, you don't make 'em twice! I want all the forgeries I can find of the stamps that I collect because from the forgeries you very often learn something more about the genuine. You don't get fooled in the same way. If it's known you specialise in a particular country, or a particular stamp, dealers offer you this stamp, and therefore if you don't know all the traps you would be very easily fooled if somebody in all innocence offered you a forgery. It's splendid to have two or three genuine stamps and two or three forgeries by various people – you learn more about your stamps that way.

Yet under the strict letter of the law in Britain, Robson Lowe must neither buy nor sell fakes or forgeries. In the United States even their possession is a crime, and this introduces a nice example of legal absurdity. An American clergyman, The Reverend Paul Freeland, had devoted much attention and a considerable fortune into amassing one of the finest collections of fakes and forgeries in the world. After his death his collection had to be transferred to Basle in Switzerland for sale, and during the filming of the auction it was ironic to see a vast number of utterly phoney stamps sold openly as fakes and forgeries fetching prices comparable to those attained by even the rarest genuine stamps.

The story of Jean-Baptiste Phillipe Constant Moens highlights another problem besetting not just philatelic collectors, but collectors of every kind. When does a *bona fide* reproduction or facsimile become a forgery? It would seem obvious that the conversion happens when someone tries to pass off the copy or pastiche as being genuine. But if, for example, you inherit some object which, in your family mythology, has always been regarded as authentic, and, in all innocence, you try to sell it as such, are you committing a felony? The law would say you are, and prosecute accordingly.

Like Stanley Gibbons and other great pioneer stamp dealers, Moens indulged in several practices no longer considered ethical. He bought original lithographic stones of *bona fide* stamps and sold prints he made from them. He even bought damaged stones which he then had repaired to churn out what he called 'private re-prints'. To confuse matters he also published illustrated books about philately containing facsimiles. His 1864 *Manual for Postage Stamp Collectors* was among the first illustrated stamp catalogues. Few would be deceived by most of the illustrations if they were cut from the book and glued to a letter – but some of the illustrations were probably made using the original stones he had bought. With subsequent forgers using these illustrations as the basis for their own copying enterprises, and the collections into which they found their way passing from hand to hand, and generation to generation, the collector today has to be highly discerning in his purchases. It should be added that Moens retired in 1900 and sold all his printing blocks. Quite where they all are now, and what use is being made of them nobody knows, and herein lies yet another dilemma which is at its most poignant for the would-be collector of very rare stamps. The best way of not being deceived by anything you wish to acquire is to compare it with what you are absolutely certain is the genuine article. In philately, as in many other fields, that is much easier said than done. The rarer the article the more difficult it is to obtain for purposes of comparison. Often all the collector can rely on is a blurry mental picture of the authentic, or an illustration, lacking detail, in some book or periodical. With stamps this problem is very acute, as Robson Lowe pointed out when asked what was the best forgery he had ever come across. He thought for a moment and then his face puckered in a strange blend of anger and delight:

To be honest, it comes in Hawaii. I was fooled because when I was shown them I was quite sure they were genuine. They weren't offered to me to buy, so I didn't make the mistake of buying them, but they were the cause of a famous law-case, and they were bought by an old friend of mine who paid a great deal of money for them. They are the most clever forgeries of the Hawaiian Missionary Stamps – if I didn't know their provenance and they were brought in and shown to me today I would start off by thinking they were genuine. The problem is that the commonest of the genuine stamps costs four or five thousand pounds and you're comparing them with photographs because you don't have the genuine available. Ninety-five per cent of the genuine exist in just three collections, two in Hawaii and one in Japan.

Robson Lowe was asked how any collector can protect himself if he comes across an allegedly rare stamp which he can only compare with a photograph. 'There will be other stamps in most issues that are comparatively common, and you compare the rarity with the common stamp of the same issue. That's usually the safest test.'

Is there any way in which the man in the street can protect himself against forgeries?

Robson Lowe's reply to this question is a theme warning for the whole world of collecting, 'If you're a bargain hunter that goes looking for bargains you're going to come across forgeries – because forgeries were made for bargain hunters.'

There is a tacit agreement, enforceable in law, that genuine currency notes shall never be shown on television. Considering the blurry image which most viewers seem to achieve on their sets, it's a rule that has always puzzled television producers. However showing pound notes on television is a classic taboo and the whole film team was nonplussed, to put it mildly, when Robson Lowe began to wax eloquent on the basic tests which every stamp collector should know.

'The simplest one of all is to look at a clean pound note!'

He immediately whisked one out of his pocket and flashed it at the camera. Fortunately it wasn't 'live' television so if necessary this demonstration could be cut from the final film. What was troubling was that his following remarks were so typically succinct and easily understandable that the 'Stamps' programme would have suffered immeasurably if they could not be included. For once, after lengthy meetings and correspondence, the heavy hand of bureaucracy lifted, and gave a friendly wave of reasonably minded approbation, and it was permitted to show a real pound note on television.

A pound note has three methods of printing. Now in the standard catalogues they always tell you how a stamp was printed – it was recessed, printed, or that it was engraved, and the colour then stands up on the surface. Now if you look at the front of a pound note and you hold it up so that the light is shining on it you will see the ink standing up like an embossing. The figures on a pound note are printed by letter press, or direct contact of the metal onto the paper – and that produces a little squeeze when seen under magnification. The ink is squeezed to the edge of the image. If you see that squeeze it's printed by letter press, or typography – stamp collectors call it surface printing. And then there is lithography: the back of a pound note is absolutely smooth, not raised at all. Study a pound note for five minutes under a magnifying glass and you've got the three basic methods of printing. Now is the stamp you're looking at printed by the method that the standard catalogue says? If it's not, it's a forgery. Somebody who knows nothing about stamps can pick out the bulk of forgeries by knowing they aren't printed by the right method. Basically the good homework of an expert is to compare what we call 'the patient', the stamp which is being surveyed, with a genuine example, even if it's a common stamp of the same issue. Is the design right, is the quality of printing right? Once you get your eye in you may tell the difference between the work of one security printer and another, even as the writings of two people are quite distinct from each other. Therefore if it isn't printed by the right man, it's wrong. This isn't science, it's knowing one's stuff, and I think that many of the scientific instruments that are used today simply conceal the lack of practical knowledge of the people using them.

Somewhat surprisingly some forgers become so enthusiastic about the process of making stamps that they outdo themselves and create stamps which are superior in quality to the originals they attempt to forge. Angelo Panelli, who ran a large-scale stamp forging business mostly from San Remo, was expert at engraving, and often used that process to forge stamps originally printed by typography. Engraving is a more expensive method of stamp-making. When asked why he engraved forgeries that were printed by De La Rue by typography, he replied,

'I think engraving is so much more artistic than typography.'

Perhaps the most difficult of all types of stamp forgery to detect are those where the official printing dies and genuine cancelling devices have been 'borrowed' to produce a discreetly small number of stamps.

In 1883 Georges Fouré, a well-known dealer, and the founder of the Berlin Illustrated Philatelic Journal, moved house to become neighbour to

H. G. Schilling, the engraver of the Prussian State Printing Office. Within months Fouré had contrived to become such good friends with Schilling that he persuaded him to use an official overprint on a stamp with faked narrow (and therefore very rare) margins. Whether the engraver complied as an innocent joke, as an equal partner, or as a result of Fouré pinning some blackmail on him, is not certain. However, he continued to assist Fouré, and with the help of the Imperial Printing Office the two men created a whole series of forged stamped addressed envelopes which were sold in good faith by several stamp dealers in Berlin. After Schilling's death in 1890 'Professor' Fouré, as he liked to be known, attempted to continue production; but, after a devastating exposure which damned his work by simply omitting any mention of it in an official monograph, thereby alerting dealers' suspicions, Fouré left his family and fled to Paris to die there in poverty in 1902.

Probably the heyday of forged postage stamps came as early as the 1860s, when the growing popularity for the new hobby of stamp collecting had begun to outstrip supply. A Hamburg lithographic company, Spiro Brothers, who printed everything from Sunday-school cards to beer-bottle labels, were soon attracted to stamps and began production in 1864. In fifteen years they turned out some five hundred varieties which were sold either as unused, or with as many as five cancellations on each sheet. Dr Tyler insists they never intended their imitations to deceive, but they were so good at their craft that many of their stamps 'delude collectors even today'. Their mass-productions of millions of forgeries threatened to erode the whole market, and dealers banded together with amateur enthusiasts in a concerted effort to inform the trade in detail about every new Spiro publication. Under the bizarre title of *The Spud Papers*, or, *Notes on Philatelic Weeds*, the *Philatelist* and other British stamp periodicals published sixty-seven detailed articles on more than four hundred forgeries. As a result by 1880 the Spiro Brothers found their 'new line' so unprofitable that they stopped marketing forgeries; but their legacy left the expanding philatelic market a more careful, suspicious trade than it had been before.

It may seem curious to those outside the stamp-world that many of Spiro's creations were bought quite knowingly as forgeries by young collectors to fill their gaps. It is difficult to commend the lack of conscience

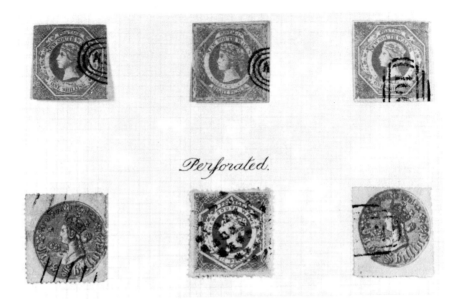

Perforated.

Crudily lithographed New South Wales 'diadem' forgeries by Spiro Brothers of Hamburg

in any collector who boasts about his priceless albums of genuine rare stamps when he knows full well that many of the key items are forgeries. However, when a stamp is so rare that it is unobtainable on the market a large number of collectors, wishing to fill a gap in an otherwise complete page, are often only too delighted to buy a forgery, and admit it as such.

Probably the most publicised, although certainly not the best philatelic forger, was François Fournier. His business was ruined by the mail restrictions and censorship of the First World War, but prior to that he boasted of having twenty thousand regular customers and his 1914 price-list offered nearly four thousand forgeries.

'My imitations are copied from genuine postage stamps by the best artists with a rare perfection which is without equal'. That was the boast of Erasmus Oneglia in his 1900 catalogue. Only three years earlier he had been arrested in England and fined twenty shillings for trying to sell imitations to Stanley Gibbons Ltd. His output of counterfeits was colossal and he indulged in every technique known at the time: engraved forgeries, photo-engravings and photo-lithography. Another member of the Italian philatelic rogue's gallery, credited in *The Stamp Collector's Fortnightly* as

'King of the Forgers', a Signor Venturini, built up much of his reputation by using Oneglia's stock. Venturini even had sufficient gall to sell publicly (after probably having over-used them) the clichés from which his own forgeries were made. Venturini and Oneglia were among the first in a long line of Italian forgers including such philatelically notorious names as Edoardo Spiotto, N. Imperato and Panelli. But the real king, if not Emperor, of them all, was Jean de Sperati.

During the preparation of our television series, 'The Genuine Article', the production team consulted a broad spectrum of authorities on all the subjects featured. Sometimes our enquiries were perhaps understandably ill-received; we were accused of trying to wash other people's dirty linen in public: doors slammed in our faces, and telephones hammered down on their receivers. More often however we faced bland, even obsequious, replies when eminent experts admitted, always 'off-the-record old chap', that 'things aren't exactly as we'd all like 'em' and that 'something should be done about it, don't you think?' But when we named names and asked very pointed, and presumably dangerously well-informed, questions we either came up against a very polite, but often unbreakable, conspiracy of silence, or such conflicting reports that within our limited resources of time and money we were incapable of ascertaining who, if anyone, was telling us the truth. Stamps, however, were the exception: admittedly no one immediately volunteered much information about Messrs. X and Y, currently forging Penny Blacks in Wigan (perhaps because they thought that giving us such knowledge might prove very embarrassing to us, making us accomplices, as parties to the crime). There was, however, universal agreement that the best forger of stamps the world has ever known was Jean de Sperati. In stamp circles, and particularly among dealers, his name conjures a combination of profound admiration, respect and fear. Even Dr Tyler, never given to exaggerated over-statement, admitted that he was, 'without question the most technically competent philatelic forger of the twentieth century.' De Sperati was literally born a forger: he learnt his craft from his mother and two elder brothers.

At the age of fifteen he and his family made a timely exit from their mail-order forgery premises in Pisa. His mother had received a tip-off about police suspicions, and left the local carabinieri with two wagon-loads of forgery equipment. Robson Lowe was just one of the many dealers who

have spent a major part of the twentieth century battling with this maestro
of illusion. It was suggested to him that his occasional mistakes over
forgeries and fakes must have cost him a great deal of money. He gave a big
smile, then said, somewhat ruefully:

'Fortunately not all on one day; I've been in business fifty-seven years
and I was a collector before that, and so it's been spread over a good many
years. At one time Sperati was costing us over a thousand pounds a year,
which is one of the reasons that we set out to break him, or close him up: it
was becoming too expensive!'

In print the latter part of that reply reads as an eminently justifiable
comment on an intolerable situation. But the way Robson Lowe said it was
as if the eventual demise of Sperati was a tragedy to all stamp-lovers, a
prosecution from which he would have preferred to be absent. He was
asked why he seemed so friendly about adversaries who engage him in
such costly battles of wits. Again he smiled mischievously, and replied,

Isn't that rather fun? Wouldn't you say the same playing bridge against a good bridge hand?

*Jean de Sperati
at his trial in 1948*

Sperati was a real craftsman. His older brother was a forger, and not a very good one because you can spot his stuff straight away. He had another brother, a great photographer, and the first man to reproduce picture postcards in large quantities from actual photographs. As a fifteen-year-old Sperati was apprenticed to his photographic brother, but living with his forger brother. He had an old relative who owned a paper mill which had been very famous in the mid-nineteenth century. Sperati got permission to go through the correspondence and he picked up the genuine papers on which many of the classic European stamps had been printed, so he started off with the genuine paper. This, with his skill in photography, is the reason he was able to do so well. At least one famous stamp collector employed him to make things he wanted in order to complete his display at exhibitions, and he even won a very high prize with the blank spaces filled with Sperati's imitations that had been made specially for him. Expert committees gave certificates that Sperati's work was genuine. Sometimes they all made the mistake. You can always pull anybody down a peg who says, 'I can always tell a Sperati' by looking in his own collection of his own pet country and saying, 'What about that?' Everybody was fooled at some time by this man. He was the grand illusionist. The perfect example of his skill was where the letters and the stamps on them were both quite genuine. They were the stamps of Sardinia with the embossed head of the king in the centre. Sperati soaked the genuine stamps off these envelopes, faded out the frames, printed new frames inverted in relation to the head [in order to create the rare error] then gummed the back of the stamp, let the gum dry, then licked it, stuck it back on the cover and in due course sold it. This work of Sperati fooled Italian experts for years. He sold them quite cleverly by putting the one or two errors in perhaps a bundle of a hundred common Sardinian covers that were worth five or ten pounds for the hundred. The dealer would spot the two errors and say, 'Oh, well, I'll give you fifty pounds for them.' Sperati might haggle and try to get him up to £75, but he was selling a hundred letters. The dealer would be selling the rare ones for three or four hundred pounds – greed would be the driving force that would get the man to buy them without looking at them properly.

Robson Lowe spoke about Sperati's eventual encounters with the law.

He had come up before the courts in France before the war. He'd tried to send an approval sheet of stamps to a man in Portugal, and it had been stopped by the Customs, and he got charged with exporting valuable genuine stamps without a licence. Well, after a lot of hoo-haa, with them gradually getting his ears pinned back, he said, 'They aren't genuine stamps! They are my imitations of them.' The French had to pull in a great expert, a Dr Lecard, and he certified that the fifteen stamps were genuine. He said, 'Look, they have the genuine water-mark, the genuine perforation,' and he explained to the judge why they had to be genuine. Finally Sperati destroyed Dr Lecard's testimony by saying, 'Well, if I produce another set of these stamps would you think that was curious?' Lecard replied, 'Well, yes I would, because some of them are quite rare.' So Sperati pulled out of his pocket another set, and the Doctor looked at it and agreed, after a few minutes, that it was almost identical.

'Now if I pulled out a third set would it be remarkable?'

Well of course it was remarkable; but it was a blooming miracle when he pulled out the sixth set! And he'd proved then that the whole case had to start all over again on the subject of forgery. He won his case: he had not been exporting valuable stamps as charged – and then they started a new case about forgery, and in all Sperati's case went on for eleven years.

For a limited period after their issue by the Post Office, postage stamps can be encashed for their face value. Thereafter they are demonetised and their value then depends wholly on their desirability as a collector's item. Forgers therefore tend to focus their interest on either demonetised stamps of low monetary denominations which because of printers' errors become valuable, or occasionally on stamps of high original value which can still be regarded as currency. In 1924 the British Post Office became highly embarrassed by the latter type of forgery, and sent Robson Lowe to Paris to acquire some for closer inspection. They included the 1883 ten shillings stamp, made by someone as clever as Sperati. It was a very clever forgery, made on the same paper on which Irish revenue stamps had been printed and the genuine design faded out. A simple means of detection was required. The genuine postage stamps had been printed on the same paper, watermarked Anchor, where the Irish revenue stamps were watermarked Foul Anchor (i.e. there was a rope around the Anchor). As Robson Lowe therefore pointed out, 'If your stamp had a rope around the shaft you knew you'd got a stinker! – but they were awfully well done.'

There are several basic tests for checking the authenticity of any stamp, many of which someone with virtually no knowledge of stamps can carry out quite easily.

The three basic methods of printing have already been mentioned, and if the stamp you inspect is not printed by the method described in the catalogue, it must be a forgery.

There are two classes of forgery: hand-drawn or hand-engraved, and photographic. Hand work is easier to detect even with the naked eye: if it includes a portrait the most cursory comparison with the genuine can show the forgery to be the wrong man or woman. However with contact photography the forgery could be of exactly the right size and look perfectly accurate. If it is a photo-engraving then the engraving will be of a different depth, and if you take a rubbing you get quite a different answer to that obtained from a rubbing of the genuine stamp. Even with photo-lithography a difference can be seen. Robson Lowe explained:

Every time you photograph an original you lose white space and the dark space grows in size. You will see that the white spaces in between letters has shrunk by twenty-five per cent although in fact the black space has only improved by five to ten per cent. You must train the eye to look at the white space and see if the white spaces have shrunk – if they've shrunk it's a forgery because every time you photograph, every time you reproduce, you slightly increase the black space and slightly decrease the white space. A lot of people don't see it to begin with, but once they've got their eye in they find this very useful.

Then one has to check the texture of the paper to see, for example, if it was made by a British mill. If the watermark is incorrect, something must be wrong. Collectors often have samples of perforations made, for example, by the Somerset House machine and the De La Rue machine. If the perforations seem to have been made by the wrong machine they too give away the forgery.

And then, once any stamp is correctly fixed to its letter, another process inviting forgery occurs. It is cancelled at the Post Office, and as the time or place of cancellation are likely to be unique that too enormously increases the value of the stamp, and the temptation of creating an appealing cancellation. Here again however, Robson Lowe explained that the forger is only likely to fool the novice or the unsuspicious.

Robson Lowe was asked about cancellations.

That's another thing that's greatly specialised in today with people forging rare cancellations. Some of them are very clever, but fortunately, if you know what the original should look like, it's very difficult for the forger to have used the right sort of ink. A forger tends to have three or four pads and he uses them for three or four hundred different cancellations, whereas in real life every cancellation has a different pad.

A very basic test on the paper of a stamp involves soaking both the genuine article and the suspect in benzine. If one stamp absorbs the liquid more rapidly than the others it can be guaranteed that they are of different origin. Even by comparing stamps under a raking light, striking surface differences can become obvious to the most untutored eye. In all there are sixteen different tests for authenticity. The trouble is that often a buyer has neither the time, nor sometimes the inclination, to carry them all out. Robson Lowe warned against making mistakes by being too greedy.

When you attend an auction there is a tendency to feel, 'Oh, I *would* like that!' – and one becomes greedy for something. I attended a French auction a few years ago and I noticed that a penny black of Great Britain was being offered, dated 6 May, 1840, which was the first day it was available for use, and this is worth a very substantial premium. But nobody mentioned this in the auction, and so I went on, and I paid four or five times what the ordinary penny black was worth in order to get the 6 May piece. When I got it back to England in the good light I found it was a beautiful bit of hand-painting and not the strike of a proper date stamp, so somebody had caught me quite easily that way. Another classic time I was taken for a ride was a Nova Scotia cover. It was a correspondence addressed to the Reverend Musgrave. Now in the original form I had all these letters in 1927, and one of these letters had an eight and a half cent stamp, and a one cent stamp and a half a one cent stamp to make a ten cent rate; this is very rare, it's the only known copy. Now some clever boy along the line took one of the common Musgrave covers and imitated the rarity from the photograph which I had illustrated of the find. He then actually submitted it to an expert committee who gave a certificate that it was genuine because they checked it with my photograph, and said, 'Oh, that's the same cover as that!' It came back to me from a famous collection, and I sold it. Then a few years later the original envelope turned up, the genuine one; there hadn't been two of them, so one of them had to be bad, and it was the one I'd sold for £360, and I had to give the money back. Well, I didn't *have* to, – but I did.

CHAPTER THIRTEEN

MISCELLANY

'The Amateur' by Honoré Daumier, 1808–1879

It has been said collectors make forgers. Acquisitive fashion drains off the genuine and the skilled craftsman in the back room willingly supplies whatever object is in short issue. Lace, playing cards, clocks, watches, even today those recent desirables that are grouped as 'bygones' are all up for asking.

Ever since the excavations started in Egypt there has been a strong demand for something from the time of the Pharaohs not only from museums but also from the private collector. So great has this been that a domestic industry amongst the fellaheen and roving Bedouin has laboured mightily to supply scarabs, small idols and the rest by the thousand. Many of these things are innocently sold to tourists or travelling dealers as reproductions, quite cheaply; but let them travel a few hundred miles and they rise drastically in price as they become 'genuine'.

These fakers won't even shrink from producing mummies, which may range from a few bits and pieces of bodies and bones, wrapped up in some gummy resinous bituminous materials, to the mummy of Queen Nitokris, which was apparently made by an old doctor in East Germany. He bought the corpse of a young girl and gave it the full treatment and then sold it for a very large sum as the embalmed body of the early queen. This fraud was discovered because the doctor hadn't quite got his chemistry right and the pride of someone's collection began to stink and rather unsavoury juices started to trickle out through the linen wrapping. Running close in this macabre trade were the gentlemen who did well in the Renaissance period with their fiddled death masks. Such objects could be taken by anybody skilled in casting from cadavers in the morgue. Most likely by working at night and then by using a kind of devilish pastiche these masks with a little skill and the use of a modelling stick were used to produce heads of the famous.

In the eighth and ninth centuries there came an overwhelming demand for sacred relics and with it frauds that spread over most of the civilised countries. There was a mass production of these relics, and it was not unknown for reverend brothers to be in on the faking. One catalogue which has survived includes the following list, some items of which should have tested the credulity of even the simplest pilgrim or peasant:

'A fragment of St Stephen's rib,
Rusted remains of the gridiron on which St Lawrence died,
A lock of Mary's hair,
A small piece of her robe,
A piece of the Cross,
A piece of the Manger,
Part of one of Our Lord's sandals,
A piece of the sponge that had been filled with vinegar and handed up to Him,
A fragment of the bread He had shared with His disciples,
A tuft of St Peter's beard,
Drops of St John the Baptist's blood.'

These items might be sold simply in a small leather wallet or in a highly decorated casket, which for top sales could be of silver, gilt or gold set with precious stones.

The Knights Templars were accused of worshipping an imaginary symbol or idol in their secret rites. In these dark practices they were supposed to be working with the impurities of the Gnoptic Ophites, the whole ritual being around this idol or baphomet as it was called. These small figures often had some form of likeness and could have been connected with early fertility goddesses such as Astarte or Demeter. The name baphomet is supposed to be a corruption of mahomet and one expert states it is also supposed to have some connection with the baptism of *Metis* or of fire. In their own time and since, there have been numerous attacks launched against the Knights Templars, often associated with these little images, but today it would appear that the baphomets are nothing more than rather crude fakes which date from around the thirteenth century and were part of a campaign of vilification against the Knights.

When Galileo opened up the heavens he also unwittingly opened up another facility for the forger. Astronomers began collecting bolides or fire-balls or meteorites and were prepared to pay large prices for them. Apparently a well-known chemist and a faker went into partnership producing imitations of bolides, although it is hardly likely that these fraudulent objects would have survived investigation if they were broken open as the crystal arrangement inside the real bolide would have been beyond the skill of the chemist.

A current fad with many collectors is for ethnographical objects: African wooden masks, native necklaces, Red Indian weaving, wood-carvings from the Pacific, even the humble little Maori *tiki*. It is likely most of these, as with the scarabs and the rest from Egypt, start out fairly innocently as tourist bait, but then after a few changes of hand become 'valued specimens'. In Germany between the wars there were a number of workshops producing small idols and native domestic-ware. Most of these objects should be fairly simple to pick up and prevent their being passed off as the real thing, because the carvers seldom bothered to import the correct wood from Africa and used local timbers, although some of them worked quite skilfully, smoking and heating the objects to cause splitting, and also staining them and generally knocking the things about to give them a battered surface to suggest age.

A rather specialised section that has daunted the forger is that of enamelling, although there have been clever frauds. One turned up in the

Metropolitan Museum in New York. It is a twelfth-century copper-gilt champlevé enamel cross and base purporting to have been of the Mosan school, which originated in the Walloon provinces and developed in Lorraine, penetrating into Austria, Poland, Switzerland and Scandinavia. Leading craftsmen included Renier de Huy and Godefroid de Claire. This little article, which stands twelve inches high, was the gift of J. Pierpoint Morgan. It had been on exhibition for some time, and had given much pleasure to viewers and been the object of a good deal of admiration; nevertheless the cross and its base had been in doubt in 1933, but then in 1936 an outstanding scholar in the field had said it was authentic, and it had been returned to a place of honour.

Later another expert had a suspicion and he gave the exhibit a very thorough examination. This brought out the fact that there were wrong names on the symbols of Matthew and John: also the inscription on the domed base of the cross had been used as the basis for the inscriptions on the cross itself; moreover whoever had done it was not familiar with the lettering or the abbreviation system used in medieval writing, or indeed with the meaning of the words themselves.

An even greater lack of knowledge was demonstrated because further mistakes were found in the inscription above Christ's head, a notable point being that the inscription, instead of being the usual I H S or I H E or I H C where there is Byzantine influence, had been put in complete; further, stylistically the figure of Christ appeared too large for the cross. Another feature that gave rise to suspicion was the contrast between the enamels on the cross which were weak and poor in colour and the stronger enamel work on the base. Chemical tests on these enamels showed that those on the cross were of recent manufacture and were quite hard and firm while those on the base were brittle and gave every indication of being of genuine age. In addition, the metal of the cross showed very little scratching; also it had a very easily removed patina; on the other hand the metal of the base had a worn appearance and patina which would be expected with an object of its supposed age. The body of Our Lord had every evidence of being genuine and in line with twelfth-century Mosan work and still bore some remains of gilding. On the feet of the figure there were signs of where a hole had been made in the left foot for a nail, then the forger had found that the angle was wrong and the hole had been filled in. What the forger had done with this crucifix was to obtain an absolutely genuine base, also a genuine figure of Our Lord: but he had faked a cross with its very crude enamelling, and then assembled the three together.

Faked glass is another of the fields that most forgers steer clear of owing to difficulties in handling and controlling the material. Genuine old glass, if examined closely, displays a very subtle greeny-yellow tinge and also it is likely there will be many minute bubbles. There have been crude attempts to produce fake Roman glass, where the deceiver has tried to reproduce the iridescent effect of age by sticking fish scales inside the glass, with either a hoof glue or egg white. Another device to try and effect ageing is to make a careful application of hydrofluoric acid or, more primitively, to bury the forged object in manure or wet peat.

There have been revivals of style and decoration with such types as Murano glass in Italy, Bohemian glass and Irish Waterford. Again, primarily these were produced to sell as reproductions, but with time, unfortunately a proportion of these take their places in the genuine division.

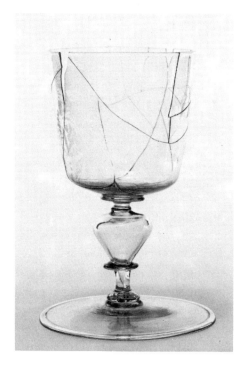

A nineteenth-century forgery of a seventeenth-century glass known as the Barnvellt glass

Excellent copies of Irish cut-glass decanters, pertaining to be around 1810, have been produced in this century. The tall but delicate wine glasses have encouraged some attempts at simulation recently. They tend to ape the decoration and the engraving, and the cutting methods of the middle of the eighteenth century. In the British Museum is the so-called Barnvellt glass which, by style and shape, is purporting to be of the seventeenth century, but is actually nineteenth century; it is a useful example to show how the forger has completed his object, then broken it and somewhat roughly put it together again. Other much sought-after objects in glass are the small round paperweights; the best of which were made in France at places like Baccarat, Clichy and St Louis in the middle of the nineteenth century. Good examples are size for size among the most valuable items that can come up in a sale room. Today there are all too many faked ones around. These come from, amongst other places, Czechoslovakia, and may be carefully scratched on the bottom to represent the abrasion and use of a hundred or more years.

Old mirrors set a problem for one bent on deceit. A genuine example has a rather hazy, dark grey reflection; also the bevels were formerly wider and more shallow than those of more recent date. The early sheet-glass was made by blowing a cylinder which was then cut down one side and flattened out. This, quite naturally, produced a glass with irregularities which can be recognised and even, at times, felt by running the finger over the surface. This combined with the dark hazy look can often point to a genuine glass, as it is unlikely that the forger has been able to compete with the early blowing process or to achieve the dark look.

The silvering of mirrors in the eighteenth century was done with mercury, which can be noted by looking at the back. In the last century the silvering was given a covering coat of a red oxide material. Attempts are made by amateur fakers to fiddle this silvering and its coating by scratching and then overlaying dark greys and near blacks. This can certainly be spotted from the back and an experienced eye will pick it up also from the front. Any mirror that has a really thick glass, which is claiming to be a couple of hundred years or more old, should be suspected at once. A simple trick to find the thickness of glass is to hold something against the surface, a finger or a pen, and note the difference between the end of the object and the reflection. This gives the thickness of the glass.

One of the nastiest provinces in the realm of faking is that of Oriental rugs, certainly from the point of view of detection. These have been a favourite with collectors for some hundreds of years, but unfortunately by their nature and the apparently simple methods of weaving and use of geometrical patterns, they are comparatively easy for the faker to imitate. He also knows that it is an area in which there are very few first-class experts who can pick up the fraud. Largely it is the knotting, the number of tufts to the inch, that governs the quality and the price of these rugs; the coarser, and generally the most hard-wearing, being the cheaper. The Caucasian is one of the better known, and such rugs are usually, apart from being coarse-knotted, brightly coloured. As opposed to this the Tabriz has elaborate arabesques in the pattern which are combined with much finer knotting. Another feature that the expert may look for is the so-called gradation. This occurs where the craftsman runs short of a particular colour and starts using a fresh batch of what should be the same colour, but there is nearly always a slight difference, and this can be picked up. It is also of course picked up by the forger who will simulate this 'gradation', but seldom is it done in such a subtle manner. As with other forms of antiques, the counterfeiter will rarely leave his piece in pristine condition and will indulge in a little 'distressing'. In Afghanistan it has been noted that the rugmakers, having completed their intricate woven imitations, will sometimes lay them out in the street for the crowds to walk over and even let cars and lorries drive over these seemingly priceless examples, leaving, no doubt, a satisfactory evidence of wear, even if it might have a pattern reminiscent of a Michelin tyre.

Very close to rug-weaving is the art of tapestry, although the production is a good deal more time-consuming and skilful, which to some degree has discouraged the forger: nevertheless there have been examples of faked tapestries which have been given the treatment necessary to 'add on the years'. What can most likely be done with tapestries is the fiddling of marks. This can also apply to rugs. What happens is that the faker will take out the signs of true origin and then weave in a mark which can multiply the value of the piece. This has been noted, particularly with the trade mark of the Brussels weaver, which is generally shown as a red shield with BB. As with the field of ceramics, there has been a fair amount of the inter-use of marks with tapestry, often done with great care and skill. An examination with an ultra-violet lamp will very speedily pick up fiddling with tapestries or rugs, as the new threads will produce considerable fluorescence.

The whole range of textiles is not one that is really attractive to the forger, owing to the difficulties from the technical angle. Imitation velvets, satin and other materials, may look quite convincing, but to the experienced eye they will be seen to have been treated to give the impression of age by subtle light bleaching and wear. Modern machines, such as the Jacquard, can never really compete with the old weaving-loom. The old materials had a slight appearance of coarseness about them; also the scientist, once alerted, can pick up the chemical processes of dyeing the threads. There is something about certain colours, especially with blues, reds and yellows, that conveys a sort of brashness, as against the more soft, fine tints of the older dyes. What can be deceptive, however, are some materials produced, for example, in the time of Louis XIII in France, which were simulating those made during the Renaissance. This reproducing of old designs has gone on in many countries in Europe. In the eighteenth and even nineteenth centuries damask, brocade and velvets resembling those of earlier times have been produced, and it can be difficult sometimes to differentiate the product of one period from that of another. Methods of ageing have included putting the textiles into a bath with a slightly tinted liquid which can, if properly done, give an overall appearance to the piece similar to that which a lightly-coloured varnish will give to a painting. Attempts have also been made to age textiles by treating velvet, brocade and other materials with steam jets and overlong exposure to bright sunlight. A further deceptive step could be for a faker to stitch on tapes before using one of the colouring methods and then when the piece is dry to take off the tapes, which would leave a convincing area of brighter colours, such as could have happened if the piece had been previously made up into a garment and then unstitched.

Illuminated manuscripts in general are well-catalogued and too well-publicised to attract the forger, although he may work around this by producing odd sheets or fragments from some work that he will have pretended to have discovered whilst actually he has invented the entire provenance of it. Some of these productions, viewed just from the front, probably artfully mounted in an antique frame, may look very convincing, and certainly before buying must be well examined from the back. As with metal sheets, the early vellum produced by hand would have certain variations of thickness and surface; whereas modern vellum has a perfect flat surface, and also an even thickness. However much the forger attempts it by the use of abrasion with very fine powders or scraping or staining, he would be unable satisfactorily to disguise a new piece of vellum.

The use of an old piece of vellum would hardly be feasible, as it would almost certainly mean the necessary removal of an early piece of illuminated work. Apart from the fact that this could have some value in itself, many of the colours used by the illuminator would have sunk into the vellum, which is extremely porous to water, and thus it is most likely their removal would so thin down the piece of vellum that the area where this happened would be readily recognisable.

There was one particular character who operated in the first half of the nineteenth century with some success in this connection. He was Vaclav Hanka, a Czech, with a strong brand of patriotism. He started off in quite a simple way, adding signatures to lesser illuminated manuscripts, and progressed from that to add 'notable works' to the artistic history of his country. In 1818 he was fortunate in being appointed librarian of the National Museum of Prague and this gave him considerable scope for his ambition. Apart from forging he manufactured a complete school of Czech painters and illuminators; the most 'famous' of these being Sbisco de Trotina. One way which Hanka thought would give everlasting fame to his fabricated school of painters was to include them in a genuine old work. He chose for this the *Jaromir Bible* and he set to work to add further illuminated embellishments to scrolls held by prophets. He added signatures, and dates, and it was one of these which stated 'PINXIT MCCLVIII' which gave the whole game away because the *Jaromir Bible* was a fourteenth-century manuscript.

A more recent attempt at forgery of the written word was by Thomas James Wise (1859–1937). He saw that there was a ready market for First Editions of works by a number of well-known English writers including Byron, Ruskin and Wordsworth. In fact he did quite well in the early part of this century until someone must have become suspicious and submitted samples of the paper he was using in his books for scientific analysis. These tests showed that esparto grass and wood pulp had been used in the paper of the books produced by Wise, which were supposed to have been published before 1861. The hard facts here are that esparto grass was not used in paper manufacture until 1861 and chemically treated wood fibre did not come in until 1874.

This production of faked First Editions had a vogue at an earlier date, because in the eighteenth century there was a workshop in Lyons which made a speciality of producing rare editions of Racine's works. Also in France, at Rouen, there were people producing early volumes of Molière: these latter going to considerable pains with the paper, type-faces, decorative detail, tailpieces and all, and with seemingly a massive amount of labour, yet somehow the figures realised made it worth while; a first edition of Molière's work dated 1669 was sold in Paris for fifteen thousand francs.

Another type of literary forgery that can be encountered is that of rare volumes which have lost pages or parts of pages which have been spuriously replaced. With added fragments it is quite amazing how a skilled calligraphic forger can successfully imitate the printed characters with a pen and brush. In damaged books it is very often the frontispiece that is missing and it is always worthwhile giving a close inspection to this part of a book when an old edition is found. There have been instances where the forger has been too clever; for example, one such edition with a faked frontispiece was detected, because the faker had added one or two wormholes which would, in his view, give a more convincing appearance of age. The only snag was that there were no corresponding worm-holes in the preceding and following pages, a clear give-away, as it would be quite impossible for the worm to reach just that one page. Close examination under magnification can also show that what had been taken for print was actually the work of a pen.

The forger has given more attention, where books have been his choice, to their bindings than to their content. Examples of fiddling and faking are numerous: the bindings often being transferred from one book to another to cause further confusion. In the latter part of the nineteenth century there was a positive plague of imitation of seventeenth-century bindings that were backed by seemingly impressive provenances and supposedly issued from various craftshops, in Paris, London and Brussels. There are a number of ways in which the fakers of bindings can work. They may try to forge the whole covering or more likely they will be content with the clever fiddling of the embellishments, the characters, the titles, the authors and the marks of celebrated bibliophiles. They may also build up pastiches, using parts of old genuine bindings and cannibalising these into a false presentation. There is plenty of scope here, what with old leathers and ancient parchments, genuine old labels that can be altered, and faked lining papers. When decorating the cover, it may be possible to secure some of the genuine old iron stamps or dyes; if not, new ones can be made in the relevant pattern. A trick that has caught many is the production of stamps that simulate a decorative coat of arms belonging to a celebrated family of collectors. This can give the impression that the book or books are from the library of a famous scholar, and it will greatly enhance the value. An example of this is the use of the original stamps which were found by the imitators of the *Sacré de Louis XV*: also those of the Rohan-Chabot family. This type of trickery has been especially successful with some American collectors.

The trick of transferring covers has made much money for the faker. This can be picked up by carefully examining the joining of the binding to the main body of the book. Any sight of new papers, or perhaps small splashes of recent glue, should arouse suspicion. Where new leathers have been incorporated, recent attempts at patination will not stand up to polishing in the same way as genuine old leather would: in fact a little trial with a slightly damp cloth should show up a fake patination.

One aspect of collecting which has gained great momentum in the last few years is that of maps, and this has brought in its wake a mass production of rather tricky deceptions. A main target has been the work of the early English cartographer John Speed. One method that has been particularly successful is that the faker first procures black and white collotype reproductions to the same size as the original Speed maps. These he may be able to buy or, if not, with the help of a co-operative printer he produces his own. Some operators may be content to work with modern papers but others, working on a bigger scale, get special papers made up to simulate those used by Speed.

When the black and white print has been processed the operator soaks it in water, lifts it out of the dish, drains off the water, puts the print between sheets of blotting paper or white towelling, places it on the floor and walks about on it. This will give a convincing battered old paper look. Next he lets it dry and attends to the edges of the paper. By judicious use of sandpaper the machine-cut edge can be made to look like a hand-made example. After this he prepares a dish of suitably toned liquid, which is made up of a certain type of Indian ink, or with liquorice, and he immerses the map in this to give it that darkish look of the early genuine examples. Further treatment can include spotting with orange/brown water colours, or coffee, and the careful placing of a few worm-holes. These he often does by using a punch, because if they have been pricked through with a needle they can easily be picked up as the side on which the needle emerges will leave a very slight coronet edge. But if he uses a punch, again he will give himself away, as the punch is unlikely to be able to reach in to the centre of the map and thus the worm-holes will be no more than two or three inches from the edge. After this treatment, the kind of colouring which would be expected with a Speed map is applied and then, as a final touch, to give that kind of withered feeling to the surface of the paper, cigarette ash or potato flour is rubbed over the whole surface. Now the example can be carefully mounted and framed; and then it becomes very difficult indeed to tell what is what. There is one way, however, that a collector can save himself a good sum of money, and that is to examine some of the lines under moderate magnification. Here it will be seen that whereas the genuine Speed engraved line will have continuity of blackness, the collotype reproduction printed line has a broken appearance with little flecks of unprinted paper coming in the line.

Outright forging of silver objects is rare. With this metal it is much more a case of fiddling, altering or tampering with the all-important hall-mark and it is with this last that the less knowledgeable faker can come adrift; for, as with the slightly ignorant collectors who look no further than the signature, the neophyte seeker for good silver just takes his eye-glass and examines the hall-mark instead of trusting to an educated eye that will pick up true, good design and style in the piece as a whole.

There are probably more good genuine silver articles still preserved in England than in any other country in Europe. In France the ravages of the Revolution brought about heavy losses and even before that time, Louis XIV was calling for magnificent pieces of silver to be melted down and used for making coinage. In Italy financial distress and changing fashion brings stories of excellent collections of antique silver also being melted down for bullion or rather stupidly being melted down to buy modern silverware. There was one lady at Sienna who did this with a beautiful old silver service, all except for one spoon, and she was somewhat horrified afterwards when she found that the value of that single antique spoon would have been more than enough to have bought the entire new set of table-silver. In the nineteenth century there were a number of large sales of silver, including the one after the death of Mademoiselle Mazencourt, where exquisite examples of the silversmith's art were sold, not by their quality, their design and excellence, but by so much a gramme, in this case twenty centimes.

The all-important hall-marking of silver was begun in England in about 1300 and this was done to guarantee the purity of silver and gold and as a protection from forgeries for the collector. He should now know that a given piece of work is by a certain craftsman, from a certain district, and made in a certain year. But, in many ways this was a come-on for the faker who is a good reader of fashion and the thoughts of the collector, and who knows how much he is governed by the right mark and the right date; after all he can fairly easily apply fraudulent marks. One way is for a cast to be taken of marks from a genuine piece of silver; but this does have a slight difficulty as far as the forger is concerned, for if he wants to, for example, deal with a whole set of silver dishes or bowls, a mark that is cast will look a little odd to the expert. This is because in each case the various marks will be absolutely regular and equidistant, whereas if they were marked honestly with a set of punches there would be some individuality and a slight variance in their setting.

A very skilled fabricator will go the whole hog and make himself a set of punches, either from a cast or from a mark which he knows and can get at. Generally he will make his punches from steel because these will tend to give the sharper impression and be more difficult to detect. But there is an even more lethal trick; if he is a skilled silversmith as well, the forger can, with care, cut out the hall-mark from a small perhaps damaged old piece and insert it into a lesser, probably more modern, article that he wants to pass as a genuine early piece.

The law in England has tried to expose these deceptive workers with silver, and sometimes they have been threatened with severe penalties:

by the early part of the eighteenth century counterfeiting a hall-mark could even bring the death penalty. In 1767 it is recorded that one ruse was to solder a bit of low standard silver to shoe-buckles or sugar-tongs and then send them for assay, so that they could get the requisite marks which they could then put on a lesser larger piece.

But the Law kept fighting back, in fact in 1884 there was an Act, section 2 of which gave the following offences which would bring severe penalties:

Forging or counterfeiting any die for marking Gold or Silver Wares or knowingly uttering the same;

Marking Wares with forged Dies or uttering same;

Forging any Mark or any Die or uttering same;

Transposing or removing Mark, or uttering them;

Having in possession knowingly any such Dies, or Ware marking with the same;

Cutting or severing Marks with Intent to effect them upon other Wares;

Affixing any Mark severed from any other Wares;

Fraudulently using genuine Dies.

The Act goes on and even includes penalties under Section 4 for dealers, which says:

Dealers to be exempt from the above penalties upon giving up the names of the actual manufacturer of such Wares of gold or silver or base metal, or of the person from whom they received them, but not from the consequence of uttering them with guilty knowledge.

In Section 9 it says:

Dealers not to fraudulently erase, obliterate, or deface any marks under penalty of £5. (Well, this was in 1884!)

It is interesting to note that sum, because even today the penalties in this country for forgery and fraudulently 'fiddling' are really ridiculously low when such large profits are to be made.

One of the attractions of old silver is the very subtle surface finish that it acquires over the years, a compound of myriad tiny minute scratches from handling and the passage of time. It is not a patination as with other materials. Today the tarnish it so often gets is caused in the present industrial atmosphere largely by sulphur in the air, but it doesn't have anything to do with the surface characteristic of old silver. For the forger, this surface does present a considerable difficulty when he sets out to ape it, having perhaps altered a piece or added to it. He may try to get away from this problem by using a rather heavy tarnish that can be chemically applied by a solution of pentasulphide of potassium – the old name for this being liver of sulphur. An even deeper tarnish can be achieved by dipping the object into a solution of mercurous nitrate. This is a trick often used when a heavily decorated piece is being fiddled around with, and it has the effect, when the piece has been polished, of leaving the upraised areas with a sheen and dark tones in the grooves and engraved areas. Another trick of the last century's operators in the field was to dip the piece into chlorine water, a solution of chloride of lime or, as it was known, *eau-de-javelle*.

Today this alteration business by an operator in silver is highly illegal, but there are many instances of it around and it is very likely still being done. Tankards are among the items that have drawn forth the skill of such men. They were a very popular form of communal drinking vessel in the seventeenth and eighteenth centuries and then they became rather more refined with the different manners of the nineteenth century. They were often converted to pitchers with the addition of a spout which might be put on at the front opposite the handle or at the side. You also get a form of pastiche, where a cover from another vessel is adapted to fit a tankard, and perhaps some piece from yet another vessel is also included in the decoration.

In America there are a number of items which have turned up with altered marks. A simple, well-proportioned silver beaker of either English or Irish origin that shows signs, although very faint, of a raised hall-mark, had the fake mark of the silversmith John Burke of Boston put over it. A silver cream-pot, which was of low quality and had been damaged, was repaired by a fake restorer: a small strip of silver was added at the top of the rim and then, to make it more saleable, it was stamped with the mark of the famous Paul Revere II. On examination, with a little magnification, this ruse becomes evident, because there is a lack of accumulated dirt and tarnish in the marking and also with the alteration. It is interesting that with the English or Irish marks there is the assay centre, the maker's initials and date. With American silver it is generally the maker's mark alone that is used.

Fake arms and armour have been in production for centuries at a variety of centres which are probably still active at producing exquisite fakes of these objects. Constantinople had a name for the production of forged oriental arms and armour, but in a way it is quite likely that anybody buying such items and thinking they had come from the Middle East will find that a beautifully decorated poniard or Turkish gun, which may be ornamented with passages from the Koran and found in bazaars in Cairo or along the North African coast, may well have been made in Germany. Nuremberg has been one of the leading centres throughout history: certainly during the Renaissance it had a thriving trade, supplying both sides in many of the battles.

There was the naïve American tourist who went to the local *souk* near Tangier and purchased what he thought to be a fine antique Moroccan dagger with a well-ornamented scabbard in brass. He took it back and showed it proudly to his hotel keeper who promptly said 'That is German', and to convince the unfortunate tourist he produced its twin which had been given him the week previously by the German commercial traveller who obviously supplied the 'craftsmen' in the *souk*.

A damascened blade has always been one of the most attractive items from Arabian and Javan armourers. It had been thought that the mere sign of this on a blade was a hundred per cent warranty of its being genuine; but no longer. The secret art of the Arabian, Javan and Persian armourers has been exposed. There is a restorer of weapons, Manfred Sachse, who lives in Germany at Mönchengladbach. After years of experimentation he has discovered a method of producing a so-called Damascene steel, a technique that was first discovered during the times of the Vikings, and he can now work excellent copies of antique weapons that even an expert will have trouble in identifying. He is hard-working, because his technique involves, as he says, 'Taking several layers of hard and soft iron, welding them together in the fire of a forge, then bending, twisting and hammering and finally the blade can have up to three hundred and twenty layers.'

Many of the imitators and forgers of warlike objects work in solitude, hidden away in their craftshops, and for this reason are more dangerous from the collector's point of view, as their often exquisite products are brought into the trade by devious and almost undiscoverable methods. In Lucca not so long ago there was a craftsman whose imitations of old daggers became famous. Somewhere in Spain there is a workshop that has been producing body armour, providing suits of knightly wear to hang or stand in the new baronial halls to provide that essential air of history and

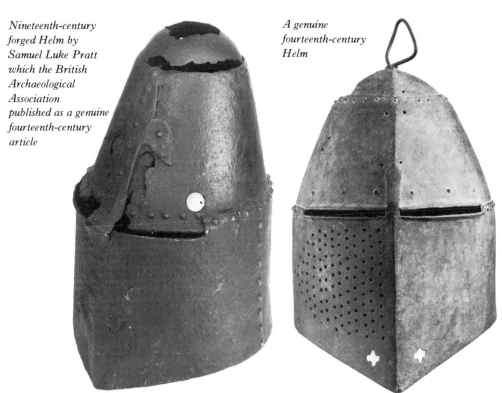

Nineteenth-century forged Helm by Samuel Luke Pratt which the British Archaeological Association published as a genuine fourteenth-century article

A genuine fourteenth-century Helm

status. There are craftsmen prepared to have a go at almost anything in this territory, even the difficult art of repoussé work on shields and armour. The fact is that almost all the truly genuine swords, helmets, shields, body-armour, daggers and the rest are either safely esconced in museums or hanging, much admired, on a collector's walls, and anybody on the prowl for bargains in this domain can view with considerable suspicion displays of beautifully ornamented swords, pikes, guns, and the rest that are offered for sale. In this category nothing shows up the fake more than the proximity of the genuine article, whether it is a pistol, a fine sword, a dagger or piece of armour; the eye can see the subtle difference, in particular of recently worked iron or steel, when the genuine article, hundreds of years old, is compared with the impostor.

As much as the fake-craftsman tries, with 'distressing' and maltreatment, he never quite achieves that complete look of age of the real thing. They may steep their objects in acid, bury them in sour ground and manure; they may scorch them with fire, bring on a pitted look with the use of a concentrated salt solution and use phoney burnishing. But still the exposé looms on the horizon. A raking light can uncover a false pitted appearance, for one thing; and besides other pitfalls, the forgers often make disastrous mistakes with their designs, such as helmets which, on close examination, show that if they had been worn and the visor had been closed, the wearer would have lost half his nose; and gauntlets which would never have fitted a normal hand. In fact, in the last century some quite grotesque pieces of armour were created with little attempt at authenticity. These appeared to have been made from rolled sheets of iron with modern round-headed nails instead of simulating the old rivets. Fake craftsmanship, regrettably encouraged by lack of knowledge, by greed and the impetuosity of some new collectors, reaps a good harvest.

The forger has had many successes with one or other of the alloys which have been used in the past for the production of various objects, the most notable of these being bronze – an alloy of copper and tin; followed by brass – copper and zinc; Britannia metal, used to ape old silver and so-called 'cock metal', a compound of copper and lead, as well as pewter made from tin and lead, which some workers use to imitate silver.

With all this duplicity with metal one of the problems that most concerns the forger after he has actually made the piece is that essential imitation of age by patination. Most of these metals, particularly bronze and brass and pewter, will acquire over the years a fine brown or greeny-grey dark sheen of patination which is one of the great attractions for the collector. There have been many genuine pieces of pewter that over the centuries have acquired this beautiful thin veiling and have had much of their value knocked off by the zealous idiots who acquired them and then subjected them to a high degree of polishing, being delighted when the pewter came up gleaming like silver.

Many are the fanciful recipes that appear in textbooks of the nineteenth century, and many are the forgery processes which are still used today to maltreat the metal surface to give it the guise of age. There are records of objects being immersed in baths of ammonia or carbonic acid and of being buried in various unpleasant substances. False green patination of bronze has been simulated by the use of powdered malachite; and this has been done by first brushing over the object with a very weak solution of cupric nitrate, which has had a small quantity of sodium chloride added to it, then bathing the object with a further mixture of weak vinegar with oxalic acid and lastly by applying the malachite with a suitable adhesive. Brass, to achieve the dull green of age, has been brushed over with or dipped in vinegar plus a little nitric acid. Alloys have been heated and treated with graphite. The list is almost endless. The only way to defeat these overtures is to study the real, appraise the appearance of that genuine aged patination and to recognise the vital difference. Here again if it is possible for a completely genuine object to be put alongside the suspect, the faults will jump out at the eye.

Not long ago the owners of a small antique business were observed at work converting some recently made Birmingham pewter ware into satisfactory antiques that could draw a buyer. Tankards, platters and measuring vessels, gleaming almost like silver with newness, were being dunked in some privately concocted corrosive and tarnishing liquid to give them a rapid ageing. This was in a little back room behind the shop. The operators worked with wooden tongs, gently lowering the pieces into the bath; whereupon as they hit the solution there was much bubbling and raising of swirling heads of vapour. The one who was dipping was heard to say after lifting out one particular piece, 'So that's put fifty years on it.' When his friend said, 'Oh, give it another two minutes,' it was replaced and when removed the conversation continued, 'That should make it about 1820, give it another few minutes.' It was lifted out once more and looked at closely and they were satisfied that it could be around 1710 or perhaps earlier.

Maybe it was of objects like this and of a similar nature that a learned expert, when asked to authenticate a large collection of 'seeming' top-grade pieces, said, 'To the best of my knowledge and ability they are original.' At the time it was reported he was partially blind.

In a still more apocryphal vein, there is that somewhat ancient tale of the man who bought the skull of Julius Caesar from a back-lane curio shop. The following year he returned to the establishment. Somewhat forgetfully the proprietor offered him another skull saying that it was that of Julius Caesar.

'How dare you,' cried the collector. 'You sold me that last year.'

To which came the riposte, 'I know, I remember well. But this one is Julius Caesar's when he was a boy.'

ACKNOWLEDGEMENTS

Page 11 Lithograph by Grandville from *Scènes de la vie privée et publique des animaux*, J. Hetzel et Paulin, Paris, 1842. 27 Punch cartoon on the Piltdown forgery, 1953. 37 H. Roger-Viollet, Paris. 41 Fortean Picture Library, Powys. 46 Metropolitan Museum of Art, Fletcher Fund. 48 Musée du Louvre. 50 Victoria & Albert Museum. 55 Dyson Perrins Museum, Worcester. 57 Dyson Perrins Museum, Worcester. 64 The Mansell Collection. 69 British Museum, London. 71 British Museum, London. 76 The Mansell Collection. 86 The Mansell Collection. 88 Mary Evans Picture Library. 92 Spink & Son Ltd. 98 BBC. 99 Spink & Son Ltd. 102 BBC. 103 BBC. 106 Simon & Schuster Inc., New York. 110 General Electric Research and Development Center, New York. 111 De Beers Consolidated Mines. 113 Alan Hodgkinson. 117 Alan Hodgkinson. 121 Henri Daumier, from *La salle des ventes*. 135 Walker Art Gallery, Liverpool. 136 Bayerischen Staatsgemäldesammlungen, Munich. 139 (top left), Italy sixteenth-Cinema-Edition, Tours, (top right) Giraudon, (bottom left), attributed to Ducayer, Giraudon, (bottom right) Walter Art Gallery. 144 British Museum, London. 146 Lithograph by Grandville from *Un Autre Monde*, H. Fournier, Paris, 1844. 159 Museum Boymans – van Beuningen, Rotterdam. 162 Rijksmuseum, Amsterdam. 165 Christies, London. 170 Mary Evans Picture Library. 176 Alain Brieux, Paris. 179 Replica Rara (London) Ltd. 181 Lithograph by Grandville from *Un Autre Monde*, H. Fournier, Paris, 1844. 183 The Mansell Collection. 191 Victoria & Albert Museum. 194 Staatliche Museen, Berlin. 195 Staatliche Museen, Berlin. 199 Gerald Duckworth & Co. Ltd. 204 Robson Lowe Ltd. 210 Robson Lowe Ltd. 212 Paul Popper Ltd. 217 Metropolitan Museum of Art, H. O. Havemeyer Collection. 221 British Museum, London. 233 The Armouries, H.M. Tower of London.